The Secured Enterprise

Protecting Your Information Assets

Paul E. Proctor
and
F. Christian Byrnes

Selected material contributed by
Bryan Nairn, Richard Barber and Thomas Waszak.

ISBN 0-13-061906-X

90000

A CIP catalog record for this book can be obtained from the Library of Congress.

Editorial/Production Supervision: *Jan H. Schwartz*
VP, Executive Editor: *Tim Moore*
Editorial Assistant: *Allyson Kloss*
Manufacturing Manager: *Alexis Heydt-Long*
Buyer: *Maura Zaldivar*
Art Director: *Gail Cocker-Bogusz*
Interior Series Design: *Meg VanArsdale*
Cover Design Direction: *Jerry Votta*
Cover Design: *Talar Boorujy*
Technical Editor: *Sue Heim*
Graphics: *Glenn Van Houten*
Composition: *Pine Tree Composition, Inc.*

 © 2002 Prentice Hall PTR
A Division of Pearson Education, Inc.
Upper Saddle River, NJ 07458

The publisher offers discounts on this book when ordered in bulk quantities.
For more information, contact

Corporate Sales Department
Prentice Hall PTR
One Lake Street
Upper Saddle River, NJ 07458
Phone: 800-382-3419; FAX: 201-236-7141
Email (Internet): corpsales@prenhall.com

Printed in the United States of America

10 9 8 7 6 5 4 3 2 1

ISBN 0-13-061906-X

Pearson Education Ltd., *London*
Pearson Education Australia Pty, Limited, *Sydney*
Pearson Education Singapore, Pte. Ltd.
Pearson Education North Asia Ltd. *Hong Kong*
Pearson Education Canada, Ltd., *Toronto*
Pearson Educación de Mexico, S.A. de C.V.
Pearson Education—Japan, *Tokyo*
Pearson Education Malaysia, Pte. Ltd.

This book is dedicated to
the victims, the survivors, and their families.

September 11, 2001

Contents

Foreword

When I started DEF CON 10 years ago, 110 people attended, wanting to share computer security information. By the time the number of participants had grown to 300, we all figured that this was the total number of people interested and willing to go to Las Vegas. We were wrong. Last year, over 5,000 hackers, students, law enforcers, and security professionals attended the conference.

I got my first taste of computers at the age of 13, and an entirely new world opened up before my eyes. The "Internet" of my early days was a 300-baud acoustic modem, the kind you see in old movies, such as *War Games*. I dialed into individual bulletin board systems and exchanged slow text messages with others interested in the same things. There were no books on computer security to speak of; without the e-commerce and Web revolution, there were no jobs, either. Things changed quickly.

The Internet was built by technologically savvy computer experts, and for a long while, they were the only ones to inhabit it. When the Net grew to the point that it was being used for entertainment and business, computer security became important. The "old-school" hackers broke into computers to gain free un*x and Internet access, but in the mid-1990s, it did not matter anymore. Linux and FreeBSD made un*x access free, computers were cheap, and Net access became ubiquitous. The new computer security threats were from not only college students hacking on the network for adventure, but business competitors, malicious attackers, angry co-workers, and foreign governments.

Web sites catering to specific technical niches of computer security have flourished, many books have been published, and an almost unlimited number of mailing lists and whitepapers are available online. Almost all of these resources assume that you know how to speak the language of security policy and technology, and they focus on the small picture. Unfortunately, the number of good security books I could recommend to people who want to be introduced to the subject of computer security can be counted on only two hands, whereas books on how to write Web pages number in the hundreds.

What Paul and Chris have managed to do with this book is to create a landscape introducing you to all of the aspects of security. From this perspective, you get to see how all the parts are related, which is no easy task. Security has gotten more complex with time; it has become more difficult to distill it down to the important parts.

After reading *Essential Guide to Information Security*, you will understand security better and be better prepared to apply it in your enterprise.

Jeff Moss
Founder, DEF CON
President, Black Hat, Inc.

AUTHOR'S NOTE:

DEF CON and The Black Hat Briefings are very popular conferences at which security professionals and corporate staff can learn from hackers, government officials, law enforcement agencies, and the top minds in computer security. The Black Hat briefings are held annually in Las Vegas and at four other locations worldwide.

Acknowledgments

We would like to thank the following people. Bryan Nairn and Richard Barber; the material they contributed was invaluable. Thomas Waszak gets a special thank you for the insight into commercial application and most of Chapter 20, "Putting It All Together," which he contributed. Sue Heim did spectacular editing, and Glenn Van Houten's graphics are top notch, as always.

Reviewers always significantly improve the quality of the end product. Special thanks to Eric Rohy, Rick McNees, Earl Perkins, Gene Kim, and Jeff Moss.

Thank you to the production team. Tim Moore at Prentice Hall is responsible for this book's existence. Russ Hall made sure it all made sense and Warwick Ford provided valuable insight. Jan Schwartz has been a wonderful and thorough production editor.

Thanks to Kay, Sherry, Heather, and Alex for all the support.

Introduction:
How to Read this Book

This book is directed to business people who are tasked with computer security responsibility, but it will also have value to security professionals looking for an overview. As such, security is viewed from a business perspective throughout the book. Topics are explored in a variety of technical depths to explain fully the impact on business and to give business professionals sufficient understanding to work effectively with their technical people. Whether you think of it as *information technology* (IT), *information services* (IS), or just *the computer people*, without a competent guide, security can go right over your head.

This book is divided into four sections.

PART 1—INTRODUCTION . . . .

This section introduces you to security, the threats you are protecting yourself from, and the basic technologies you will need to protect yourself.

PART 2—PROTECTION METHODS . . . .

This section explains the protection methods used commonly in today's business environment. This is where you will read about firewalls, virus protection, intrusion detection, etc.

PART 3—IMPLEMENTATION . . . .

This section focuses on implementation methods and choices for different sizes of businesses. In Part 3, you will read about risk assessment, configuration, deployment, and managed security services.

PART 4—ODDS AND ENDS . . . .

This section includes discussions of legal issues, company politics, and other factors necessary in your success with information security.

To help you, the authors have provided plenty of examples, anecdotes, and technical descriptions to guide you. The following icons help to organize topics in the book.

 TECHNICAL DEPTH

This icon lets you know that the section you are about to read digs deeper than most of the rest of the book. It is intended for people with some computer background. Read these sections to understand the technology behind your security, impress your IT department, and keep vendors honest.

 KEY POINT

This is usually a one- or two-line repetition of an important point in the text, intended to make it easy to skim the book for relevant information and to emphasize important facts.

Example

This icon denotes an example or anecdote that emphasizes a point made in the main text of the book. These are used to enhance the information you're reading and to put it into the context of your business.

The authors understand that businesses are not created equal. To accommodate different sizes of businesses, we offer the following guides to help you find the information relevant to your situation.

Large Enterprise

A large enterprise is one with more than 1,000 servers, more than $1 billion in revenue, and more than 2,000 employees. Large enterprises are usually characterized by multiple worldwide sites and special requirements, such as "follow the sun" management. Large enterprises will likely require more security expertise than is offered in this book.

Medium Business

Medium-sized businesses have over $100 million in revenue, more than 100 servers, and over 500 employees. Medium businesses usually have multiple sites. This book will be especially useful to executives and managers of medium-sized businesses.

Small Business

A small business has less than $100 million in revenue, fewer than 100 servers, and fewer than 100 employees. Although most of the information in this book will have value to small businesses, some of it may be more than is necessary.

Security is a journey, not a destination. There will not be a point in this journey when you can say, "Now I'm secure." This book will be your road map.

Part 1

Introduction to Security

1   Introduction to Security

In this chapter . . .

- The Four Objectives of Security: Confidentiality, Integrity, Availability, and Nonrepudiation

- Roles and Responsibilities

- Security Policy

- Security Technology

Most of us understand how locks, barred windows, lit parking lots, and loud barking dogs can be used to make our office buildings more secure. Computer security can, in many ways, be compared with these physical security approaches. But, as with anything else that we translate from the real world to the computer world, we find that we must very firmly define our terminology and our business needs before the computer version can either be understood or made to work. In this chapter, we will define what computer security is and how it is achieved in a successfully secured organization. If you have no experience with computer security, you probably think that your computers already include solutions to these problems. In fact, most business people believe that. They are wrong.

OBJECTIVES OF COMPUTER SECURITY . . . .

If you are new to computer security, you will soon learn that there is a lot more to it than keeping "evil" hackers out of your systems. Computer security has four objectives: confidentiality, integrity, availability, and nonrepudiation (NR). Securing information is equivalent to ensuring that computers keep your secrets, hold valid information, are ready to work when you are, and keep records of your transactions. Figure 1–1 shows the four objectives.

These first three objectives are the "motherhood and apple pie" of Information Technology (IT) departments. Unfortunately, too much apple pie can make you sick (or at least overweight), and too much security can be bad for business. We hope that this book will prepare you to understand how much security is enough for your business and why it is (and should be) up to you. The fourth objective becomes especially important when you transact business using computers for activities such as online sales or securities trading.

The three objectives of confidentiality, integrity, and availability can never be completely separated. The definitions and solutions overlap among the three. That is not a problem. We just need to keep the end goal in mind: computers that do what we want, when we want because we are the business owners of those computers. But they must do nothing for anyone else.

Confidentiality

The first objective of security is confidentiality: keeping information away from people who should not have it. Accomplishing this objective requires that we know what data we are protecting and who should have access to it. It requires that we provide protection mechanisms for the data while it is stored in the computer and while it is

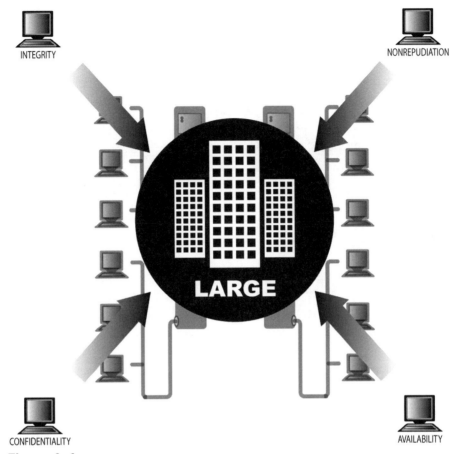

Figure 1–1
The four objectives of information security.

being transferred over networks between computers. We will need to know the application programs that we use (or could use) to manipulate the data and control the use of those applications. Luckily, the Chief Security Officer (CSO) and the IT team will handle the mechanics of doing all this—just as soon as we tell them how to figure out who should have access to which data and applications and how far to go in providing confidentiality (see "Relative Security," later in this chapter).

 *KEY POINT*

Confidentiality mechanisms keep information from being read by unauthorized people.

In the Internet world, confidentiality has taken on an expanded meaning in the form of privacy controls. For some industries, such as health care and finance, privacy is now a regulatory issue. The U.S., European, Canadian, and Australian governments (with others following) have legislated privacy controls to varying degrees. Even U.S. companies in other industries are now governed by privacy legislation of other countries if they have employees or customers in any of those other geographies. We will cover the legal requirements for security in much more detail in a later chapter. In addition, public demand for privacy has forced many companies to formulate clear privacy policies to prevent their customers from going to competitors.

There are numerous technologies available to provide confidentiality for computer applications, systems, and networks. They will be described with their strengths, costs, and weaknesses in later chapters of this book.

Integrity

The second objective of security is integrity: assuring that the information stored in the computer is never contaminated or changed in a way that is not appropriate. Both confidentiality and availability contribute to integrity. Keeping data away from those who should not have it and making sure that those who should have it can get it are fairly basic ways to maintain the integrity of the data.

KEY POINT

> Integrity mechanisms assure that information stored in the computer is never contaminated or changed in a way that is not appropriate.

But many security failures happen despite reasonably strong controls on who has access. Sometimes, the people we trust are not trustworthy. Sometimes, we need to extend levels of trust to people about whom we know little or nothing, such as temporary workers, third-party business partners, or consultants. Integrity constraints have to go beyond the simple "who" definitions and handle the "what" conditions. Once someone has been granted access, what operations can they perform on our computers? This leads to requirements for detailed constraints on different types of access within the computer system and, thus, to much of the complexity of a modern business computer system. If a typical end user can change the behavior of the operating system or network, anyone inside our company can stop business from being processed—intentionally or not.

The need for data integrity connects computer security to a closely related discipline: business continuity planning and data recovery. Data will eventually be damaged by hardware failure, software failure, human errors, or security failures. Recovery processes are a necessary part of any business IT plan and frequently are under the control of a security department.

Availability

The third objective of security is availability: ensuring that data stored in the computer can be accessed by the people who *should* access it. Availability is a broad subject addressing things such as fault tolerance to protect against denial of service and access control to ensure that data is available to those authorized to access it. Most computers can at least differentiate between two classes of users: system administrators and general end users. The major exceptions to this rule are the desktop operating systems that have become common on personal computers.

If you read, you'll find references in most IT publications describing Microsoft Windows 95/98, in all its versions, as being insecure. One of the reasons for this is that the operating system has no ability to discriminate between system administrators and general end users. Many other desktop operating systems have this same shortcoming. Anyone who uses one of these computers can change its security environment and can, in fact, turn security off. A few users in an enterprise deciding to turn off security can open the network to attack in some cases. Of course, these operating systems also have many other security weaknesses, even when security is turned on.

KEY POINT

Availability means ensuring that the data can be accessed by all authorized people.

Authorization should extend well beyond discriminating between system administrators and general end users. In a well-secured computer system, each user is assigned a series of corporate roles, typically by the Human Resources department, based on his or her job description. The computers determine exactly what each user is allowed to do, using those roles. This "role-based authorization" allows even system administrators to be limited in their control of the computers. This is frequently used to stop the otherwise powerful administrators from turning off security or auditing and, thus, providing themselves with unreasonable and undetectable power over their employers.

In the Internet world, availability has also taken on an expanded meaning. One of the most common forms of security problem for Internet applications is the "denial of service" (DoS) attack. This is a focused attempt by a cyberattacker to make a computer system and its data unavailable. This can be done in two ways. First, the attacker may try to damage the target computer or some network component on which the computer depends. Second, the attacker may simply send so many messages to the target computer that it cannot possibly process them all. Other people attempting to use that computer for legitimate purposes find that the computer is too busy to service them.

Nonrepudiation

Security is a large enough task just trying to meet the confidentiality-integrity-availability objectives. Technologies used for those objectives are also used to create business-related functions for NR, which allows the formation of binding contracts without any paper being printed for written signatures. NR is new and not broadly used, but most security experts agree that it will be based on digital signatures, which are described in Chapter 13, "Digital Signatures and Electronic Commerce." The use of security-related technologies and the need for a strongly secured and trusted instrument for creating digital signatures have led to NR becoming a new security objective.

NONREPUDIATION BENEFITS

NR has many valuable goals, including assuring that messages came from the person whom the message claims sent it and that the message has not been altered in transit. One of the beneficial side effects to these mechanisms is the ability to prevent users who send messages from denying that they were sent. This has significant value in many business situations.

For example, in a business-to-consumer (B to C) transaction, consumers place orders. Sometimes, they change their minds and decide they don't want what they ordered and will claim that they never ordered merchandise or that the order was not what they requested. NR mechanisms keep consumers honest and protect businesses in these situations.

Another business that benefits significantly from NR is the online auctioning business, where clients of varying integrity and intent exchange merchandise, using the business as a go-between. In this environment, it is mission critical to have mechanisms that keep everyone honest.

WHO IS RESPONSIBLE FOR SECURITY? WHY ME? . . . .

Most business, government, or nonprofit organizations have an IT department. Large organizations have a person or a department devoted to information security. Recently, many organizations have created a Chief Security Officer (CSO) executive position. These internal security people tend to be one of two types. Some of them want to handle all of the security issues themselves. This may result in a comfort level from having a central expert who handles these decisions for you, or it may cause intense anguish because someone who seems unconnected to real business needs is making business decisions.

Security professionals who demand the definition of requirements as the first step in information security populate the second category of CSO. These demands are intimately tied to the business and the people who operate the business. They can be challenging to business people with little understanding of computers or security. Whether you like it or not, these people have the right idea.

Only the smallest groups and federal defense organizations can have a security policy set by a central person or organization without consultation with the business managers. The CSO who tries to dictate security policy to a modern, complex organization inevitably fails. The policy becomes ineffective through active subversion by the peers of the CSO or by passive noncompliance by midlevel management and the employees.

Why is this inevitable? An executive with good intentions trying to protect the computer systems so as to improve confidentiality, integrity, and availability surely ought to be able to work with the rest of the company to everyone's mutual benefit. Security people working in harmony with the rest of the company are critical to success.

RELATIVE SECURITY . . . .

Security is never just "on" because it is relative to your requirements and the time and effort you apply to it. Unfortunately, due to a number of factors, security can actually be off. Once security is being invested in, there are many questions to answer about how much security is enough. Too much security can get in the way of doing business. The amount of security that your organization has is a balancing act between business needs and levels of protection.

Key Point

Security is never just "on." Unfortunately, it may actually be "off."

Security can impact profitability in a positive or negative manner, depending on how it is managed. Improving security to reduce risk may cost money, and as with most of life, the last 20 percent of risks to be eliminated will cost 80 percent of the money. Once basic security needs have been met, it is important to balance risk reduction costs against the potential for loss if security fails. Most business plans contain some allowance for downside risks. Many security-related risks exceed these allowances, but a case-by-case analysis should be done before large security investments are made.

Too Much Security Can Get in the Way of Doing Business

In a typical well-secured company, an access policy may state that any employee granted access to internal computer applications must pass an external security check (such as a search for a criminal record or prior employment problems). But that policy could make it impossible to bring in temporary staff to cover short-term needs. The external security check could take longer than the period of employment. Then is the policy appropriate? For some companies it is. A similar problem arises when the policy requires, for security reasons, that a central department add all computer users.

In some companies, the time to add a new user from the central administration department exceeds the time that the temporary employee will be needed. Instead of re-evaluating these policies and fixing the processes (or technology), many managers design bypass mechanisms that undermine security. A typical bypass to the latter problem is to define a pool of unidentified user accounts on the computer that can be assigned and reassigned locally. Eventually, these accounts become the property of someone who should not have them, and his or her access can neither be audited nor controlled. Security has failed.

Lower security levels result in increased risk to the business. But higher security levels may result in business being hurt. Both business and security managers need to find the appropriate middle ground that provides adequate protection with minimal

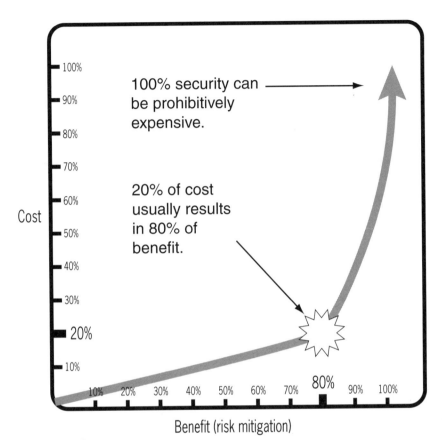

Figure 1–2
Cost/benefit of security.

business impact. Figure 1–2 plots the benefits of security versus the costs of security. As with many business projects, 80 percent of the benefit is derived by 20 percent of the cost. The last 20 percent of the benefit will become much more expensive.

There is no such thing as perfect security. In fact, good security doesn't cost that much, and trying for really high levels of security may be cost-prohibitive.

ORGANIZING SECURITY:
ROLES AND RESPONSIBILITIES . . . .

Making computer systems secure requires a variety of skills. It is common business practice to organize a complex set of tasks along required skills. Unfortunately, many large IT organizations organize around technologies. Computer security, which should be more business oriented than technology driven, is easier to achieve if we follow good business practice.

ADVICE FOR A SMALL BUSINESS

Small companies need to make their computers secure using staff who have a long list of other responsibilities. But it can be useful to understand the various roles involved in securing computers in large companies.

Common computer security-related roles are shown in Table 1–1. A single person may perform multiple roles if they require similar skills.

One of the basic security principles is separation of powers: One group of people or managers should not be allowed both to set the rules and to manage compliance to the rules. If all of the functions listed above were placed with a single person or organization, there would be no separation. Even placing them all within the IT division would be much too close. A few of the roles are easy to see as being fully separated from IT. The internal auditor and the resource owner are the first two to be handed to other managers.

Within IT, it is important that the roles associated with security policy formation (officer and manager) be isolated from those concerned with the deployment of enforcement mechanisms (network and system staff). Two roles, security operator and forensic analyst, are relatively recent additions. As tools for monitoring policy compliance have matured, these roles have developed to operate the tools via security

Table 1–1   Common Security-Related Roles

Role	Critical Skills
Security officer	Executive communications, business negotiation, staffing and budget.
Security manager	Business negotiation, communication with technical staff.
Security operator	Technical system operation, information research and analysis.
User administrator	Administrative skills, customer interface.
Network technician	Technology deployment and management.
System administrator	Technology deployment and management.
Internal auditor	Detailed analysis of business and technology.
Forensic analyst	Detailed investigative analysis of technology.
Resource owner	Understanding the value of the information, the risks that exist in the business environment and the appropriate level of investment in security required to meet business needs. This can never be an IT role.

consoles, to analyze the information that these tools provide, and to enable recovery from successful security attacks.

Fitting all of these roles into an organizational structure results in two common solutions, depending on one outside influence: the government. Some industries are subject to computer security regulations. Health care, financial services, and state and federal agencies need to organize computer security as a parallel organization to IT. Typically, the CSO reports to a regulatory and compliance executive who has a legal background. In other industries, the CSO (sometimes referred to as the Chief Information Security Officer, or CISO) reports to the corporate Chief Information Officer (CIO), in parallel with—and at the same level as—the head of IT.

In organizations that have done a poor job of implementing computer security, there is no CSO or CISO, and computer security functions are handled by technicians buried within the IT organization. This approach to computer security is rapidly waning in publicly traded companies, due to extreme pressure from external auditors and federal government agencies responsible for critical infrastructure protection.

ADVICE FOR A SMALL BUSINESS

Smaller companies do not create "officer"-level positions. In this case, it is important to separate the policy and execution roles as much as possible. Although an IT department—no matter how small—may retain all responsibility for configuring, installing, and maintaining the computer equipment, security policy, which governs many details of those tasks, should be assigned outside of IT.

WHAT DO YOU NEED TO KNOW? . . . .

The absence of a recognized loss due to a computer security failure may help you feel that your computers are comfortably secure. Making your computers secure may, in fact, be very disturbing. When computers are made secure, a common result is the discovery of losses that had been taking place undetected. One company discovered that its email was being routed through a server at one of its competitors. Every business plan, inventory report, and new order had been visible to this company's most significant competitor, and there was no way to know how long it had been going on or who did it. This loss occurred because security had not previously been in place.

Security does not just detect outside hackers. The majority of computer-related losses are caused by insiders, sometimes with malice but often through misunderstandings. When we talk about protecting the confidentiality, integrity, and availability of the information stored in our computers, we do not discriminate between outsiders and insiders. Making an erroneous change to the information needs to be stopped, no matter who is trying to do it. We cannot use technology to force people to type numbers correctly, but we can at least assure that anyone able to type numbers in is fully authorized (and presumably trained).

 KEY POINT

> The majority of computer-related losses are caused by insiders, sometimes with malice but often through misunderstandings.

Companies that focus on protection from outsiders are making a serious error in their security strategy. The most common form of serious attack by an outsider is to pose as an employee. By guessing or stealing an account name and password for any employee, the attacker becomes, to all appearances, just another employee. Security is effective only if it provides oversight of all activities, whether by an outsider or by the most trusted employee of the company.

So how can you know that your computers are secure? Remember that security is relative. There is really not a condition that is totally secure. There are levels of security. So the correct question to ask is, How secure are we? The best answer is "as secure as (or slightly more secure than) other companies like ourselves." Unfortunately, interpreting this answer requires that you know how secure your competitors are.

Most companies treat their security posture as a competitive advantage (or disadvantage) and are reticent to discuss it. That leaves most of us at the mercy of third parties to evaluate our security and decide whether it is sufficient. Many of those third parties are consulting companies that make their money by making the computers more secure, so, surprisingly, they infrequently find that computers are sufficiently protected. Large companies try to use more independent means of finding the right levels of security and get involved in user groups or use technical analyst firms, such as META Group or Burton Group, that have no expectation of profit from setting the bar too high.[1]

THE ROLE OF THE BUSINESS MANAGER ....

Business unit managers have a critical role in computer security. If this is you, then you are the resource owner. The IT staff can never understand how important the information stored in a computer is to the business, because they cannot fully understand the business. Only a business person can judge just how important a set of data is to the business operation. And only a business person can judge the importance of the threats to that data. The people who are involved in security (such as the CSO) and the people who are involved in the technology (IT) can provide the business resource owner with information and guidance. But they should never have to make the final decision. How much security is enough? That depends on the value of the information and the risks. And those are up to you.

The process by which you dictate the appropriate security investment is called *risk assessment*. If you are in a large organization, this is what the CSO is asking you to do. If you are in a small or medium-sized organization, you need to take this bull by the horns yourself. Clearly, assessing the value and risks of information assets is a key business skill in the twenty-first century.

THE NEED FOR POLICY . . . .

Security is not the result of wishful thinking, nor is it the result of well-intentioned technical staff members who believe they know how to secure computers. Because security is relative, it can be achieved only by setting goals to measure it against. Those goals become security policies. More formally, a policy is a guidance statement, endorsed by an executive, which provides clear but flexible guidance for determining technology and operation-specific security standards. Standards are supported by procedures. Chapter 3, "Security Policies," describes the structure and content of security policies, as well as the manner in which they should be determined.

 KEY POINT

> Security is not the result of wishful thinking, nor is it the result of well-intentioned technical staff who believe they know how to secure computers.

ENFORCEMENT TECHNOLOGY . . . .

Figure 1–3 shows how enforcement technology acts as a set of walls and barriers that protect your assets. Although this is a very simple way to describe enforcement, think of it as a shield preventing your assets from being affected by unauthorized activity. Technologies that enforce security are typically implemented within the computing

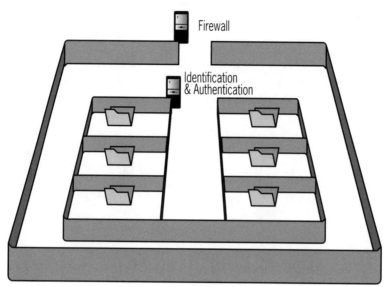

Figure 1–3
Enforcement technology protects business assets with barriers.

infrastructure. They become extensions to the network, server, and desktop computers. Part 2 of this book is dedicated to describing security technologies, including enforcement technologies. Here are some of the terms you will become familiar with:

Access Control. Access control is a generic term for a broad set of security technologies designed to restrict computer access so that only people with permission will be able to use the computer or get to the stored data. In this book, we will use the term *access control* to refer to the control mechanisms that are built into the computer operating systems (such as Microsoft Windows, UNIX, or MVS) by their vendors. Chapter 4, "Authentication, Authorization, Access Control," provides more information on access control.

Identification and Authentication (I&A). These two terms are frequently used interchangeably. Although technicians may wish to quibble, we will discuss all of the technologies that allow us to identify an individual under this heading. There are a lot of different approaches that can be used to identify people. When you type in an account name and a password, you are invoking an I&A system to grant you access to the computer or application. But this category also includes credit-card-sized electronic devices, known as *smart cards*, which can be used to store a stronger equivalent of an account and password combination. This category also includes a set of technologies known as *biometrics*. A computer set up for biometric authentication might allow you access based on your fingerprint, your voice, or simply the way you look. Unfortunately for the moment, you still have 24 passwords to remember. Chapter 4 provides more information on authentication.

Firewalls. A firewall is simply a filter that stops some network traffic from passing through, while allowing others to continue. If your organization is connected to the Internet, you almost certainly already have a firewall. If, for any reason, you suspect that you may not have a firewall, immediately turn to the chapter on firewalls, read it, and take action to correct the situation. A firewall is a mandatory filtering device that provides a minimal but necessary level of protection from Internet-based attacks. Firewalls are also used to isolate areas of a company that have differing security requirements from one another. A research department may have either very high or very low Internet connectivity requirements, depending on the industry being researched. The sales and marketing areas, on the other hand, typically need a moderate degree of access and reasonable security. An internal firewall separating sales from research is an expedient solution to these varying security needs. Chapter 5, "Firewalls," is dedicated to the topic.

Virtual Private Networks (VPNs). Messages traveling between computers can be intercepted and read. They may be altered without the changes being detected. When all of the computers and all of the communication links are inside our own organization, we tend to ignore those risks. When the internal environment becomes less stable or less secure, we may need to make the communications between computers more secure. When our workers start accessing computer systems from outside of our own facilities, we must ensure that communications are well secured. The dramatic increase in telecommuting has driven the use of VPN technology. VPN uses advanced encryption technology to make computer messages unintelligible while they are moving between computers. This also makes them impossible to change or forge without detection. Chapter 10, "Encrypted Communications," provides more information on VPNs.

Public Key Infrastructure (PKI). This is a means of enabling security across large, open systems, such as the Internet, such that users who have never met will be able to develop trust. PKI requires a broadly deployed infrastructure. Unfortunately, the ability to use bits and pieces of PKI from multiple vendors is still a challenge. In a fully realized PKI system, all users are fully identified in a guaranteed manner, and every message they send or application they use is clearly and completely associated with that individual. PKI is designed to scale up to millions of participants. You need to plan for PKI but it is still several years away from being fully realized. PKI is addressed in Chapter 9, "Public Key Infrastructure and Encryption."

Secure Sockets Layer (SSL). SSL is a slightly different subset of the requirements addressed by PKI. SSL is a Web security protocol that encrypts and authenticates Web communications and uses PKI as the basis of authenticating servers and clients. It works primarily with World Wide Web (WWW) servers and is well proven. It comes in multiple flavors, but the simplest implementation (SSL2) is the one most widely used. SSL3 is much more secure, in that both parties involved (the end user and the server) must prove who they are in order to start communicating, but it is much harder to manage. SSL is discussed in Chapter 10.

Single Signon (SSO). Everyone wants to get by with a single password. Every vendor has promised to make it happen. SSO is difficult or impossible because we have so many varied computer systems. Any company that uses only one type of computer can create an SSO environment. Very few companies qualify, due to the history of uncontrolled acquisition of computer systems. One subset of SSO is Web SSO. Because all Web servers are based on some common technology, we can create an SSO capability for all Web-based applications. But this capability is available only if it is designed into the applications. Chapter 12, "Single Signon," provides more information on SSO.

OPERATIONS TECHNOLOGY . . . .

In addition to enforcement technologies, security systems must be administered, monitored, and maintained. Figure 1–4 shows your enterprise with the addition of video cameras to alert you to problems and give you the information necessary to manage those problems.

User Administration. Most organizations use the tools delivered with each type of computer to add user accounts to each computer or to all of the computers of that type. In large organizations, that may result in hundreds of actions needed to add or delete the accounts associated with a single employee. Many organizations, lacking a central control mechanism, simply leave accounts in place after an employee has left the company. This results in a huge security risk. Some employees are unhappy when they leave. Others become unhappy after they leave. Former employees pay little attention to keeping information, such as passwords, secret.

Intrusion Detection. It sounds obvious that, if you are not looking for intruders, you are unlikely to see any that trespass on your computer systems. Unfortunately, most computer security failures remain undetected for long periods of time—some forever. Intrusion detection tools let you know when something suspicious is going on. Chapter 8, "Intrusion Detection," addresses intrusion detection.

Vulnerability Scanners. Any computer can be configured to secure or insecure. Simple changes while a computer is in production may compromise the security of the computer unintentionally (or intentionally). Scanners investigate the configuration of your computers and tell you whether any security holes have been opened. Chapter 6, "Vulnerability Scanners," provides more information on vulnerability scanners.

Virus Controls. A virus is a computer program that was designed to (1) move rapidly into many computers and (2) typically do some damage. The rapid movement

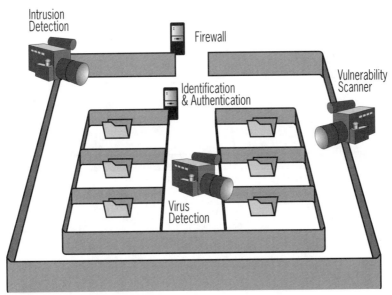

Figure 1–4
Operations technology helps monitor and administer your network.

from one computer to many of the computers to which one is connected is the behavior that caused these programs to be compared with viruses. The damage they do
may vary from trivial to very serious. Controlling them requires a multipart antivirus
strategy. Virus scanners are discussed in Chapter 7, "Virus Detection and Content
Filters."

SECURITY SERVICES . . . .

Finding and keeping qualified staff to manage computer security is difficult. If done
carefully, many security tasks can be outsourced to service providers. In any case,
people are an important component in information security. Figure 1–5 completes the
simple security picture by adding people to enforcement and monitoring. Part 3 of
this book, "Implementation," describes these services in detail.

    Risk Assessment. Estimating the value of your information assets and the risks
they are exposed to is part of your job. But it really is an ongoing process, and it requires that some IT security staff be devoted to working with the business community
to maintain the risk assessments. An outside organization can supply short-term or
continuous assistance to the IT security team in the form of consultants to work with
business leaders such as you to create and maintain those assessments. Please note

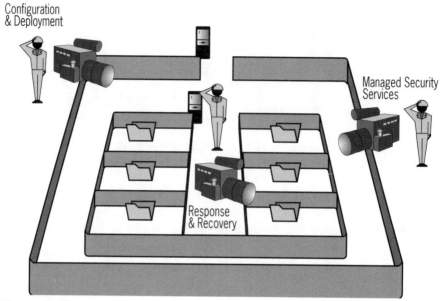

Figure 1–5
Enforcement, monitoring, and people protect your enterprise.

that if you are in financial services or health care, you are required by regulation to maintain a current risk assessment. Chapter 15, "Security Assessments," addresses risk assessments.

Architecture. Understanding all of the technology options for security can be daunting. An outside consultant who has expertise in security architecture can help build the base document that is used by your IT and application development teams to create secure computer systems.

Configuration and Deployment. Installing and configuring security software can be a large job. If IT staff is not available, much of the work can be outsourced to a systems integrator with security experience.

Managed Security Services. Once security software is installed and operating, someone needs to operate it. Console (control room) operations frequently require 7-day/week, 24-hour/day staffing. Outside organizations can provide that as a service more efficiently than many companies can do it for themselves. Typical managed security services are firewalls, VPNs, and intrusion detection.

Response and Forensics. What do you do after you detect an intruder? In the physical world, one good answer is to call the police. Although we may want to do that for a computer intruder, it is important that we also take immediate actions to limit damage and identify the culprit. Having the plan in place will always be the responsibility of a single person in your company. But an outsourcer may provide the staffing to execute that plan.

Lastly, you will need to use the information in this book to establish a security program within your company. Chapter 14, "Establishing a Security Program," will guide you in creating that program. Like life, security is a process, not a destination. You may believe that you only need to do a few discrete things needed to "secure" your enterprise such as installing a firewall, implementing virus scanning, and training your people. The reality is that enterprises are living, breathing entities that are always changing, as is the danger of a security breach. You will always be working on security and the security program is your guide for on-going improvement.

 *KEY POINT*

Security is a process, not a destination.

SUMMARY . . . .

The four objectives of information security are confidentiality, integrity, availability, and nonrepudiation. Confidentiality is making sure that unauthorized people can't read your sensitive data. Integrity makes sure that unauthorized people can't change your data. Availability means that your computers and data are available when you need them. Finally, nonrepudiation means that you can form a binding contract between parties over a computer link that can't be denied (repudiated) by either party.

A good security officer will endeavor to work with business unit managers to determine security requirements that mesh effectively with business objectives. Policy is created from these requirements and a classification of mission-critical data within the organization. Policy drives implementation, including technology, process, and procedures, to create an effective information security program.

Enforcement technologies include access control, identification, authentication, firewalls, PKI, SSL, SSO, and VPNs. Operations technology includes secure user administration, intrusion detection, vulnerability scanners, and virus controls. Security services include risk assessment, architecture, configuration, deployment, response, and forensics.

Technology is not the most important aspect of computer security, and outside hackers are not as much of a threat as internal misuse. Security is a process, not a destination. Security is relative and effective only when it is balanced with business requirements, cost, and risk mitigation.

ENDNOTE

1. Chris Byrnes, one of the authors of this book, is an analyst for the META Group.

2 Threat Briefing

In this chapter . . .

- A List of Threats Against Which You Should Consider Protecting Yourself

- Return on Investment (ROI) for Security

- Quantifying Risk

The first step in implementing security is to justify it to executive decision makers. You may be that executive decision maker. What elements should you be looking for to know that your security team is addressing issues important to your organization? The ultimate goal of this information is to construct a business case for implementing various types of security in your organization.

Every organization will have slightly different justification needs. The key is to understand the threats that affect your business and be able to quantify the cost, time, and business savings that will be realized by mitigating those threats. A good way to fail is to try to protect against every threat. Another good way to fail is to chase threats made popular by the press, as opposed to analyzing your organization's specific requirements.

CSI/FBI STUDY . . . .

The Computer Security Institute (CSI) conducts a study each year in cooperation with the San Francisco Federal Bureau of Investigation (FBI) Computer Intrusion Squad to quantify losses to computer misuse. The 2001 survey[1] (see Figure 2–1) was based on responses from 538 security practitioners in U.S. corporations, government agencies, financial institutions, and universities. This study should carry considerable weight in your efforts to justify intrusion detection systems in that it quantifies losses and validates the threat through a third-party survey of organizations just like yours.

The study found that 186 respondents were able to quantify their financial losses and reported a total of $377,828,700 in financial losses due to computer misuse. Slightly fewer respondents admitted that financial loss had occurred but that they were unable to quantify it. Over 40 percent reported intrusions by outsiders, and 94 percent reported some form of abuse by insiders. Theft of proprietary information was experienced by 18 percent, but this constituted the highest financial loss. Denial of service (DoS) was detected by 36 percent and financial fraud by 11 percent of the respondents.

It's important to differentiate between the number of respondents and the amount of losses. In most CSI/FBI survey years, losses to insider threats have been over 80 percent of the total losses, even though only 55 percent of all respondents claimed insider misuse. Although there have been continual increases in the number of outsider attacks, the losses are still overwhelmingly attributable to insiders.

Web site and e-commerce attacks were cited as an increasing trend. Ninety-seven percent of respondents have Web sites, of which 23 percent said they had experienced unauthorized access within the last 12 months. Of those who reported

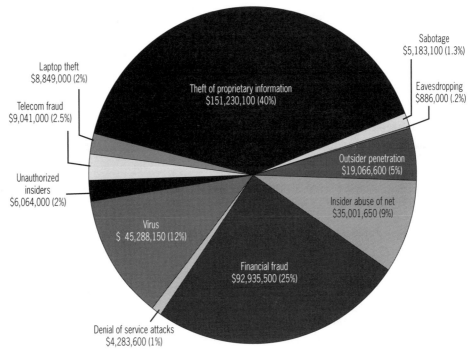

Sabotage
$5,183,100 (1.3%)

Laptop theft
$8,849,000 (2%)

Eavesdropping
$886,000 (.2%)

Theft of proprietary information
$151,230,100 (40%)

Telecom fraud
$9,041,000 (2.5%)

Outsider penetration
$19,066,600 (5%)

Unauthorized
insiders
$6,064,000 (2%)

Insider abuse of net
$35,001,650 (9%)

Virus
$ 45,288,150 (12%)

Financial fraud
$92,935,500 (25%)

Denial of service attacks
$4,283,600 (1%)

Figure 2–1
Breakdown of losses attributable to information security breach.

unauthorized misuse, 21 percent reported 2–5 incidents, and 58 percent reported 10 or more incidents. Twenty-seven percent said they "don't know."

CSI also points out that most people think of hackers as the primary threat to their security. However, it isn't necessary for criminal intent to be involved for serious financial losses to occur. As an example, in 1999, the study cites a report from Net-Partners Internet Solutions, suggesting that employees reading about the Monica Lewinsky scandal on the Internet may have cost companies as much as $500,000,000 in lost productivity. This figure is based on 13,500,000 people downloading the Starr report at work.[2]

The total number of intrusions and the total amount of losses can't be derived from the survey exclusively because it represents only the respondent's experiences. The survey contains significantly more data. One trend is clear: Computer crime and information security breaches pose a growing threat, and the financial cost is tangible and alarming. In preparing your case for intrusion detection, be sure to get the latest copy of this survey.

THREATS . . . .

Fear, uncertainty, and doubt (FUD) are a time-honored tradition in justifying security. Even though unseen threats are not sufficient justification by themselves, understanding threat is an important piece of the puzzle when constructing a business case for security.

Misuse Examples

The following is a list of threats and losses that many organizations suffer. This list was compiled from the authors' experience with actual corporations' actual losses. How many of these scenarios has your company experienced and how many could be mitigated through the use of additional security?

Abuse of Privilege

- An administrator gives unauthorized elevated privileges to a contractor so that the contractor can install an application.
- An ex-employee uses an old account that should have been disabled.
- An administrator creates back-door accounts.
- Privilege is inadvertently propagated as a result of adding new domains.

Mission-Critical Data Access and Modification

- An employee changes his/her performance evaluation.
- The pricing page on the Web site is modified.
- The message of the day is modified.
- A maintenance foreman embellishes activity records.
- A contractor gains access to preliminary proposal evaluation results.
- A project manager accesses a contracting officer's competitive bid data.
- Medical records are stolen.
- A hacker clears the security event log.
- The home page on the Web site is modified with hate messages.

Changes in Security Configuration

- Users disable locking screensavers.
- The legal notice text is modified, welcoming hackers into your system.
- A new system is deployed with guest account enabled.
- Systems are hastily rebuilt with the registry open to the network.
- Users with laptops connect to the network with compromised systems.
- Anonymous users browse critical files.

Attempts to Gain Access

- Brute force login via modems.
- Terminated employee attempts to log in using expired accounts.
- After-hours login attempts by regular employees.
- Successful logins at strange hours.

Insider Threats

Insiders are individuals with trusted relationships. This includes everyone with authorized access to your network. Access means both physical access to computers and logon access, so insiders include everyone from the CEO to the janitor.

Government has long understood the threat of malicious insiders, and industry is beginning to feel the effect of insiders through industrial espionage. In June 1998, Booz, Allen, and Hamilton hosted a National Security Information Exchange (NSIE) workshop on insider misuse. The U.S. government and the National Security Telecommunications Advisory Committee (NSTAC) sponsored the event. Information on this conference may be found in the June 1999 paper, "NSTAC Network Group Report."[3] The objective of the workshop was to increase the understanding of the complexities involved with the insider threat issue and to offer strategies and best practices for organizations making plans to address the threat.

The NSIE workshops were established to identify what actions should be taken on the part of the government and industry to protect critical national security telecommunications from the threat of computer intruders. Government member organizations include departments and organizations that are major telecommunications users, represent law enforcement, or have information regarding the network security threat. Industry member organizations include telecommunications providers, equipment vendors, system integrators, and major users. The workshop defined six basic categories of malicious insider, each with its own motivation:

Disgruntled Employees. These people feel that they have been mistreated in some fashion. They may have been passed over for promotion or believe that they are underpaid or discriminated against in some manner. They are motivated by revenge.

Paid Informants. These are industrial spies, information brokers, criminal organizations, or intelligence services. Stolen data can range from unpublished phone numbers to personal information stolen from computers. These people are motivated by financial gain. They are growing in number as a result of cultural changes: the reduction in employee loyalty and the increased focus on personal gain.

Compromised or Coerced Employees. Employees may be coerced by past experiences or personal connections, such as threats to themselves or family members. Coerced employees act as agents for criminal or terrorist organizations seeking information. They are motivated by fear.

Former Employees. Former employees sometimes retain their access to their old employer's systems. They already understand the security system and its vulnerabilities. They also maintain relationships with former co-workers that can lead to additional insights about how and where to attack. Money or revenge can motivate former employees.

"Pseudo-Employees." Corporations have long relied on temporary work forces, including outsourcers and contractors. These people usually have all the access and privileges as real employees, without the same obligations and scrutiny. Revenge, money, or fear can motivate pseudo-employees.

Business Associates. Customers and partnerships with other companies result in an entirely new concept of "insider." As the Internet advances, more companies are working to extend their e-commerce sites as far as possible into customer homes. This is commonly called business to consumer (B to C). Also, as businesses expand, they expand their networks into areas such as supply chain management, which places their networks together with suppliers who also use their competitor's networks. This is known as business to business (B to B). In both cases, there are numerous opportunities for insiders to take advantage.

Several factors have increased the insider problem. Cooperation between traditionally competitive businesses has increased the likelihood that you will also have competitors with authorized access to your systems. This practice has led to another industry buzzword—*co-opetition*. Outsourcing has also resulted in an increased number of non- or pseudo-employees who have access to your network. E-commerce has put the customer straight into your network through the Internet.

The traditional network boundaries separating the insider from the outsider are starting to blur, increasing the list of potential insiders. The following is a short list of potential insiders. How many of these have access to your network?

- Employees
- Contractors
- Business partners
- Competitors (on contract teams)
- Customers (through the Web)
- Janitors (by walking into a locked office)

Hacker Threats

A hacker is someone with the technical knowledge to surpass the barriers you have put into your computer network (firewalls, intrusion detection, and so on) to be able to log in to computers without authorization and gain privileges that give them access to sensitive information. Hacker threats are real. However, the press feeding-frenzy that has romanticized the likes of Kevin Mitnick has left organizations with an inappropriate perception of just how bad the problem has become.

INSIDER CASE

"Ex-employee nabbed in $10M hack attack"

Company: Omega Engineering, New Jersey

Date: February, 1998

"A fired engineer doubling as his company's network administrator acted out corporate America's worst security nightmare when he allegedly launched a logic bomb that wiped out all the firm's software, inflicting $10M in damages."[4]

The specifics in this attack include the following:

- Timothy Lloyd, the fired engineer, was the network administrator while employed.
- Lloyd had all the privileges to make network additions, deletions, and changes.
- He used his privileges to embed a logic bomb.
- Omega had audit trails.
- The audit trails led back to Lloyd.

In reality, any hacker good enough to break through a nominal defense (reasonably configured firewall, good policy, and monitoring) is not a real threat to your organization. There aren't that many good hackers out there, and the really good ones are doing it for the excitement—not the profit. There are much easier ways to get information if you really want it. There are three basic types of hackers: script kiddies, serious hackers, and information merchants.

Script Kiddies

Script kiddie is the term given to hackers who use the veritable plethora of automated attack tools available on the Internet. These tools (known as scripts) usually exploit a number of common vulnerabilities in computer systems to give their users unauthorized access and privilege.

A script kiddie is usually characterized by his or her lack of knowledge of the underlying mechanisms of exploitation and the vulnerabilities that are being exploited. This lack of knowledge means that the script kiddies are usually unsuccessful; however, it also means that they do not understand the damage that can occur when they do succeed. This makes a script kiddie somewhere between an annoyance and a serious danger.

Script kiddies are the lowest form of hacker, and there are millions of them. They are best defended against by keeping your computer systems up to date with the latest patches and using monitoring (intrusion detection) to detect their presence.

White-Hat Hackers

A serious hacker is someone who understands the underlying mechanisms of the computer system and the vulnerabilities they are exploiting. A serious hacker attacks computers by hand and does not use scripts, so that he or she can overlap techniques and break through even the most sophisticated defense mechanisms.

Hackers obviously have a wide range of skill levels. Luckily, the most intelligent are usually "white-hat hackers," which means they have all the skills but they use them to help companies become more secure or to expose vulnerabilities so that they can be fixed. The reason for this phenomenon is that, to become the very best, you have to immerse yourself in the art, and you begin to understand the implications of what you are doing. You also begin to realize that there is considerably more profit in using your skills to secure organizations than there is in breaking the law and bragging about it.

Hackers and Their "Benign" Intentions

Whenever you read about the prosecution of a hacker in the press, you will almost inevitably read one of two excuses from the accused. Either the hacker was "just having fun to see how far he could get into an organization," or he or she was attempting to "help" the target organization by showing them where their security vulnerabilities existed. In any case, the hackers insist they "never meant any harm."

At a recent security conference, in a session focused on hackers and their intentions, there was a particularly heated exchange between two participants regarding the harm hackers can do, regardless of their intentions. One of the participants was a hacker on a panel, essentially making the arguments above. The other was a person who had a family member in the hospital with a heart condition. The point was that hackers could inadvertently alter data relating to prescriptions or care, resulting in someone with a critical condition receiving a medication that could kill him or her, or affect life-sustaining machinery hooked into the hospital's computer system.

Considering that most "hackers" are basically kids looking for the thrill of breaking into computers, it is easy to understand that they may do inadvertent harm because they have no vested interest in the organizations they break into. Whereas the heart patient has his or her life at stake; small mistakes can have disastrous consequences. There is no such thing as "I never meant any harm" when it comes to breaking into someone else's information.

Black-Hat Hackers and Information Merchants

There is a class of hackers who lack a social conscience and either don't care about the profit motive or decide to ply their skills in a blatantly illegal manner for profit. These comprise a very small group of hackers known as *black-hat hackers*. Many of these "black hats" spend days hacking to break into organizations and steal information—not for profit but for social status within their peer groups.

The most dangerous group of all is a subgroup of the black hats that steal information for blackmail or hire. These hackers are known as *information merchants*. This is the group you need to fear the most; however, to fall victim to this group, you have to be targeted. If you are targeted, your perimeter defenses are only a small part of the protection measures you will need. These people will use dumpster diving, social engineering, and even taking a job as a system administrator (SysAdmin) at your company to get information.

Hacker Conferences

Hacker conferences are events where hackers of all types and skill levels get together to exchange information. The best publicized of these is DefCon, held in Las Vegas each year, where several thousand hackers meet. These are mostly social events where script kiddies get to exchange the latest scripts and the serious hackers get to brag to each other about their latest conquests. They run hacking contests and sell a variety of paraphernalia, from black boxes for unscrambling cable signals to T-shirts touting their presence at the event. There are also workshops held on how to write hacking tools and exploit vulnerabilities.

Individuals on your staff may want to attend these events in hopes of gleaning useful information about the security risks. You should send only your most technical people associated with security. Many of the workshops have value, but they are usually technical details on exploiting a vulnerability that can be fixed with a simple patch from the vendor or a hacking technique for which there is no defense except staff training and good policy.

Social Engineering

Social engineering is a technique whereby individuals can gain access to your computers by talking staff members into giving them the information directly or providing access codes to your computers.

One of the perennial examples of social engineering is calling one of the least technical people in your company and pretending to be a system administrator. The attacker explains that he or she needs to do a password reset on the victim's computer but the victim will need to give the "administrator" the victim's current password. Most people (believe it or not) give the attacker the password without a second thought, at which time the attacker says that the victim will receive an email with a new password later that day. The email never comes, and the nontechnical victim never gives it another thought.

Social engineering is an insidious threat and can be countered only with a good security awareness program and good policy that prevents these types of attacks.

Network Vulnerabilities

Network vulnerabilities are either flaws in configuration or flaws in software that make it possible for individuals to access information or gain unauthorized privilege. Most of these vulnerabilities have fixes (patches) available so that your organization is no longer subject to the vulnerability. Vulnerabilities do not cause loss for your organization unless someone intending you harm exploits them, such as hackers (see above). The only way to keep up on these vulnerabilities is to subscribe to one or more of the many services that track vulnerabilities and to keep your operating systems up to date with the latest patches.

There are tools available to help you determine how vulnerable you are. Known as *scanners*, these tools will "attack" your computers from a central location, then list all the attacks that were successful. These tools have advantages and disadvantages. For more information, see Chapter 6, "Vulnerability Scanners."

Loss of Brand Equity

In a meeting with a security officer from one of the world's largest banks, the topic of internal misuse versus external threats came up. He agreed that his bank lost millions each year to internal embezzlement, but the bank still wanted to focus its security solutions on the external threat. He explained that, although an individual may get away with over $10 million, this was peanuts compared with what the bank would lose if the bank lost credibility in its ability to protect its assets. He explained that the bank believed that its customers were more concerned about external threats because they knew nothing about the internal losses. Internal losses are never published and, in effect, never happen, as far as the public is concerned.

One of a company's greatest assets is its credibility. This is known as *brand equity*, the measure of a customer's faith in a company. It is one of the most valuable assets that a company has, and it can be damaged severely by incidents that shake customer faith.

· ·

 *KEY POINT*

> One of a company's greatest assets is its credibility or brand equity.

Information security incidents can result in the loss of credibility and brand equity. Even though 80 percent of losses are attributable to internal misuse, most people are only familiar with threats from "hackers" and other outside threats popularized by the press. Companies must protect against the well-known external threat to protect brand equity, even though the real losses are internal.

Brand equity is one of the key reasons that a security professional will never release the name of a client. Just the fact that a company has engaged a security consultant may affect the public's perception of the company's credibility. However, in the last few years, this effect has almost reversed. As the public becomes more aware of information security issues, the public favorably perceives companies engaging security experts. This can actually raise the trust in a company's credibility. As the public perception changes about internal versus external threats, we will see a reversal of company focus.

Graffiti (Web Site Defacing)

Organizations that offer e-commerce or Web sites should be particularly concerned with a class of attacks that involves changing Web site information. Graffiti attacks are relatively easy to launch, because most Web sites are poorly protected. Firewalls allow external access because most Web sites are designed to support use from the Internet. Most Web site graffiti attacks use this "normal" access path to compromise the Web server and allow unlimited access to server resources (see Figure 2–2). Any Web site secured by the network services department is subject to compromise. Network staff do not know how to secure system or application-level constructs. Virtually all graffiti compromises result from assigning security responsibility to the network staff.

Denial of Service

DoS attacks are named because they result in a resource not being available to "service" its users. For example, when disks fill up, the service of storing data is denied. When CPUs slow down, the service of timely processing is denied. When an account is locked out, all the services of a computer are denied to the locked-out individual. When computers crash, all the services associated with the computer are denied to all users.

DoS attacks come in many flavors and at different levels of severity. Most of us have experienced minor annoyance at a slow network. One of the most well-known and severe cases of denial of service was when amazon.com, E-trade, and other e-commerce pioneers were shut down by a distributed DoS in February 2000. The damage estimates range from a few hundred thousand to several million dollars for each site.

Insiders can cause DoS attacks, as well as outsiders, but these types of attacks usually leave many clues, so malicious DoS attacks are usually initiated by anonymous outsiders. This is why network intrusion detection is so effective at detecting these attacks. The packets that deliver the attack usually carry many telltale character-

Figure 2–2
A Web site that has been attacked and defaced.

istics that can be detected with network intrusion detection. Many times, the attacks span multiple days and effectively shut down all business for their targets during the attack.

Malformed Packets

Most DoS attacks come in the form of dummy transaction requests that overload the target server with counterfeit work requests. Another form of DoS attack attempts to destroy the target system. Malformed packets come in a variety of shapes and sizes, with the intent of causing a protocol stack to crash. Network protocols are complicated pieces of code, and it's difficult to handle all the different types of error conditions that can arise. In most cases, programmers do not attempt to handle impossible situations, such as null arguments in critical fields. Hackers take advantage of this by creating these very situations, causing the protocol to fail. Results range from hung networking to machines that crash. There are a number of DoS tools available on the Internet that use this technique. These go by names such as *land, bonk*, and *boink*.

Packet Flooding

Packet flooding is a simple DoS technique that involves sending as many packets as you can at a single network device until it either crashes because it can't handle the load or becomes so slow that legitimate user requests can't get through. This is not a very sophisticated attack, and it is fairly easy to detect and defend against by denying access to the source computer sending the packets. However, if the attacker is spoofing the source address, it may be very hard to find out where the packets are originating.

Distributed Denial of Service

A special case of packet flooding is the distributed denial of service attack in which a number of computers are used to attack all at once. If the source IP addresses are spoofed, it can be difficult to both shun and defend against. Network intrusion detection is not a panacea against this attack, but it is a vital tool in both detection and response.

SECURITY AND RETURN ON INVESTMENT . . . .

Most organizations think of security as an insurance policy. In reality, security can be an enabler of business. Although this may seem like a buzzword-compliant, content-free statement, let's examine it a little closer. Security provides credibility and improves brand equity.

Return on investment (ROI) implies that you will invest X amount of dollars to implement security and get some multiple of X dollars back in the course of conducting business. How does security help us do things better, faster, or with more quality? More importantly, how can we quantify those advantages to represent an ROI?

A good security program provides many ways to save money. It allows you to focus limited resources on actual, measurable threats. It helps to balance the workload across systems and people. It reduces the time and effort necessary to deploy and maintain consistent policies across the enterprise. It significantly reduces the time and resources necessary to assess the extent of compromise after a security incident. All of these advantages add up to saved time and money for your company, in addition to reduced risk.

Quantifying Risk

Classic risk assessment is a process that quantifies potential losses. In building your business case for security, it is vital that you show an ROI. Quantitative risk assessment allows you to put dollar figures on potential losses to justify the costs of implementing a security system.

Dr. Stan Kaplan of Bayesian Systems, Inc. is very well known in the field of risk analysis. In his article "Words of Risk Analysis,"[5] Dr. Kaplan defined *risk* with three questions: 1) What can happen?, 2) How likely is it?, and 3) What are the consequences? Answering these simple questions helps to quantify risks.

James A. Cooper defines *risk analysis* as "a technique for quantitative assessment of relative values of protective measures."[6] Cooper defines annual loss expectancy (*ALE*) as projected costs for identified risks. First, assets are identified and valued. Next, the expected value *e* is equal to the probability of loss of the asset per year times the value *v*.

$$ALE = e = p \bullet v$$

There are nine steps in Cooper's risk analysis methodology:

1. Identify and value assets.
2. Identify threats. (Kaplan's What can happen?)
3. Identify vulnerabilities. (How can threats be realized?)
4. Estimate risks. (What is the probability of realizing a threat?)
5. Calculate ALE for each vulnerability. (What is the statistically expected loss?)
6. Identify protective measures.
7. Estimate ALE reductions for each vulnerability due to each protective measure.
8. Select cost-effective protective measures.
9. Respond to experience by modifying protective measures, by recovering from disasters, and by prosecuting transgressors.

Risk assessments are a black art. However, risk assessments are a valuable tool to make a business case. Although it may not be possible for you to do a comprehensive risk assessment of your network (some have suggested that it's not possible, anyway), do not discount the power of showing selected examples of risk mitigation with ALE calculations. It will show that you've done your homework and have thought the problem through. Also, listing your risks is necessary for your requirements analysis in any case.

Quantifying risk is one of the best ways to convince management to spend money on security. Unfortunately, protection against unseen adversaries does not make a great business case by itself. Assessments of different types are further covered in Chapter 15, "Security Assessments."

SUMMARY

You need a strong business case to justify security to executive decision makers. This business case is constructed from multiple elements, including the following:

A Threat Briefing. The FUD principle is a time-honored tradition in information security. Presenting a threat briefing as part of your justification will help you to explain the threats that a security system will counter. Just when you thought it was safe to go back in the water…

Quantifying Risk. Traditional risk assessment helps us to quantify threats into actual money losses. This section provides a thumbnail sketch of one risk assessment process for use in a business case analysis for security.

ENDNOTES

1. CSI/FBI Computer Crime and Security Survey 2001, www.gocsi.com.
2. Ibid.
3. www.ncs.gov/nstac/NSTACXXII/Reports/NSTAC22-NG.pdf
4. *Computerworld*, February 23, 1998;32(8):6.
5. Kaplan, Stan, "The Words of Risk Analysis," *Risk Analysis*, 1997;17(4).
6. Cooper, James A. *Computer and Communications Security: Strategies for the 1990s*, New York: McGraw Hill; 1989.

3 Security Policies

In this chapter . . .

- Why Policies Are Important

- How One Policy May Not Work for Everyone

- What You Need to Include in Policies

- What a Security Policy Looks Like

- How Policies Are Applied and Enforced

- Who Is Responsible for Security Policies

Many security professionals began their careers in technology-related positions. This frequently leads to an overestimation of the role of technology in computer security. Technology is necessary but it meets only some security requirements. Information security consists of many things other than technology. In fact, by most measures, only around 30 percent of security is covered by technology. The single most important nontechnical subject in computer security is security policy.

NONTECHNOLOGY-RELATED SECURITY TOPICS . . . .

It's important that you understand the role and relative importance of technology in security. Much of this book focuses on technology, rather than nontechnology-related aspects of security, for two reasons. First, many relevant nontechnology topics are concepts that you already understand, such as the need to set requirements relevant to your own business. We'll touch on many of these aspects and explain how your current knowledge can be applied to computer security. Second, the details of some of these nontechnical topics require a book of their own. We'll settle for providing a level of practical knowledge that you will need to understand and that will contribute to the creation of a secure computing environment.

BUSINESS POLICY . . . .

Every business has policies by which it operates. In small organizations, many of those policies may be unwritten and informal. Larger organizations cannot rely on peer influence or corporate culture to control behavior, so policies become more formal. Most businesses design policies so that the people they impact easily understand them. The policy may describe the way in which the organization meets a goal or may forbid some activities or approaches to handling business activity.

KEY POINT

The single most important nontechnical subject in computer security is security policy.

In regulated industries, policies may show how the organization interprets a legal requirement. Virtually all organizations have some set of human resource (personnel) policies. These describe appropriate behavior by both management and non-management staff to ensure that legal restrictions are met and that people are treated fairly. In other words, policies often exist to stop inappropriate behavior.

Security policies are a special case of business policies. They follow the same rules and perform the same function. Security policies document how your organization will create a secure business environment by minimizing the risks associated with using computers. Most security policies are about human behavior.

WHY ARE POLICIES IMPORTANT? . . . .

It is possible to install and configure computers and apply technology-based solutions to security problems without developing any security policies in advance. You may even end up with a secure environment. This is not recommended. In many organizations, the network technical staff selects, configures, and deploys most of the security technology. If you ask the firewall technician whether policy applies to him or her, the answer would probably be no. But some of the most common security failures result from firewall misconfiguration. This is not because the network staff is incompetent or poorly trained. It is far more likely that, in trying to respond to the needs of the business, the network staff will configure the firewall in ways that inadvertently open security holes. Many of these mistakes can be averted with clear policy statements.

Clear policy statements about what traffic may and may not be allowed through various firewalls provide the network staff with a benchmark that allows them to rapidly identify the configuration options that create security weakness. This benchmark also provides network staff with the ammunition they need when they should say no to a request to open the firewall in new ways. Technicians should never be required to make judgments about what is or is not appropriate for the business. Someone who has an understanding of the business, as well as the level of security needed by the business, must make those decisions. That is the role of the security officer. Security policy is how we document those decisions.

 KEY POINT

It is the security officer's role to understand the business, as well as the level of security needed by the business, and it is the security officer who must make those decisions. Security policy is how we document those decisions.

HOW CAN ONE POLICY WORK FOR EVERYONE? . . . .

The alternative is to view the organization as a set of isolated business units, each with its own security requirement. Rather than treat the units as being on a common network, we look for ways to isolate each unit, to the degree appropriate, from the central network and from one another. Once the business units are isolated via filtering routers, network topology, or internal firewalls, each business unit can operate by somewhat different rules (policies) without changing the risk profiles of other units.

This approach to policy formation can quickly get out of hand if every business unit claims to be unique. A better approach is to establish broad levels of security, then to classify each business unit into one of the levels. Policies for all units within a level will be consistent. We refer to the group of business units with similar security requirements as a *security domain*.

Some policies will be consistent across all business units within an organization. Typically, these have to do with the philosophy or culture of the organization. A policy specifying activities that constitute appropriate use of computers is one example. Your company might decide that minimal usage of company computers for non-business uses is acceptable. Examples of such uses might be personal email,

 ADVICE FOR A LARGE ENTERPRISE

In many cases, no one policy works for everyone. Larger organizations frequently find that the degree of security needed by different business units varies widely. Security costs time and money. A business unit that can absorb risk should be able to operate with a lower security investment than a more sensitive business unit. If both business units are connected to the same corporate network, any weakness in the low security unit will be a threat to the high security unit. If one security policy applies equally to everyone, all business units must invest in security to the level required by the unit with the highest security requirement. Higher levels of security cost more. Setting the level of security across the entire organization to meet the highest requirements drives the cost of security too high for most organizations. The solution can be the use of policy groups (see Figure 3–1).

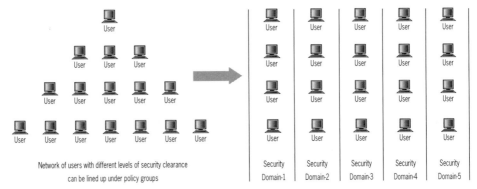

Figure 3-1
Disparate organizations can be lined up under policy groups.

calendars, and small databases. The policy could specify that such uses must take place during work breaks or outside of work hours. This type of policy should be consistent across all business units.

Another consistent policy might be one that defines the method of doing a risk assessment. Risk assessment is the process by which a business unit identifies the impact of potential security failures. Managers within the business unit, working with guidance from the security officer, determine business impact, which is then used to decide on appropriate steps to take to ensure security. The method for measuring risk should be the same across the organization. Additional information on risk assessment can be found in Chapter 15, "Security Assessments."

Policy that determines when risk assessments will be performed may vary among business units. The policies that determine which risks require additional investment in security and what those investments might be are specific to the business unit. This arrangement of central and local policies is referred to as a *policy structure*. To build a policy structure, you will:

- Collect the central, common policies into a base policy document.
- Produce an outline of the policies that will be needed in each security domain.
- Negotiate with the business managers so that the details of the policies will be specific within that domain.
- Present the threats and the cost and impact of various mitigation approaches. This may require the assistance of a knowledgeable security officer.
- Create a risk assessment and a set of requirements that reflect the business response to the threats. The business manager may create this.

Negotiated policy statements are the solution to balancing security requirements that reduces risk against both required investment (costs) and the potential business impacts on the business. Business people and security people have to work together for effective security.

KEY POINT

> One incorrect act can open the company to severe damage from loss of confidentiality or integrity.

POLICY GUIDANCE . . . .

Policies dictate when a security technology must be used in order to protect computer data. They also dictate the IT processes that will be used to manage and maintain a secure computing environment. The most important thing dictated by security policies is the behavior of people within the company who use the computers. Computer security is never perfect, but even if we had the ability to perfectly protect the information held in our computers, people would be able circumvent all of the protections.

By specifying security-related behavior in policies, we tell people what we expect of them. If we do not provide that guidance, we should not expect our employees to consistently act correctly. One incorrect act can open the company to severe damage from loss of confidentiality or integrity. Moreover, if we provide no guidance, we have little recourse against deliberate acts to undermine security.

There are many areas subject to either central or negotiated policy controls. Some of the more important areas include secure communications, isolation infrastructure, identity infrastructure, permission infrastructure, configuration management, user management, threat management, conformance monitoring, and application architecture.

Secure Communications Policy

One of the clear and present dangers to information security is the unauthorized disclosure of sensitive information as it is transferred between computers—on internal computers and the Internet. There are conditions under which you should protect all of your data while it is moved between computers:

- You will probably want to hide everything before it is passed over the Internet. There are some types of data that should be protected, even if the movement is between two computers inside your company headquarters.
- Your patent or prepublication financials might need to be protected as the data is moved. There are some activities that should never be undertaken unless the communications involved are highly secure.
- SysAdmin functions typically need strong protection.

For all of these cases, you should have a secure communications policy that indicates the conditions under which communications should be protected.

Your policy may limit the ways in which employees can access some information, so it may have behavioral or even work efficiency implications. If you require that company email be encrypted when it is accessed via the Internet, you may be stopping some employees from working from home. Or you may be dictating expensive changes in your email system that the IT team will find difficult to implement. That does not *necessarily* make the policy wrong, but it does mean that the implications have to be well understood before the policy is published.

Isolation Infrastructure Policy

You need to isolate your internal network from the Internet, while still allowing acceptable business transactions to take place. The tool commonly used to achieve this is a firewall. Large companies now divide their internal networks into segments, using additional firewalls. A standard connection to the Internet that allows e-commerce transactions may use four to six separate firewall functions (interfaces), although they may all be contained in a single firewall computer. A company that performs a lot of e-commerce may have a "server farm,"[1] with many application server computers protected from inappropriate access from the Internet by a complex of dozens of firewalls.

Individual computers that might be considered high risk, either due to their connection to insecure networks or due to the critical nature of the data that they store, can be isolated using a "personal firewall." Figure 3–2 shows a possible large corporation isolation design.

In the figure, each of four business operations has been isolated from the rest of the company. This diagram assumes that these four functions do not share any server-based applications except those that have been located on computers in the Web server area. The Web server in this diagram would be considered to be in a "DMZ" network segment, because it is accessed from the Internet and internal systems but is

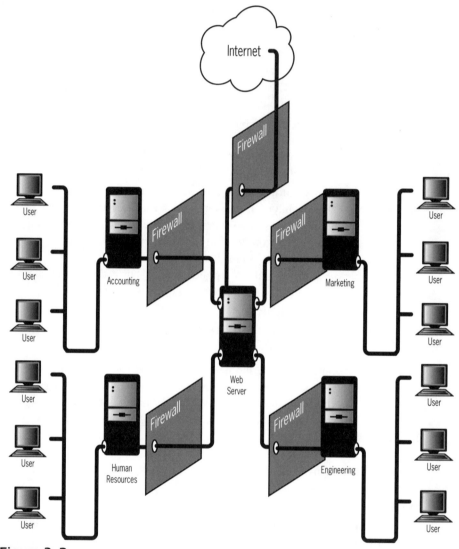

Figure 3–2
Isolation policy governs the separation of groups from each other and the
enterprise from the Internet.

isolated from everything by firewalls. More information about using firewalls and
constructing a DMZ is contained in Chapter 5, "Firewalls," and Chapter 18, "Implementing Web and Internet Security."

A firewall should never be installed without business specific configuration. The
configuration of a firewall is critical to its success. Misconfigured firewalls are use-

less. They allow penetration by hackers with little or no effort. The placement and configuration of firewalls must be dictated by policy. This security policy sets a basic level of protection that must not be compromised. Shifting business needs can cause demands for firewall reconfiguration. IT staff members need the policy to tell them when (and why) they must say no to some business requests in order to protect the rest of the business units.

KEY POINT

The configuration of a firewall is critical to its success. Poorly configured firewalls are useless.

Identity Infrastructure Policy

Many organizations built their computer networks from many different generations of hardware and software. Frequently, different groups within the company acquired and managed those computers. Now the same computers have been connected to a corporate network and are being accessed by many employees. In some companies, a typical employee may have 10–20 passwords. The passwords change on different schedules, and each has different rules about its formation.

It seems obvious that an identity policy would immediately fix this problem by dictating a common structure for user account names, password formation, and

When employees want to use a computer, they identify themselves to the computer or network. The most common way of doing this is to type in a user account name and a password. The simplest identity policy dictates that everyone must use a unique account name and a reasonably long password to get access to computer facilities. System administrators have very powerful rights once they have identified themselves to the computer. A typical identity policy will have special conditions for system administrators. Many passwords are easily guessed, so a good policy will require that certain rules be followed in password length and structure. Passwords are easily compromised, so frequent changes of password should be required.

password change cycles. Unfortunately, most companies find it difficult to make the changes. A combination of inertia, local control issues, computer system short-comings, and the cost of change make this sensible policy unachievable for many companies.

New technologies require new policies. Many organizations are developing all new applications and are redeveloping the user interface of older applications, using a browser front end to a Web server application host. An identity policy that covers only new application development could specify that all identity information must be held and processed in a standard manner so that, at least, the password proliferation prob-lem will not get worse. Without such a policy, application developers will continue to build identity management into the application logic, and this problem will remain unsolved.

Permission Infrastructure Policy

Most computers have a built-in ability to control access to the applications installed on them. Employees identify themselves via account names and passwords, and the computer system allows them to access only the applications and data that have been assigned to them. Each computer has its own list of who can do what. In a complex environment with hundreds of computers, each computer has to be managed in its own way. In a large Web farm with hundreds of servers and hundreds of applications, the task is virtually impossible.

One company that the authors have assisted studied its top 10 applications to see where the application maintenance costs were highest. They found that 14 pro-grammers were dedicated to maintaining permission tables and code for those appli-cations. Setting a common policy and moving those 10 applications to centralized permission management allowed 10 of those 14 programmers to be reassigned to new application development. In Web application development, a common permission policy allows the application to scale more easily at significantly lower cost. Without policy application, developers continue to build solutions into the application logic.

Configuration Management Policy

The term *Configuration Management* (CM) is used in a number of different ways within IT. For security policy, CM refers to two policies, dictating:

1. The setting of some operating system parameters in servers and work-stations that are required to make those computers secure.
2. The restriction of changes to applications (and Web site content) to only those that have been tested, documented, and approved.

Having a policy that dictates the security configuration settings of servers and workstations is similar to the need for an isolation, or firewall, policy. Without it, the entire company is subject to the lowest security environment in the company. Any one misconfigured server will provide illicit access to the entire company.

Maintaining control of application configuration is equally necessary. Simple changes to an application program can open severe security holes. If there is no control over which changes are made and no record of what changes are made when, there can be no consistent security. There are many reasons other than security that can cause a business to need to maintain control over application changes.

User Management Policy

A policy for identity infrastructure is a good start. But as long as social engineering techniques can be used to acquire a valid account and password, all the security in the world becomes useless. A very clear and detailed policy should dictate how an employee becomes authorized to use the computer systems and which systems he or she can use. Exception conditions with escalated management approvals should be included.

The user management policy should be extended with a clearly defined process definition. As with most other processes, this process should be audited on a regular basis.

Threat Management and Monitoring Policy

If you install all the right security technology pieces, define and execute perfect processes, and get everyone in the organization to behave according to security policies, a residual threat still remains. In most cases, imperfections in technology alone leave very significant holes, and insiders can always threaten an enterprise. A threat management and monitoring policy can help to deal with this residual threat.

A typical threat management and monitoring policy specifies how to identify and counter the threats that cannot be completely prevented. Technologies such as vulnerability scanners and intrusion detection can be deployed. We use the policy to specify when and where these tools will be used.

Conformance Monitoring Policy

Security policies are not beneficial if they are ignored. If you do not know whether your policies are being ignored, you will be unable to perform an effective risk assessment. This results in improper controls that can cause inappropriate investments in security—either too high or too low. It can also result in significant losses if a security breach occurs. The conformance monitoring policy lists the technologies and processes used to measure the degree to which everyone complies with other security policies. Many of the tools used for conformance monitoring overlap with threat management tools but are applied in a different manner.

Application Architecture Policy

Organizations that build their own applications, such as trading floor applications, back-office applications, and inventory control applications, know that trying to put security into an application after it is deployed is very difficult. Thirty years of development history have taught us that designing security into applications at the architecture level improves security and reduces long-term application maintenance costs. Basic policies should be set forth for building hooks for elements such as logging, authentication, authorization, and access control. All developers should use a common facilities set to gain operational efficiencies.

WHAT DOES A SECURITY POLICY LOOK LIKE? . . . .

Security policies have no specific form. They do not have to be large, monolithic, and comprehensive volumes that gather dust on the shelf of the security officer. Security policies need only to be easily understood. Employees need to know which policies apply to them. A simple and understandable policy will be more effective than a comprehensive, detailed policy that no one can read.

Some general principles for policy creation are:

- Policies are created by consensus, not edict.
- Policies should be brief and easily understood by the people who are expected to conform to them.
- Everyone who is expected to know the policies must be able to access them easily.

HOW ARE POLICIES APPLIED AND ENFORCED? . . . .

Chapter 14, "Establishing a Security Program," describes how security is marketed and sold to the organization (an important step for funding, support, and success). Ideally, enforcement is the responsibility of every person in the company. A good way to make this happen is to make information security compliance part of every performance appraisal. People with management responsibility should be trained and have formal responsibility for security policy enforcement. To succeed, you must have executive sponsorship. Executive teams in publicly held corporations need to place sufficient stress on creating and maintaining a secure computing environment. If there is a failure to do so, the executive team will eventually be censured by the corporate auditors and their own board of directors.

WHO IS RESPONSIBLE FOR SECURITY POLICIES? . . . .

We all are. Business leaders must determine the appropriate level of security investment through effective risk assessments and negotiated security policies. Security officers must define and refine policies and measure compliance. Executives must appropriately prioritize security concerns to keep risks to manageable levels.

Policy is the basis of all security. Without it, security will fail.

SUMMARY . . . .

Policy is the most important nontechnology-related aspect of computer security. Policy defines the who, what, where, and when of security, including processes and procedures. Policies are negotiated between the people knowledgeable in security and the business unit owners. Good policies are based on specific business objectives; they support sound business practice as well as mitigate risk.

Some policies can be centrally administered and applied across the entire enterprise. Some policies are business unit specific. Be careful to avoid every business unit claiming to be unique but take special requirements into account. Monitoring for conformance is an important part of enforcing policy.

Every individual in the organization should have ownership and understanding of the policies he or she is expected to follow. A policy does not have any specific form or format other than it should be understandable by the people it affects.

ENDNOTE . . . .

1.   A server farm is a room with hundreds or even thousands of computers (servers) providing data and application services to the business.

4 Authentication, Authorization, Access Control

In this chapter . . .

- Authentication
- Authorization
- Access Control

Information security is all about ensuring that only the good guys can use the data stored in computers. At one level, everything in this book is about separating the good guys from the bad guys. Firewalls keep the bad guys from using our network. Intrusion detection tells us when a bad guy is trying to use our systems. Everything in information security starts from the assumption that we can identify good guys and that anyone we cannot identify is a bad guy.

THE AAA DISCIPLINES . . . .

The tools that we use to identify the good guys, figure out what they are allowed to do (because not all good guys are equal), then limit the behavior of everyone to only those actions that are permitted are called *AAA*: authentication, authorization, and access control.

These three disciplines were the original basis of all information security. They still form the basis on which all other security mechanisms depend. The AAA disciplines are also among the most dynamic, with new technologies being introduced and proposed as standards every year. The sequence of authentication first, authorization second, and access control third is commonly used because it describes the sequence of computer actions that take place in order to grant a good guy use of the computer. But to best understand what these disciplines are and how they relate, we will describe them in a different sequence.

ACCESS CONTROL . . . .

The mechanism to stop unauthorized people from gaining access to data stored on a computer is the access control function. Computer operating systems have access controls built in. That is why you need to log in, or sign in to a computer, before using it. The login process proves to the computer that you are authorized, then the access control function lets you in. In theory, anyone who tries to use the computer without a correct login will be unable to use the computer or its programs.

Figure 4–1 shows the different steps of access control. The first gate is identification, where you simply show who you claim to be. In this diagram, it is represented as your picture. The next gate is authentication. This is where your identity is confirmed, where you prove that you actually are who you claim to be. In this case, authentication is shown as a passport that proves you are who you say you are. The next step is authorization, shown here as visa stamps in your passport. These visas actually

Figure 4–1
Access control.

allow you access into the different computers and applications for which you are allowed access. This is access control.

A perfect access control function would be infallible. It would always stop any unauthorized access. There would be no way to bypass it. Computer operating systems are very complex, and their access control functions are one of the most complex areas of the system. As a result, access control functions generally take 10 years to mature. Virtually every operating system ever built had security problems during its first decade. Vendors tend to change the name of operating systems every few years to escape the taint of past security failures. It is important to know the "heritage" of operating systems in order to understand their maturity and, therefore, their security.

In some cases, the access control function of an operating system can be improved by adding third-party enhancement products. In other cases, the operating system vendor may provide options that enable stronger access controls. In either case, the changes in the access control function will probably impact other software. Many management and control tools that are commonly used will fail when confronted with strong access controls. Their programmers assumed weaknesses in access control that would allow their programs to gather and pass data without constraint. The stronger access control functions block those actions and cause the management and control programs to fail.

So, as with many areas of computer security, access control is a balancing act. Strong access control reduces the risk of unauthorized use of the computer, but it may make managing the computer much more difficult. In general, if you use a mature operating system and configure its access controls well, you will be at the balance point. Immaturity shows in the number of patches and fixes issued for relatively young operating systems (for example, Linux and Windows 2000). To achieve a reasonable level of access control in these systems, significant investment is required in researching and installing patches. Failure to make this investment results in steadily declining security as hackers learn new ways to bypass the access control functions.

Not all access controls are built into operating systems. Some database systems and applications contain their own access control functions. But most applications rely on the operating system to provide their access control.

AUTHENTICATION/IDENTIFICATION . . . .

The most common way for someone to learn your password is to look under your mouse pad. The second most common way is for them to ask you (as in social engineering). Third is guessing. All three work amazingly well. Security policies that dictate the minimum length of a password (at least six characters), its composition (at least one numeric but also at least one alphabetic character), and the frequency with which all passwords must be changed (30–45 days) are critical parts of any security program. Some computer systems allow these password policies to be enforced automatically.

Stronger security is achieved by using technology in addition to passwords. In general terms, identity can be established through something you know (such as a password), something you have (such as one of the tokens described below), or something you are (such as your finger and its fingerprint), which is known as a *biometric*. Strong authentication (more certain than a password, which could be known by multiple people) is achieved by using two or all three identification methods. The combination of a password and a token or a token and a biometric give high identification surety.

Almost all authentication today is performed by typing in a user account name and a password. The password is called a *credential*, and it has value only as long as it is kept secret. If anyone else learns your password, they can impersonate you and use all of the computer facilities that you are authorized to use. There would be no way to tell that someone else was impersonating you. Everything they did would be attributed to you. If they use your computer identity to gather child pornography from the Internet, you would be implicated. This is not an idle threat. It has happened in U.S. corporations.

The terms *authentication* and *identification* are tightly intertwined throughout the security literature. We consider them to be interchangeable for the purposes of this book.

Who Are You Really?

There are two conditions that commonly lead a company to look for stronger methods of identification than a simple password. Some information stored on the computer may be very sensitive. Disclosure of the financial data of a publicly held company prior to its formal report could endanger the company. Access to that data may need to be secured more tightly than other data. The second condition leading to the use of strong authentication results from varying access paths. When an employee who uses sensitive data works from home, access must be granted through some outside network connection.

Outside networks have varying degrees of security. Many home workers were using strong authentication devices before the Internet was in business use. Even though the network connections they were using were relatively secure, the strong authentication approach was considered prudent. Now that most companies are using the Internet for home access, the use of strong authentication for at-home workers is virtually universal.

Strong authentication is accomplished using four types of technology: Kerberos, tokens, biometrics, and certificates. Other technologies have attempted to make market inroads into solving the tricky issues of authentication. These are the current winners. As we said above, these are used in various combinations. Each technology type is described separately in the following sections. We bring together these technologies, as well as access control and authorization, at the end of this chapter.

Kerberos

One of the first problems that needed to be solved in order to strengthen authentication was that of password safety. If you send your password over a network, it could be intercepted by anyone and used to impersonate you. In addition, many computers may need to know who you are and that you have already successfully signed in. The technology for transferring your password securely and using it to connect to many computers is called Kerberos, named for the mythical three-headed dog that protected Hades.

Because Kerberos exists, you may wonder why you frequently need to type in account names and passwords to many computers and applications separately. Although the technology has been available for a number of years, computer manufacturers have been slow to adopt it. But Microsoft decided to include Kerberos as a default technology in Windows 2000. As a result, we expect that the plethora of passwords that many organizations require their staff to memorize and change constantly will shrink rapidly over the next five years.

Tokens

The first step above "something you know" is "something you have." This is known as two-factor authentication. Simply having possession of an item augments your password because only one person at a time can have that item in his or her hand. There are two conditions that must be met: The item must be totally unique and there must be a reliable method of determining that you do, in fact, have that item. Tokens are those items.

Each token is unique. It contains some form of electronic logic that makes it unique. Most tokens look like a credit card, although a few manufacturers have found ways to shape them into key fobs and other form factors. There are three ways that vendors have devised for you to prove that you really do have the token when you sign in.

1. The token has a small LCD display on its face. A number is displayed on the LCD, and that number changes every minute. To sign in, you tell the computer your account name, your password, and the number shown on the face of the token. If all three are valid, the sign-in is successful.

2. The token has a small numeric keypad on it, in addition to the LCD panel. To sign in, you tell the computer your account name and password. The computer responds with a short number for you to type into the token keypad. The token then displays another number. You tell that number to your computer, and if it matches, the sign-in is successful.

3. The token slides into a reader attached to your computer. You tell the computer your account name and password, and the token takes care of the rest. There are two very different generations of this token type. The older ones are used primarily for government work and are very expensive. The newer ones are described in the "Certificate-Based Authentication" section later in this chapter, because they use something called a *certificate* to establish strong authentication and secure communications.

Biometrics

Why doesn't the computer already know who I am when I walk up and give me what I want? Why do I need to remember passwords and account names when the computer is much better at remembering details? These are valid questions, but the technology to deliver instant and reliable recognition is still immature. Biometrics is the science of identifying you by something that you are. A wide variety of biometric technologies has been constructed, and a few of them are ready now for small-scale or specialized deployment. The major biometric technologies are:

Fingerprint. Fingerprint readers use fingerprint characteristics to perform authentication procedures (see Figure 4–2). They are small and moderately reliable. Some fingerprints are difficult to read, due to worn finger surfaces after doing manual labor. Readers need to be cleaned frequently.

Iris Scan. This uses a small video camera. Poor office lighting and sunglasses cause failed sign-ins. This requires no action by the user.

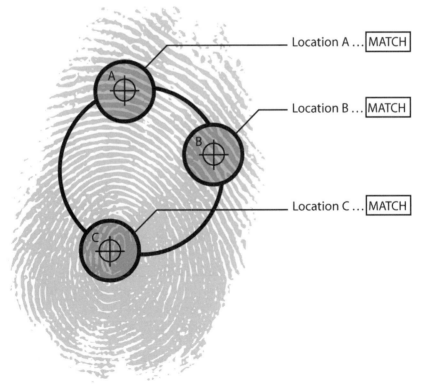

Figure 4–2
Biometric thumbprint readers use fingerprint characteristics to authenticate.

Facial Recognition. This technology also uses a small video camera. Poor office lighting or dramatic appearance shifts cause failed sign-ins. This requires significant computer processing power and disk storage.

Voice Recognition. This makes use of a microphone. It is moderately reliable, but uses a lot of computer processing power. Failed sign-ins can be caused by a bad head cold.

Hand Geometry. This requires a large, bulky reader, but is very reliable.

We included hand geometry in the list to demonstrate that some biometrics may be very good but have purposes other than authentication to a computer. Hand geometry scanners are in use by the U.S. Passport Office at major airports. Frequent travelers can register their handprints and use the scanners instead of standing in long lines at passport control. The scanners are built into kiosks the size of a desk. Scanner size does not matter to this application.

THREE-FACTOR IDENTIFICATION

> Three-factor identification is ostensibly the strongest level of authentication available. It requires three pieces of information for you to prove who you are. These include:
>
> - Something you know, such as a password.
> - Something you have, such as a unique token.
> - Something you are, such as hand geometry or iris scans.

The biometric technologies listed above work beautifully when their vendors demonstrate them. In fact, they may meet the needs of some groups. Each has conditions under which its reliability is reduced. Many of those conditions are controllable. The most serious problems with biometrics arise when a large organization tries to use them across a large audience. To be valuable in most business organizations, the biometric technology must be centrally managed.

When a technology such as a biometric is demonstrated, all of its components are in the computer being used for the demonstration: the fingerprint reader, the software that drives it, the stored finger image, and the sign-in program. In the typical business environment, great care has been taken to ensure that some of these elements have been moved away from the computer so that an intruder cannot compromise everything simply by stealing or invading a single computer. To make biometrics work in a business environment, the stored finger image (or its equivalent) must be maintained on a central directory. When you press your finger to the reader, the central directory must approve you. Today, your password is handled in this manner. Biometrics cannot be allowed to reduce the security level.

Many organizations have been disappointed by biometrics because the tools to manage them via a central directory are not yet mature. There are two possible solutions to this problem. The first solution is to wait for the vendors to deliver strong tools for handling biometric data in directories. The second solution is discussed in the section "The Ultimate Solution" later in this chapter.

Certificate-Based Authentication

The state of the art in authentication is Public Key Infrastructure (PKI). This is a "something you have" authentication technology, in that something called a *certificate* is issued to you, and your possession of it, together with your password, constitutes proof that you are who you claim to be. The certificate is really nothing more than a pair of computer records, but they have a special relationship to one another, based on an unusual kind of computer encryption. The technology behind PKI is described in Chapter 9, "Public Key Infrastructure and Encryption." In addition to authentication, PKI technology is also used in Secure Sockets Layer and virtual private networks (SSL and VPNs, described further in Chapter 10, "Encrypted Communications").

The part of your certificate that you use to authenticate is called your *private key*. Although this key can be stored directly on your computer disk, this has two disadvantages. First, anyone using your computer might copy it. They would still need your password to unlock it, but with a copy, they could take a long time to work out your password and then start to impersonate you. The second problem is that you could sign in only at your own computer. Many people need to connect to the company network from other computers—from public kiosks or from home. So when a certificate is used for authentication, it should always be stored in a smart card.

Smart Cards

A smart card looks like a credit card. Looks are deceiving. This card has a complete computer built into it. The computer holds your private key. To use the smart card, you must have a smart card reader attached to or built in to your computer. You slide the smart card into its reader, then type your account name and password in to your computer. Your password never gets sent to a central directory. Instead, the password gets sent to the computer in the smart card.

The smart card computer reacts by allowing your private key to be used. The private key never leaves the smart card. Rather, your computer uses the smart card computer to set up a secure communications session with the network. The session works only because your private key has an associated certificate holding your public key at the central directory. The existence and use of your private key via the smart card proves who you are.

Smart card PKI is just coming of age. The cost of a smart card reader will soon become insignificant in the construction of a computer keyboard. The standards that allow easy integration of smart cards, PKI, and existing operating systems are in place. The processes that a business needs to manage certificates and store them in directories are rapidly being solved. We expect PKI to grow rapidly in acceptance from 2002 to 2005.

AUTHORIZATION . . . .

Recall that authorization works like visas in a passport. It defines authorized places that you are allowed to visit. Figure 4–3 shows how the visas in the company president's passport allow more access to computers and applications than the visas in the Web designer's passport. The Web designer is authorized to see only marketing and outbound Internet applications but the company president is allowed to access the entire network.

The development of Web-based applications for business-to-consumer (B to C) use made authorization difficult. The use of portals, which provide a common starting point for access to many Web applications, made authorization nearly impossible. In response, vendors have built a new generation of centralized authorization engines. These are frequently referred to as Web SSO (Web single signon) tools.

Once a security system is sure of who you are because you have satisfied the need for authentication, you still need to define and control what users are allowed to do. This is known as *authorization*. In distributed computing, the decision of what you may access is left to every computer and every program. In the days of the centralized mainframe computer, authorization was well understood and controlled. In the transition to distributed computing, authorization got lost and is just recently being rediscovered.

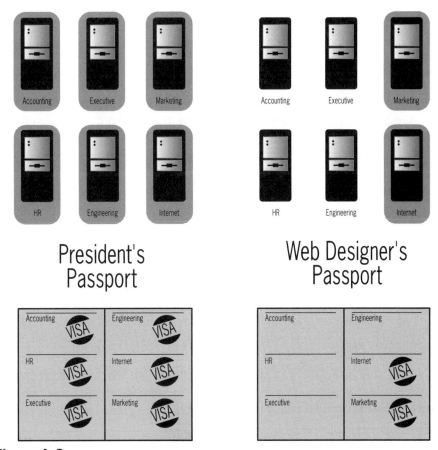

Figure 4–3
Authorization defines access for different job roles.

Having an authorization tool allows you to solve the problem of keeping track and enforcing the rules of who can do what on the computer system. There are two ways to handle authorization. The most common is to keep track of everyone who can authenticate in a directory, then to list in their directory entry every computer and program they have a right to access. This works well for small groups of users or small collections of computers and programs. As the number of users and computers increases, this solution becomes difficult to manage.

The second approach to authorization is called *role-based authorization* (RBA) or *role-based access control* (RBAC). We will use RBA. Constructing a list of standard roles for your company and assigning authorizations to those roles can dramatically simplify the administration of any authorization system. Assume that 80 percent of the authorizations in your company could be described by standard roles. Work toward defining a number of roles equal to 25 percent of your number of employees.

Each employee should have multiple roles assigned. The overall number of authorizations will fall dramatically, as will the cost of administering them. In addition, gross changes, such as the restructuring of a division or a change in job descriptions for a class of employees, can be implemented in hours instead of days or weeks. You can gather more information on RBA from the Web site of the U.S. National Institute of Standards and Technology (NIST) at *http://csrc.nist.gov/rbac/*.

ASSEMBLING THE PIECES . . . .

Authentication tells the computer who you are. Authorization tells the computer what you are allowed to do. Access control stops you (and everyone else) from doing things that are not allowed. All three of these functions must work together. And, in the typical network, they must work across multiple computer types, operating systems, and programs. Given that computer vendors compete instead of cooperate, creating a secure network can be close to impossible. The resulting compromises leave us with weak security, successful hackers, and numerous passwords for every employee to manage.

But the picture is improving. We will describe where we see AAA going from a strategic perspective and will then describe how things will actually be for the next few years.

The Ultimate Solution

Jane, a worker, approaches her computer and takes her smart card from her wallet. The card has survived the journey in a wallet quite well because it is as flexible as any other credit card. Jane slides the card into a slot on the right side of her computer keyboard. A message pops up on the computer screen that says, "Please press your right thumb on the fingerprint scanner." Each day, the message may request a different finger. The fingerprint data never leaves the computer. Instead, it is sent into the smart card, which recognizes the fingerprint and allows the use of Jane's private key.

The combination of who Jane is (from her fingerprint) and what Jane is carrying (her smart card) has provided sufficient authentication so that Jane can now access many, but not all, of the computer programs she needs. By storing the fingerprint data in the smart card, we eliminate the need to manage that data in the directory. We also allow Jane to connect to the network from any computer that has a smart card reader.

Now Jane's computer is showing a list of all of the programs she is currently authorized to use. In addition, there is a button on the screen labeled "High Security Applications." Jane cannot see that list until she has provided one more level of authentication—her password.

Every computer and program in the network is prepared to accept a message and to validate it as being from Jane—so long as she has been listed in the central directory as having that right. Her directory entry says that she is an employee (as opposed to a customer, prospect, or contractor) and that she has an accounting role in payroll. Because she is listed as an employee, she has access to the email system and the Human Resources department home page.

Because she is in the payroll department, she can access the pay management program. But that program will allow her to see and modify only nonexecutive payroll data. To process executive salaries, Jane will need to type in her password. Making a change to an executive salary takes yet another action. The program requires Jane to submit a digital signature, along with the salary change request. Jane types in her signature password. This is another password that never leaves the computer. When Jane types in her signature password, it is sent to her smart card, which unlocks another certificate. This certificate is used only for creating signatures. In effect, Jane is providing a legally binding signature that could be enforced in court if it were attached to a contract.

When Jane leaves her desk to go to lunch, she takes her smart card with her. Removing it from the reader automatically logs her out from all of the computers and programs. She remembers her card because she cannot get into the women's room without it. It unlocks the door. She would also not be able to get back to her desk because it opens the office employee entrance. She could use the main entrance, but security personnel there will want to see her ID card, and that is printed on the front of the smart card. It took Jane only a week to start remembering her card.

The Real World for the Next Few Years

A few companies are approaching our ultimate solution scenario for small groups of users within the next year. For most of us, a less elegant solution with more compromises and weaker security will suffice for a few years. The wide installation of Microsoft Windows 2000, Windows XP, and Windows .Net Server will install Kerberos as an improvement on basic password authentication. Many other computers and programs will be adapted to accept Windows Kerberos authentication. As a result, you will need fewer and fewer passwords.

Adapting those computers and programs to Kerberos is not a waste of time. The same interfaces will allow PKI authentication to work, replacing Kerberos as PKI matures. You may already have your first smart card in the form of a credit card. Your work smart card may arrive within two years. Its use as a digital signature device will follow shortly thereafter. Connecting it to biometrics will come last. That could be as late as 2006. But one vendor issued a product that could do exactly that in 2001. The company was in Germany and it may not have the ultimate solution. But someone will. Perhaps sooner than we think.

SUMMARY . . . .

The basic technologies of Information Security are identification, authentication, and authorization. Access control is a set of steps, including identification (presenting an ID), authentication (proving it's really you), and authorization (visa stamps in a passport that define where you are allowed to visit).

Access control is built into many operating systems but many do not have access controls. In this case, access control can be built into applications such as databases. Perfect access control would allow only legitimate users in and keep others out. Perfect access control does not exist because of limitations in technology and the expense of trying to control "everything."

Authentication is usually enforced by usernames and passwords. Passwords are flawed because they are easy to discover. Other methods of authentication include certificates, tokens, and biometrics. Three-factor authentication includes something you know (a password), something you have (a token), and something you are (biometric verification).

Authorization is a complicated problem because of the large number of roles and tasks that must be managed in a company of any size. The key to successful role-based authorization is to be able to limit the mission-critical roles and tasks to a manageable number.

Part 2

Security Technologies

5 Firewalls

In this chapter . . .

- What Is a Firewall?

- What Are the Uses of Firewalls?

- What Are the Types of Firewalls?

- How to Architect a Firewall Solution

- How to Manage Your Firewalls

- Business Practices

The practice of putting walls around assets to secure them predates history. Man has used doors, fences, walls, and other methods to accomplish this task. In the computer world, firewalls fulfill this role. Firewalls are considered one of the critical information security technologies required for any business. However, they are not a panacea. In fact, firewalls are the source of considerable security risk in many organizations.

WHAT IS A FIREWALL? . . . .

Firewalls separate your valuable assets from dangerous threats. The word *firewall* didn't come into use until the 1700s by forest rangers to describe gaps cut into forests so fires will have a place to stop. The firewall keeps the fire from spreading to protected parts of the forest. The word was later used in the machine era where, for instance, a firewall is built between an engine and a cockpit to protect occupants on one side from the dangers on the other side. There is even a firewall between car engines and the interior. Firewalls are also used in the architecture of houses and in the oil storage industry.

In medieval times, castles often used moats, high walls, and drawbridges to control access to the interior. This was done to protect the inhabitants, as well as the assets of the kingdom. Internally, large doors, secret passages, and gates were used to segregate areas of access from one another. In the digital world, firewalls serve the same purpose because they are intended to keep out unwanted intruders (see Figure 5–1).

Firewalls, or gateways, help to control access. They do this by acting as an intermediary configured with a set of rules to allow or deny communications between one network, group, or host and other entities. Firewalls are a combination of hardware and software, which act as gateways. Consider a property surrounded by a fence. There is a single point of access, or gate, that controls access between the interior and exterior of the fence. Firewalls are routinely used to separate business networks from the Internet to keep hackers and other unwanted intruders from entering.

Firewalls can also provide segmentation between internal resources. Like doors that separate different rooms within your building, firewalls can separate people and resources within your digital organization. In this way, firewalls can be used to separate mission-critical business units from each other, such as the trading floor and the insurance unit. People from one unit should not be looking at the data in another.

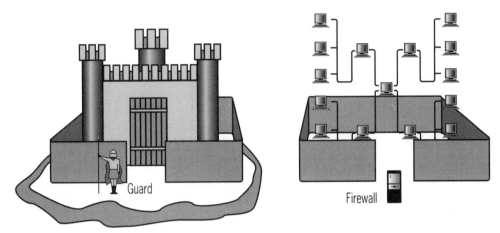

Figure 5–1
Firewalls act as guards to control information in and out of your network.

USES FOR FIREWALLS . . . .

Firewalls in their simplest form control access to, from, and between your networks (see Figure 5–2). However, there are many more uses for firewalls, including regulating communications flow, controlling communication types to Web servers, supporting VPNs, and authenticating, using third-party products. This is more than "keeping people out."

Figure 5–2
Firewalls can be used to separate operating groups from each other.

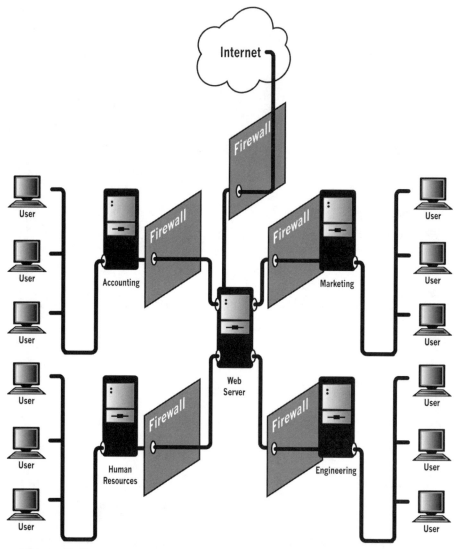

Figure 5–3
A single firewall can be used to create logical partitions within your
enterprise.

Firewalls can allow a Web server to be accessed from the Internet. Firewalls can
also limit the types of communications that users have to a Web server. They can also
be used to authenticate users into your network. Some firewalls have native authentication or support third-party products. This allows you to authenticate users prior to
allowing them access to information resources. This increases the level of security, in
addition to providing a tangible audit trail.

Depending on the firewall, it can be used to support VPNs. VPNs encrypt network transmissions between two points. Some firewalls can act as termination points for this encryption. The firewall can be configured to encrypt traffic between itself and another firewall or even between itself and VPN client software residing on a user's workstation. This is useful in environments where communication is sensitive, such as patient or client records. VPNs are covered in depth in Chapter 10, "Encrypted Communications."

There may be a requirement to segregate one network segment from the rest of the environment (see Figure 5–3). A commonly used example is a research and development network. Due to the sensitive nature of activities transpiring on this type of network, greater security may be required. Another example is the need to separate the engineering department from the sales department. These two departments have different access requirements and require segregation so that engineering can have unrestricted outbound access to the Internet while sales is protected by restricting access.

TYPES OF FIREWALLS AND HOW THEY OPERATE . . . .

There is a variety of firewalls commercially available. As firewall technology became mainstream in the late 1990s, the functionality evolved significantly. There are three fundamental technologies behind firewalls:

- Network layer
- Application layer
- Hybrid

Other terms commonly used to describe these technologies include packet filters, application gateways, and stateful packet inspection. These terms are described below.

Network Layer Firewalls

Network layer firewalls operate at layer three of the Open Systems Interconnection (OSI) model. This type of firewall acts as a packet-filtering router, meaning that it inspects the incoming packets and does not forward packets matching specific criteria. Network layer firewalls are very fast, relatively inexpensive, and the least robust of all firewalls. Simply put, these firewalls are concerned only with source address, destination address, and port information.

KEY POINT

> Network layer firewalls are very fast, relatively inexpensive, and the least secure of all firewalls.

Consider a firewall protecting a Web server accessible to the Internet. The Hypertext Transfer Protocol (HTTP) and its secure variant (HTTPS) are used to allow clients utilizing Web browsers to access information from Web servers. To reduce exposure, the packet-filtering firewall limits the number of services users can access to TCP port 80 (HTTP) and TCP port 443 (HTTPS). See Table 5–1 for an example of a firewall rule that implements this requirement.

This is accomplished with an access filter or rule that configures the firewall. A firewall access rule restricts types of network outbound traffic and also restricts inbound destinations using "actions" that are taken based on packets that match selected rules. Commonly, these actions are "allow or deny." "Allow" actions pass matched packets on to their destination. "Deny" actions do not forward matched packets. To the destination computer it is as though the denied packets don't even exist because they have been filtered out. A rule enforcing this type of action would look something like this:

Table 5–1   *An Example of a Firewall "Rule"*

ACTION	SOURCE	PORT	DESTINATION	PORT
Allow	Any	TCP 80 TCP 443	Web Server	TCP 80 TCP 443

This is an effective method of controlling access based on source and destination information, but network layer firewalls are still considered the least secure. These firewalls do not monitor more detailed information, such as the state of communications or application information. In addition, working with and managing filters or access control lists can be cumbersome, leading to simple mistakes, such as allowing access to clearly threatening packet types. These are mistakes that can leave your systems vulnerable, and many organizations do just this. Having a poorly configured firewall is worse than having no firewall at all because it gives you a false sense of security.

Application Layer Firewalls

Application layer firewalls are also known as *application gateways* or *proxies*. These firewalls are generally considered the most robust and possibly even the most secure. However, this level of security can cost in the form of decreased performance, lack of application support, and scalability, depending on the complexity of configuration. These are valuable devices that may be worth the trade-offs.

 Key Point

> Application layer firewalls are also known as *application gateways* and *proxies*.

A packet-filtering firewall is usually implemented as a router with access control lists. An application gateway firewall, on the other hand, is commonly a server, with routing enabled and firewall software installed. These firewalls address ordinary packet filtering but can also address security for individual applications because they operate at all layers of the OSI model, with specific emphasis on the application layer.

Application gateway firewalls work as proxies. A port is opened on one side of the firewall, connecting the incoming data stream to the appropriate proxy. Another port is opened, leaving the proxy to the destination host on the other side of the firewall. A specific proxy must exist for each application you want to use through the firewall. Vendors are continually adding new proxies for new applications. However, you may experience problems using new applications, because the firewall doesn't have an existing proxy. Please note applications without existing proxies can be passed using packet filtering, instead.

This type of firewall allows you to create extremely granular security and access rules. You can tie user privileges and access rights to specific applications. For example, to allow a business partner administrative access to your network, you can configure the firewall to allow access from the partner's network to yours and identify specific devices and ports to be used for communication. Remember, this does not authenticate the user before allowing access. It only controls whether the packets can access a device. You will certainly want to have users authenticated before allowing them access. This is usually controlled at the device itself.

Performance degradation can be an issue with application layer firewalls. The added functionality of tying applications to specific packets requires increased processing. It's true that packet filters are faster than application gateways, because there is less processing involved. For those willing to trade some performance for enhanced security, an application firewall may be the right choice.

And finally, the Application layer interacts with software applications. It is responsible for determining resources and synchronizing communications.

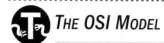 THE OSI MODEL

The OSI model was developed in the 1980s by the International Standards Organization (ISO). While parts of the OSI model have helped to form Internet protocols, the original OSI protocols are somewhat obsolete or unused. The OSI model is commonly used to explain and compare network technologies.

Implemented in seven layers, the OSI model includes a physical, data link, network, transport, session, presentation, and application layer. The following is meant as a brief overview of each layer's responsibilities:

The Physical layer is best known as "the wire." This layer defines the electrical and mechanical specifications for handling the physical link between communicating network systems.

The Data Link layer provides media access control. It specifies characteristics pertaining to networks and protocols including physical addressing, error notification, and flow control.

The Network layer tends to be the most familiar to everyone. It provides routing and related functions enabling networks to communicate with one another through connection-oriented and connectionless protocols.

The Transport layer provides reliable data transport to the upper layers. This layer typically provides error checking and recovery.

The Session layer establishes, maintains, and terminates communication sessions.

The Presentation layer is one of the most difficult to envision. It is responsible for ensuring the compatibility of information sent from the application layer of one system to the application layer of another system.

Hybrid Firewalls

Hybrid firewalls perform the functions of both a packet filter and an application gateway. The term can also be used to describe a firewall that is state- or session-aware and performs packet filtering but does not act as a proxy. By *state-aware*, we mean a firewall that can monitor a session and maintain information regarding said session. This includes source and destination IP and port information, as well as sequence numbers at layer four of the OSI model. In addition, it may also keep track of authenticated users. Although it may not perform as an application gateway, it possesses increased functionality over a standard packet filter. Hybrid firewalls provide adequate security and tend to perform faster than application gateways and slower than packet filters.

KEY POINT

Hybrid firewalls may perform the functions of both a packet filter and an application gateway. They can also be used to describe a firewall that is state- or session-aware and performs packet filtering but does not act as a proxy.

Figure 5–4 compares the three different firewall technologies using the OSI seven-layer network model.

WORKING WITH FIREWALLS . . . .

Once you've decided on a firewall technology and begin to build or configure one, you will be faced with many decisions. You'll soon discover that there are many useful security practices that the owner's manual neglects to mention. Here are a few ideas to help you successfully architect and build a firewall solution.

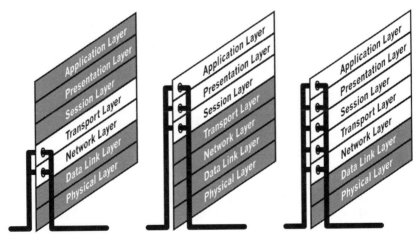

Figure 5–4
Comparing different firewall technologies using the OSI model.

Access Rules

Access rules are the lifeblood of your firewall. Carefully consider how these rules should be constructed and the order in which they should be placed. This may seem obvious but failure to set access rules properly is one of the most significant weaknesses in most organizations. Start building your firewall's rule set by allowing nothing. This immediately places you into a posture of heightened security. As you determine services and resources that require access, modify the rules.

In the interest of enabling business, an uninformed administrator might initially allow everything through the firewall, then scale back. This is the wrong approach! You wouldn't allow strangers free access to your home and tighten security after the fact, so you shouldn't take this approach with your firewalls.

 NETWORK ADDRESS TRANSLATION

A key function of today's more robust firewalls is the ability to perform network address translation (NAT). Explained in detail in RFC 1631,[1] NAT was originally created to solve the Internet's dilemma of IP address depletion and routing scalability. Our current scheme uses 32-bit IPv4-based IP addresses. In short, this means there is a total of 4,294,967,296 possible addresses. Although this sounds like a lot of addresses, it is not. For the sake of scalability and administrative ease, IP addresses are assigned in blocks to very large organizations or Internet service providers (ISPs). Considering the number of companies with Internet connections, not to mention home users, the world would certainly have run out of IP addresses, had it not been for NAT.

Although many additional uses for NAT have been identified, the one that relates most directly to your organization is HideNAT. This allows networks possessing large pools of nonroutable IP addresses (RFC 1918) to masquerade behind a single IP address. In simplest form, Hide-NAT is a many-to-one relationship. This is advantageous, because it alleviates the impact on IP address depletion and adds a level of protection to your environment because users cannot directly access nonroutable IP address space from the Internet. Although VPNs can also provide this type of protection, it is more complicated and requires software and authentication (we'll discuss this concept later in this book).

There is also a one-to-one relationship found in NAT. More specifically, this is known as *static NAT*, and it is useful for other functions. Static NAT is helpful when you need to mesh overlapping IP space in non-routable environments. A prime example can be found when two organizations construct a partner-to-partner connection where both parties are utilizing the same internal IP scheme. To resolve this conflict, one or both organizations can map IP addresses to alternate assigned addresses, thus eliminating overlap.

It is also helpful to map addresses to public service network (PSN) devices. Some organizations may use a public pool of addresses for their PSNs, but using RFC 1918 and static NAT allows for added security. For example, if an access rule is misconfigured but contains no accompanying NAT rule, internal networks and resources will remain inaccessible to Internet users. This can be a double-edged sword when configuring access to devices on non-Internet-routable network segments. Exercise care. Configuring NAT correctly may be more complicated, but for the paranoid, it can provide extra security.

Figure 5–5 depicts implementations of static and HideNAT. For a static NAT, such as the one seen in the Web server relationship, the firewall advertises the address of the publicly available resource and ultimately routes traffic through to the nonInternet-routable address. In the HideNAT configuration, users masquerade behind the public IP address of the firewall in order to allow access. The firewall keeps track of these connections and allows solicited traffic back to the point of origin.

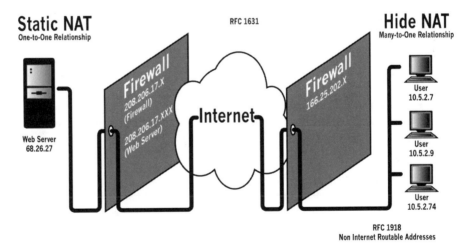

Figure 5–5
Static and HideNAT implementations.

ARCHITECTING A FIREWALL SOLUTION . . . .

Before you place a firewall into your network, you'll need to make a few decisions regarding the protection of resources, controlling access, the importance of high availability, and whether you're interested in supporting a traditional system or an appliance.

What do you want to protect? At a minimum, you want to protect your internal LAN from the Internet. Do you have the need to construct an extranet? Do you have a PSN or other remote access? Many of these questions can be answered by existing information security policies, so long as your organization has them.

Internet Firewalls

The most common of all firewalls is an Internet-facing firewall. By placing a firewall between the Internet segment and all other networks, you protect yourself against inbound assaults, as well as limit other networks—such as an internal LAN, extranets, and PSNs—from attempting to initiate unauthorized outbound connections through your ISP. This is a key point, because many organizations overlook the liability they face from outbound traffic.

Extranets

Extranets are an extension of your network that is outside your model of trust. This is where you allow partners to connect to your business. It's easier to consolidate all partners onto their own network with a separate interface on your firewall. There is liability associated with building an extranet. More specifically, you have an obligation to protect individual partners from one another on your extranet. This is most commonly done by employing packet filters or Access Control Lists (ACL) on the router(s) that aggregate(s) partner connections. An ACL is a list of people or devices, and permissions that apply to them.

Extranets help businesses and larger organizations contain vendors and partners to a sandbox. Because all traffic to and from the extranet must now traverse the firewall, access controls can be utilized to construct privileges that are granular and specific to individual partners or transactions. If you have networks connecting into your LAN, now is the time to consider migrating them to an extranet.

The DMZ

The name *demilitarized zone* (DMZ) advertises a semiprotected area that you do not completely control. A DMZ created by one or more firewalls creates a PSN meant to allow the general public access to network resources and services (for example, Web, email, and/or domain naming services). These resources must be protected to maintain integrity and availability.

Generally, one or two firewalls make up your DMZ setting up two logical partitions: one between your servers and the Internet and one between your servers and the rest of your private network. The partition or firewall pointed toward the Internet is configured with rules that allow outside people access to your public service servers. The partition or firewall pointed at your inside network is typically very restrictive, allowing almost no traffic through (see Figure 5–6).

Firewalls and Dial-Ups

Another point of entry into networks is through remote access or dial-up connections. You may consider placing the remote access connectivity piece of your network on its own interface of the firewall. This allows for tighter controls and a concrete audit trail for those connecting remotely. In the event that you must economize, consider making remote access part of your extranet.

Placing your LAN on its own firewall interface is a good idea. It allows you to limit any and all access to your LAN from outside or untrusted users. It also allows you to control the types of access traveling outbound from your network and ultimately limits your liability from internal users who may be attempting to access resources that they shouldn't. Most frequently, organizations will limit outbound Telnet or FTP access. Additionally, other components can be used in conjunction with a firewall to ensure that users are not accessing questionable material via the WWW.

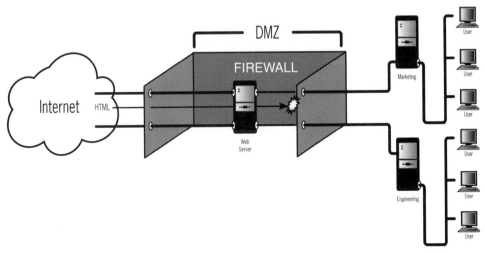

Figure 5–6
A DMZ with one firewall creating two logical partitions.

In Figure 5–7, all network segments are separated from one another by using a firewall. With a properly constructed set of rules, you can adequately secure access to these segments.

High Availability

You may want to consider operating your firewall in "high availability." This means implementing a pair of identical firewalls. Although this can be cost-prohibitive for smaller organizations, others depend on network connectivity to conduct commerce. In this scenario, a disruption in service can be costly, so the added expense of redundancy becomes a business imperative.

High-availability architectures can be constructed in a number of ways. Fail-over and load balancing are the major schemes. In fail-over, a piece of software is used to link two firewalls. The software allows the devices to send "keep-alive" messages to one another. In the event that the primary firewall becomes disabled, the secondary device assumes control. Load-balancing architectures are built on the same concept as fail-over; however, both devices remain online at all times, and network

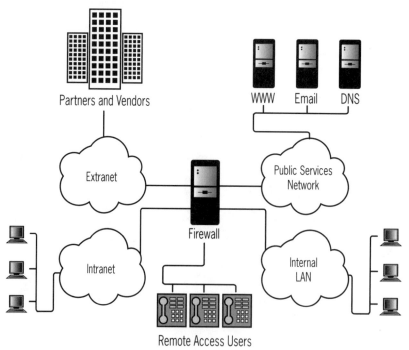

Figure 5–7
Firewall placement architecture.

traffic is evenly distributed between the two. Often, the firewalls will operate using Virtual Router Redundancy Protocol (VRRP). In effect, this allows the devices to share a common IP address, making the redundancy transparent. Furthermore, an algorithm is used to measure cost in order to distribute the load.

Implementation and integration of your firewall(s) is not an overly daunting task, but it helps to have a plan in place before making any changes. You should schedule the integration in conjunction with a maintenance window because, in all likelihood, you will be disrupting network service.

MANAGING FIREWALLS . . . .

Depending on the size of your organization and the complexity of your firewall(s), firewall maintenance can be a full-time job. Keeping up with log files, operating system patches, auditing, and access rules can be daunting.

As previously mentioned, traditional firewall systems are built on server technology. Whether this means some variant of the UNIX or Windows operating systems is entirely up to you. Performance, scalability, ease of administration, and security are all factors to consider. Regardless of platform, the final product consists of an operating system, firewall software, and access rules. Let's analyze the operating system first.

Firewalls and Operating Systems

The operating system is the program that runs the computer. Firewalls are software that runs on top of the operating system. The firewall is critical in protecting your perimeter and segregating your networks, so it is essential that you harden your operating system on which your firewall runs. Securing the device involves turning off services that do not need to be used. These might include, but are not limited to, rlogin, ftp, and lp in a UNIX environment. In a Windows environment examples include, but are not limited to, computer browsing and messengers. If you're not using a service, there is no sense in continuing to run the service. Not only does it increase the number of tasks the device has to do, but it opens up the machine to more vulnerabilities. Think of a house with three entryways and half a dozen windows. There are many ways into or out of the house. Should you board up all but two windows that you frequently use and nail all but one door shut, you've maintained functionality that you use but limited the security exposure elsewhere.

In addition to limiting services, auditing should be enabled and reviewed. In Windows, these would be items you'd see in the Event Viewer application. In UNIX, there are various auditing mechanisms. Often, files exist in the */var/audit*, */var/log*, and */var/adm* directories. Auditing allows you to review important system and operating information. Who has been accessing the machine? From what source did remote users come? Have key files been touched?

You can do other things to secure the operating system, including modifying TCP/IP stacks and performing kernel hacking. Depending on your level of comfort with the chosen operating system, these may be beyond the capabilities of your organization. You must weigh the balance between complete security and functionality. You may want to modify or replace existing software applications that reside on the machine designated as your firewall. Keep up with the latest security patches. Subscribing to an advisory service that can inform you of vulnerabilities will help in educating you, and visiting a vendor's Web site should arm you with fixes and/or workarounds.

Prime examples of secure software package substitutions are Secure Shell (ssh) and Secure Copy (scp). Without going into great detail, ssh and scp can be thought of as secure versions of Telnet and FTP. The latter are remote access applications that operate in clear text, thus making any and all communications vulnerable to interception. The former, however, are encrypted and instill confidence that the communications taking place are secure. Although someone may be able to capture the stream of transactions, they would not be readable.

Firewall Appliances

Maintenance can be controlled somewhat by using a firewall appliance. A firewall appliance is a hardware device that is specifically built and tuned to perform as a firewall. Appliances come in a number of forms, depending on the level of functionality they possess. For instance, a packet-filtering firewall can be implemented as a router. In this case, you would have an appliance that contains interfaces, processor, memory, and so forth, but no hard drive. The operating system and access control list would remain in read-only memory. The same could be done with the UNIX platform, although now you're dealing with the operating system, hard drive, interfaces, and so on.

Manufacturers and engineers start with an operating system and remove all unnecessary software packages, files, and services to create a firewall appliance. Most frequently, they develop a menu-driven or Web-based interface for the purpose of configuration. Although some shell access may be permitted, this is usually quite restricted, and changes are overwritten upon reboot. One of the advantages of this device is that configuration files can normally be saved to a diskette. In the event of a system failure, it is relatively easy to install another system and load the configuration from the diskette.

When purchasing an appliance from a manufacturer, system maintenance is reduced. The manufacturer should handle items requiring attention, if they are reputable. This is often handled by releasing another image that can be easily loaded.

This does not mean you are released from total obligation. Depending on the type of firewall, you will still have log files to review, in addition to auditing user accounts on the device and other activities. Appliances are an efficient way to deploy and redeploy firewalls.

The decision to deploy an appliance is not for everyone. Some organizations are more comfortable working with a system with which they are familiar. Additionally, appliances tend to lack the same scalability that a UNIX system has. It isn't always possible to upgrade RAM or processor speed, or to add interfaces to an appliance without purchasing a new system. The benefits include a vendor relationship that can be leveraged for support and the ability to allow the vendor to deal with the responsibility of ensuring the device's security from a hardware and software perspective. However, it is important to note that the vendor is not liable for misconfigurations of the system in your operating environment.

Access Rules

Each firewall has a set of access rules. If you employ someone to manage your firewalls full time, caring for a diverse set of distributed rule bases may not be of high concern. On the other hand, you may have limited resources, and central administration can be important. There are firewall products that provide for distributed management, and you may consider purchasing one of these. If your budget limits you from doing so, extra care must be given in creating a management environment for which to handle rules, log files, user accounts, availability, or status information.

Firewall rule bases can range from simplistic to extremely complex—from a limited number of rules to great numbers of access, authentication, and NAT rules. When dealing with multiple firewalls, it may be easiest to keep all rule bases with their associated firewalls, but is essential that you save a copy of these rule sets in a secure location for disaster recovery purposes. Again, using a product that includes central management functionality or creating a space for such purposes can accomplish this.

Firewall Logging and Reporting

Log files provide assistance with a number of key items, including transactions, reporting, and prosecution evidence gathering. When faced with connectivity problems, log files can provide valuable information regarding what is happening between point A and point B. For example, consider your network connecting to a business partner and allowing the partner access to your inventory system. You've made the proper access and NAT rules. You've ensured that routes exist and everything is in place to conduct business.

If you receive a phone call from the business partner, stating that they are unable to access the inventory system, one of the first places you'll look is your firewall. After verifying that the rules have been applied, take a look at your log files. Do you see the partner trying to initiate a connection? If not, this is a good indicator of faulty routing between the two parties. If so, did the firewall allow the transaction or did it drop the connection? A dropped connection could mean misconfiguration of the rules, and a passed connection could indicate either a different type of misconfiguration or lack of routing between the firewall and inventory system. Perhaps the initial connection was made, but it couldn't be passed back to the originator. A number of things can occur. It is fair to say that nearly 75% percent of the time, the problem will be routing and/or firewall rules but, regardless, your log entries will act as an excellent resource in resolving issues.

The ability to provide comprehensible reporting is key if you are to make the best use of your firewall. It's helpful to have a central log repository because it consolidates your information and allows you easy access to all information, as opposed to running different reports on multiple firewalls and crossreferences reports. This isn't to say that there aren't situations where you'll want to run reports specific to a single firewall, but having a central repository is helpful, if only to isolate processing to one device.

....

 KEY POINT

> The ability to provide comprehensible reporting is key if you are to make the best use of your firewall.

Firewall vendors provide reporting with their products; in addition, there are third-party products that also do a very nice job. If you're going it alone and wish to create usable reporting, you could take a simple approach, including Perl scripting or Microsoft Excel. Of course, given the right skills, you could create a database and write reports using a database front end. The choice is yours and largely depends on your specific needs.

Reports can tell you a number of things about your operating environment. You may want to create reports specific to dropped connections, or perhaps you are troubleshooting and require a report that is time-based. You can filter on specific devices, networks, and even services. You may be interested in who or what utilizes most of your firewall resources. In this case, you'd report on "top-talkers." Depending on your requirements, the level of skill possessed within your organization and the tools you're using, you could report on anything!

Your reports and the log files themselves provide you with valuable auditing information. Armed with this information, you can refine your firewall rules to implement more granular access controls. Although you would need to exercise extreme caution, you could potentially block a problem network. If you see someone regularly causing mischief, you could block his or her specific IP address. Remember that this is only an example and that ignoring specific IP addresses is easily circumvented by using a different IP address. The point is that you can use your logging information to improve security.

Log files also provide prosecution support. Your log files will give you information regarding access. In the event that you discover suspicious-looking transactions, you can further monitor or, if confirmed, take appropriate actions. The course of action you choose will be based on the incident response policies your organization has in place. If you don't currently have these policies, you should consider creating them. A specific incident may warrant contacting the abuse department of an ISP or it could cause you to seek legal assistance. Your policies will help define this, and logged information will help to substantiate your claims.

Managing firewalls is similar to managing servers, routers, or any other information resource, with an emphasis on security and asset protection. As with all new concepts, it just takes a little time to become acclimated to how everything works and what the best practices, tricks, and tips are for making your job easier.

BUSINESS APPLICATION · · · · · · · · · · · · · · · · · · ·

Have you heard the phrase, "A chain is only as strong as its weakest link"? The same principle applies to business partnerships and connectivity between information resources. Think about the following scenario. You have taken great pains to secure your perimeter; you've even begun to secure all of the information resources within your organization. Furthermore, you're working to raise awareness, and you've earmarked funds for security policies and procedures. Let's also imagine that a partner of yours is connected to your network, because it enables the transfer of important client information that is updated nightly.

Many times, your connecting partner lacks commensurate security controls. Unfortunately, this scenario is seen all the time. In many cases, organizations allow business partners a direct connection to their internal LAN. To the point, you could have a seemingly secure environment, but trusting an insecure partner could mean ruin.

It is no more difficult to terminate a partner connection at your firewall than it is your LAN. Segmenting these connections allows you to control the level of access your partners receive and limit the liability faced from internal users.

At times, security is seen as a business inhibitor. Firewalls play a large part in shaping this perception, due to the fact that they control access. *Control*, rather than *limit*, is the key word. Although it may take extra time and money to ensure that a business solution is secure, you will be enabled to conduct transactions and exchange information without leaving information systems completely vulnerable. Although it is difficult to quantify, you'll foster customer confidence and protect your brand, which ultimately saves you money.

It is important to integrate security and, more specifically, firewall changes into your mainstream project planning and change management process. This will raise awareness among those involved with networking initiatives and will bring possible deviations to light. From time to time, the benefits of business and network connectivity may override the security needs of the organization. In this case, you must weigh the merits of the situation to ensure that they outweigh potential risks. Keep in mind that any time you're dealing with security that it makes no sense to spend more securing an entity than the entity is worth.

SUMMARY . . . .

Firewalls separate your valuable assets from threats. Firewalls control access to your network but they also regulate communications flow, control allowed types of communications, support encrypting traffic between cooperating firewalls (VPNs), and can authenticate users.

There are three basic types of firewalls. Network layer firewalls may be implemented as filtering routers with minimum overhead and less protection. Application layer firewalls use proxies to provide a higher level of protection with more overhead. Hybrids try to provide the best of both worlds.

Firewalls use access rules to enforce policy. Although simple, many organizations fail to implement these rules properly, leaving themselves open to attack.

Firewalls can be used to create nonaddressable network segments, allowing a company to have private network segments that don't require more Internet addresses. Firewalls can implement extranets and a DMZ to protect a PSN and remote access mechanisms. Firewalls are routinely configured in a high-availability architecture, where two firewalls work together to back each other up and share traffic load.

Firewalls are a necessary part of any security infrastructure.

ENDNOTE . . . .

1. An RFC is a Request for Comments from the Internet Engineering Task Force (IETF). This is essentially a draft standard for Internet operation.

6 Vulnerability Scanners

In this chapter . . .

- Why Your Machines Are Configured Insecurely

- What Is a Vulnerability?

- What Are Vulnerability Scanners?

- How to Integrate These Scanners into Your Security Process Effectively

Your machines are not configured securely, leaving you open to unwanted intrusion from the Internet and other security threats. This is the case for a variety of reasons, and enterprises are constantly working to improve the situation. Vulnerability scanners are the front-line tools for finding and eradicating vulnerabilities of all types.

YOUR COMPUTERS ARE *NOT* CONFIGURED SECURELY . . . .

No matter how much effort you invest in keeping your computers up-to-date with the latest patches, you will still have improperly configured machines in your enterprise, leading to an increased level of risk. This is for multiple reasons.

Proper Configuration Is Difficult

Secure configuration requires a highly educated staff with access to the latest vulnerability information, patching techniques, and software. The more machines you have, the more diverse your network will be, making it harder to know exactly what you have to do. It's rare to have all of the latest information for all the different platforms that comprise your network. Even if you have this information, your staff has to be able to interpret it and determine the proper way to roll out the fixes to your network without impacting the availability or reliability of your mission-critical applications.

It is normal for enterprises of all sizes to have very complex environments. One large international bank has over 15,000 computers using seven different operating systems, including Solaris, Linux, HP/UX, Windows 3.11, Window NT 3.5.1, Windows NT 4.0, and Windows 2000. In the bank's Windows NT 4.0 environment, there are six patch levels available. In total, there are over 40 combinations of operating system and patch levels. This bank has a staff of seven tracking security vulnerabilities and fixes on these computers.

Smaller organizations may have less complexity, but there are fewer people to do the research, make the judgments, and apply the patches. The result is that the relative complexity of the smaller environment (relative to the ability to manage the systems) may actually be higher than that of a large international bank.

Consistency Is Hard in Large Enterprises

The complexity of multiple sites, diverse business unit requirements, and diverse skill levels in the staffs across your business will almost guarantee that your entire enterprise will never be at exactly the same level of protection. Tracking this consistency level is an important metric in determining your risk level.

The same bank mentioned above has 30 primary office locations around the world and over 100 business units with their own applications and IT support personnel hired locally. Some staff members are aware of security but there are no enterprise-wide standards. There are procedures in place for central reporting of patch levels but the information is uneven.

Enterprises Are Living, Breathing, and Changing Things

Business requirements change every day. Machines move in, machines move out. People are hired, and people leave. Companies are acquired, and business units are spun out. These daily changes assure a level of inconsistency and multiple opportunities for the introduction of poorly configured systems.

The bank has purchased several other banks in the last few years. Each of these new businesses is being integrated over time. Each arrived with its own security expertise and weaknesses. The expertise can be used to the advantage of the acquirer, and the weaknesses usually introduce new security vulnerabilities into the enterprise. One interesting note is the cultural clashes that occur when a smaller company is acquired with higher security standards than the acquirer and the new unit is asked to "dumb down" its procedures.

Vendors Delivered Insecure Software to You

It's true. Historically, security is not built in to most software applications and operating systems. This means that you may have legacy applications with few or no software controls. These days, security is a hot topic, and many software vendors build security features right in. This is great until you realize that most configuration defaults are not secure, and these have likely been deployed all over your enterprise. Your legacy applications have probably been configured poorly for years.

These problems go beyond blank administrative passwords. Routinely, auditors review the bank's controls and realize that there are significant security issues with legacy software applications. However, it is always "officially" determined that the threat is acceptable, as long as it is addressed in the future. This cycle goes on for years, mainly because the operational costs of fixing these problems can be prohibitive. A good example of this is collecting and reviewing audit data. Everyone is supposed to be doing it. Very few are.

Keeping Up on Patches and Updates Is Very Difficult

Operating systems such as UNIX and Windows 2000 have special security requirements because all of your software applications run on top of them. Vulnerabilities in these complex systems are routinely programming errors that require patches (Microsoft calls these *Service Packs.*) Patches require testing and significant deployment efforts, leading to inconsistency and risks spread throughout your network.

The bank has excellent procedures, measured by any standard, for patch testing and rollout. However, the sheer magnitude of the effort and the inconsistency of the various installed systems pushes significant patch rollouts to six-month cycles or longer. Each of the applications has to be tested by a central IT department, then by each business unit to ensure that it doesn't break any of their applications. No business unit is willing to risk its trading floor going down for several hours just so it can be safe from the latest DNS vulnerability. However, this means that the trading floor *is vulnerable* to this threat until the patch is rolled out. It's a simple cost/benefit analysis.

Poor Administrators Change Things Unintentionally

Most administrators know how to administer a system according to their job description and typical duties but many of them are not security experts or even aware of security. These people are asked to install software with features they don't understand; they make changes to permissions to get applications to function correctly, and they sometimes make configuration changes just to make their lives easier. Each of these changes can introduce risk into your systems, and it happens every single day.

This scenario plays itself out every day when administrators of different skill levels are rolling out new applications that are not part of the standard build process. A business unit may be setting up a new application and require a relational database to be installed. The person who usually does this is out that day, so they send one of the new people. The new person doesn't know how to set it up securely, so they do the best they can, opening up several vulnerabilities on the way. No one notices, and soon this new application becomes mission-critical, based on an insecurely configured database.

Hackers and Insiders Change Things Intentionally

Even if you have solved most of the challenges of keeping your systems configured securely and your staff is brilliant enough never to make mistakes, you still have to worry about malicious changes from the inside and outside. If these threats didn't exist, you wouldn't need to worry so much about security.

The bank has excellent procedures for establishing privileged accounts, including the filling out of forms and approval by management. One administrator found this procedure to be too much trouble, so he created a set of privileged accounts across a number of mission-critical machines for his own use without going through the procedures. Because no one knew about these accounts, he also used very insecure passwords leaving the enterprise vulnerable to outside attack. By bypassing controls, he also left the enterprise without any record of his actions, so that these accounts could not be monitored and administered, also raising risk.

Ultimately, you have to accept that, no matter what your process and procedures for change control and secure configuration are, you will still suffer from some number of systems being configured incorrectly. Worry if your staff tells you otherwise. So what can you do about this situation?

KEY POINT

> Viruses are a clear and present danger but they can also be dealt with very effectively, using protection techniques in conjunction with detection and eradication software.

By regularly scanning your network for improper configurations, you can gather important information about the state of your security posture and know exactly what areas of your network need which types of fixes. This will lower risk overall in your network and help direct your limited resources to actual risk areas rather than "shotgunning" fixes at the network in general. Scanning helps you accomplish the following tasks:

Access Control. Scanning assures that file systems use "least privilege" access permissions and ensures that all network shared drives require password authentication.

User Accounts. Confirm that authentication policies are enforced on user accounts defined on all servers and that unused accounts are not retained.

Patch Levels. Scanning is used to confirm that every operating system has the most recent security patches, service packs, and software to track known vulnerabilities, including HTML, XML, script, and CGI exploits.

Services. Confirm that servers and client desktops run only necessary network services and that these services are properly configured, with access controls to restrict use.

VULNERABILITY SCANNERS . . . .

A vulnerability scanner is a piece of software that scans your network for poor configurations and other "holes" in your security. Scanning software sits at a central location in your network and essentially lobs "attacks" on your machines in a sequential fashion. When an attack is successful, the scanner makes a note of this in its database and continues the scan. At the end of a scan, a report is generated that indicates which machines were vulnerable to which attacks. This report can be used to understand which machines need patches or configuration changes to lower risk.

Discussing vulnerability scanners can be difficult due to their nature. The terms in the last paragraph (*holes, attacks, vulnerable, success*) are not definitive in their usage. In other words "attacks" aren't really attacks because they are not malicious and are not executed in the same manner as a malicious attack, in many cases. Here are some more qualifications of these terms:

Holes can be the presence of malicious software, a version of software with a security vulnerability (that may or may not have a patch), poor configurations, incompatible applications, or many other potential problems. Scanners look for a wide range of vulnerabilities.

Attacks are executed only so far as to determine that a real attack would have some ability to succeed. In many cases, network Application Programming Interfaces (APIs) are used to check configurations directly without actually trying to exploit a hole. A variety of techniques are used to scan systems and networks for vulnerabilities.

Successful is qualified because many of the attacks fall short of actually exploiting the vulnerability. Many of the results may not be completely definitive in their conclusions.

Vulnerable is qualified for the same reason that successful is qualified. A conclusion that a system is vulnerable to an attack because certain conditions are found to exist is not always a definitive conclusion that such an attack would succeed.

These qualifications mean that scanners are not always definitive in their conclusions, influenced by the types of vulnerabilities for which they are scanning and the quality of the test. However, these are still very good tools for assessing security posture and determining segments of your enterprise that require attention.

Most vulnerability scanners test a host computer and let you know what network services are running on that host. The better scanners will do not only that, but also tell you whether the services running are susceptible to a known vulnerability or are poorly configured. For Windows NT Servers and Workstations, scanners perform an extensive list of tests including the following:

- Network port scanning using UDP
- Network port scanning using TCP SYN, ACK, FIN packets
- Scanning of Network Neighborhood
- DNS and SNMP vulnerability testing
- Scanning for known Trojans and backdoors, e.g., Back Orifice
- Server Message Block Querying
- Transport protocol and session enumeration
- Active Services testing
- Ability to establish NULL IPC$ session to host
- Service Pack and Hotfix enumeration
- User account details and privilege enumeration
- Share enumeration, including Admin($)
- Testing for ability to query NT registry
- Checks for known Vulnerable URL structures and CGIs
- Vulnerability to known DoS attacks
- SMTP, FTP, POP3 banner grabs and service-specific vulnerabilities
- MS SQL Server vulnerability checks

There are two basic approaches to vulnerability scanning: network-based scanners and host-based scanners. Network scanning is by far the most popular because it is the easiest to implement, but it has several risks associated with it if used improperly. Host-based scanners are more stable and supply unique information, but they require an agent to be installed on each computer that will be scanned.

Network-Based Scanners

Network scanners are software tools that run from a central location and launch "attacks" over the network to test for various vulnerabilities. A central console is used to map the entire network and send network packets to machines that are being scanned to gather information. The console can be directed for specific attacks to scan and on which machines.

Figure 6-1 shows how a network scanner integrates with your network. The central console sends out packets and receives responses from the scanned machines. These packets mimic the network attacks to check for vulnerabilities. A database of results is created, from which reports are generated.

Network scanners are easy to use because all you have to do is load them onto an available machine, point them at your network, and shoot. However, they have associated risks, including:

- They can be "chatty" on the network, draining valuable bandwidth.
- Some tests can cause scanned machines to crash. Network scanners discover vulnerabilities by trying to exploit them. Some of these vulnerabilities, if successful, will cause the machine to crash. In some cases, the tests alone—successful or not—can cause an end-user system to crash.
- Some combinations of tests can take a very long time, using considerable resources on your network.
- Hackers and curious employees can use this same "point-and-shoot" ease to discover vulnerable parts of your network.

To use network scanners safely, you should understand each of the tests, including its risks and resource requirements. Scan selected parts of your network and control the types and frequency of the scans. We'll talk more about this later.

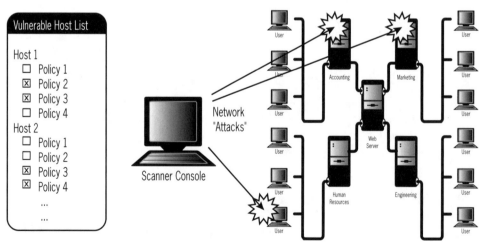

Figure 6–1
A network scanner in your enterprise.

Host-Based Scanners

Host-based scanners differ from network scanners primarily in architecture. Host-based scanners are agent-based, which means that a message from a central console will cause a vulnerability to be checked locally, rather than over the network (see Figure 6–2). The only traffic on the network is message traffic between the agent and console. Another primary difference is that a local agent can check for the existence of an insecure configuration without actually trying to exploit the vulnerability.

Host-based scanning doesn't suffer from many of the problems associated with network scanning. Network traffic is significantly reduced because there is no attack traffic on the network for each scan. Host-based tests are not likely to crash end-user systems because the tests are just checking for the existence of the vulnerability, rather than trying to exploit it. Host-based scanners can't be used by others to scan your network because they are usually activated through a secure channel between the console and scanned computer that can be used only by authorized people.

Port Scanners

Port scanners are a special type of vulnerability scanner used to detect and "map" machines in a network and the ports those machines are using. A port is an address within the computer that listens for network traffic. Computers have over 10,000

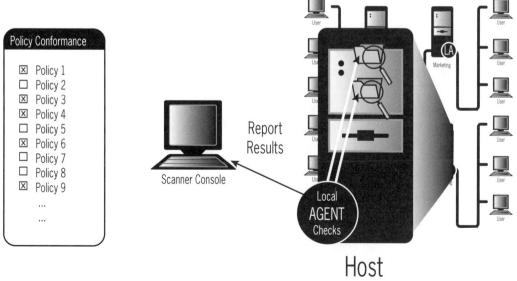

Figure 6–2
Host-based scanning in your enterprise.

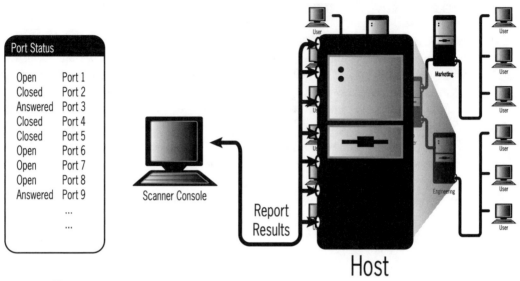

Figure 6–3
A port scanner.

possible ports. Many of them are idle but many of them have applications listening that will respond to the port scanner. Figure 6-3 shows a computer with multiple ports on the network.

Most vulnerability scanners have some kind of port-scanning capability to find computers on a network but there are tools available that specialize in this capability. One of the most well known of these is a freeware tool called *NMAP*. NMAP ("Network Mapper") is an open source utility for network exploration designed to scan large networks rapidly. NMAP uses IP packets to determine what hosts are available and what services (ports), operating systems (and operating system versions), and firewalls are in use. NMAP is free software, available with full source code under the terms of the GNU GPL. For more information on NMAP, go to *www.insecure.org/nmap*.

COMMERCIAL SCANNER PRODUCTS . . . .

A number of scanner products are on the market. Each has its own advantages and disadvantages. A scanner is typically an enterprise-class software tool with network system identification, data management, user-defined vulnerability rules, and security reporting capabilities. They test the network infrastructure for security vulnerabilities and provide recommendations on how to fix them. Some use root-cause and path-analysis to illustrate the exact sequence of steps taken to uncover vulnerabilities, enabling administrators to identify exactly where to correct vulnerabilities. We recommend that you go through a requirements analysis and acquisition process to select the right product for your enterprise.

FREE VULNERABILITY SCANNERS . . . .

There are a number of free scanning products available for smaller enterprises that don't want to bear the expense of acquiring and operating a commercial scanner. Buyers beware, however. These tools can be effective in the hands of an expert but you should realize that they may have poor user interfaces, little or no support, and are kept up to date less frequently than their commercial counterparts.

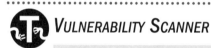 *VULNERABILITY SCANNER*

> The GNIT scanner for Windows NT produces an HTML report that can be viewed with your browser and performs certain checks. It can be downloaded at *www.security.ellicit.org/programs*. GNIT scanner checks:
>
> - NBTStat scanning
> - Null IPC Session establishment
> - Net View scanning
> - Lists all Global Groups
> - Lists all Local Groups
> - Lists all User Accounts
>
> GNIT gives the following details for each account:
>
> - Global and local group membership
> - Account expiration date
> - Full name
> - Bad password attempts
> - Comments
> - Last login date
> - Last logoff date
> - Login server
> - Successful logins

- Password age
- Primary group ID
- Privilege level
- RID (relative identifier)

GNIT performs the following functions:

- Lists numbers of network adapter cards installed on remote machine
- Lists which protocols are bound to which NICs
- Displays Web server type and version
- Scans for 84 known vulnerable URL structures (easily modified)
- Grabs FTP banners
- Attempts to log in anonymously via FTP
- Grabs SMTP banners
- Grabs POP3 banners
- Checks Telnet connects
- Checks WINS connects
- Checks DNS connects
- Checks NNTP connects
- Checks LDAP connects
- Checks SOCKS connects
- Checks Microsoft SQL Server connects
- Checks pcAnywhere connects
- Checks Wingate Log File Service connects
- Checks AltHTTP connects
- Checks Netbus (default) connects
- Checks VNC connects

Winfingerprint

Winfingerprint scans your hosts and returns information about NetBIOS shares, users, groups, transport protocols, date and time, and services. It will scan systems in your Network Neighborhood, attempt to establish Null Sessions, and query the Win-

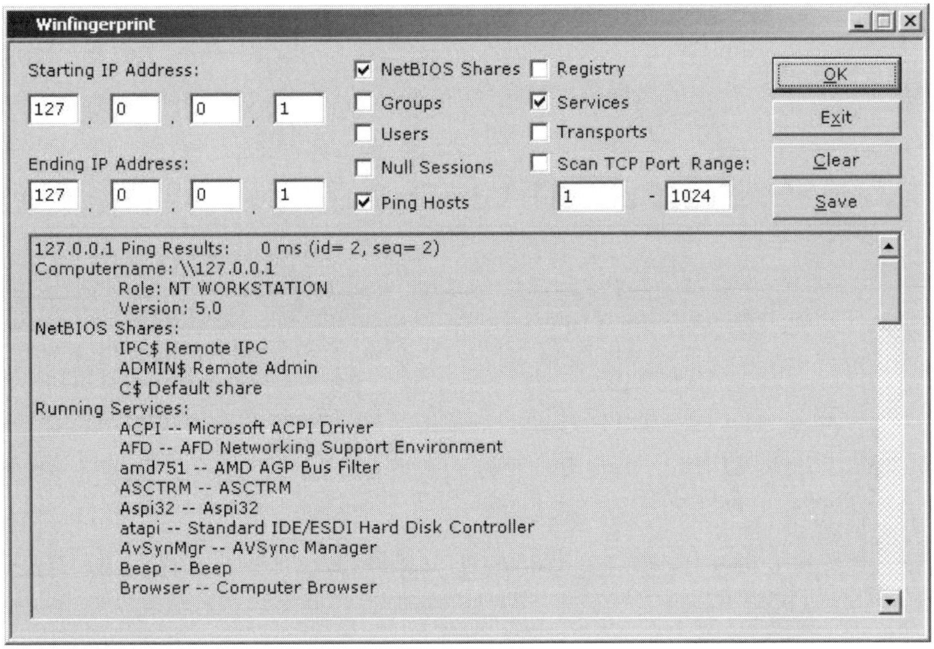

```
Winfingerprint                                                    _ □ X

Starting IP Address:        ☑ NetBIOS Shares  ☐ Registry        ┌──────────┐
                                                                │    OK    │
 127  .  0  .  0  .  1      ☐ Groups           ☑ Services       └──────────┘
                            ☐ Users            ☐ Transports        Exit

Ending IP Address:          ☐ Null Sessions    ☐ Scan TCP Port Range:   Clear

 127  .  0  .  0  .  1      ☑ Ping Hosts        1    -  1024       Save

 127.0.0.1 Ping Results:    0 ms (id= 2, seq= 2)                          ▲
 Computername: \\127.0.0.1
        Role: NT WORKSTATION
        Version: 5.0
 NetBIOS Shares:
        IPC$ Remote IPC
        ADMIN$ Remote Admin
        C$ Default share
 Running Services:
        ACPI -- Microsoft ACPI Driver
        AFD -- AFD Networking Support Environment
        amd751 -- AMD AGP Bus Filter
        ASCTRM -- ASCTRM
        Aspi32 -- Aspi32
        atapi -- Standard IDE/ESDI Hard Disk Controller
        AvSynMgr -- AVSync Manager
        Beep -- Beep
        Browser -- Computer Browser                                      ▼
```

Figure 6–4
Winfingerprint interface.

dows NT registry. It reports in HTML. Figure 6–4 illustrates how freeware interfaces have improved significantly over the last few years. Winfingerprint can be downloaded at *www.winfingerprint.sourceforge.net*.

SAINT

The Security Administrator's Integrated Network Tool (SAINT) is designed to assess the security of computer networks. Older versions of SAINT are available for free. Customers can purchase the report writer and autoupdate products to receive the latest versions for free. SAINT is better than most freeware tools because the income stream from the optional products maintain an employed and focused development team. The latest free version can be downloaded from *www.wwdsi.com/saint/index.html*.

Cerberus Information Scanner

Cerberus Information Scanner (CIS) scans the network to detect running services (such as HTTP, SMTP, POP3, FTP, and Portmapper). CIS checks Windows NT systems to see whether any accounts, shares, groups, driver- and user-mode service checks, and registry checks are accessible to unwelcome visitors. It also scans for MS

SQL Server vulnerabilities. CIS was recently acquired by @stake, Inc. (*www.atstake.com*), and a commercial version has been promised. It can be downloaded at *www.cerberus-infosec.co.uk/cis.shtml*.

VULNERABILITY DATABASES . . . .

There are several sources for both vulnerability assessment vendors and your security team to gain access to vulnerability information. A vulnerability database usually includes elements such as a description of the vulnerability, the platforms that are affected, and what the corrective actions are to eliminate the vulnerability. The following is a sampling of the better known vulnerability databases.

BugTraq (*www.securityfocus.com/bid*). Sponsored by Securityfocus.com, this is a very large database of vulnerabilities, including description, exploit details, and fix details.

CERT (*www.cert.org*). The Computer Emergency Response Team (CERT) is a federally funded research and development center operated by Carnegie Mellon University.

X-Force (*xforce.iss.net*). Internet Security Systems (ISS) is a scanner vendor that maintains a team of people to uncover and track vulnerabilities.

CIAC (*www.ciac.org*). The Computer Incident Advisory Center (CIAC) is sponsored by the U.S. Department of Energy. It includes virus alerts, news, and an extensive vulnerability database.

NtBugTraq (*www.ntbugtraq.com*). This database is run by an individual, Russ Cooper, but is one of the more definitive sources for tracking Microsoft vulnerabilities.

SECURITY PROCESS
AND PROCEDURES FOR SCANNERS . . . .

Scanners should be used in conjunction with security processes and procedures based on policies appropriate for your organization. Generally speaking, you should scan mission-critical and high-risk systems more frequently and spend more time fixing vulnerabilities on those systems. Having said that, here are a few tips for different sizes of organizations:

ADVICE FOR A SMALL BUSINESS

For small organizations, scanners can be used once or twice a year and after major system upgrades to confirm that your servers are hardened with the latest configuration changes. This should be possible to accomplish with a few days of work on fewer than 100 servers. The amount of work necessary to bring your systems up-to-date will depend on the severity of the detected vulnerabilities and the value of your mission-critical assets.

ADVICE FOR A MID-SIZED BUSINESS

For medium-sized organizations, scans should be regularly scheduled on mission-critical sections of the network and areas of high threat (such as computers in the firewall DMZ). Other systems may be scanned less frequently. It may be necessary to engage one person at 50 percent of his or her time to scan and disclose that information to the system administration staff.

ADVICE FOR A LARGE ENTERPRISE

Large enterprises should take scanning very seriously. Realize that maintaining current patch levels alone will be a significant undertaking. An independent staff (depending on the size of the enterprise) should be responsible for scanning mission-critical systems on an ongoing basis. Many fixes will require large rollouts of patches and significant testing before rollout. Scanning doesn't solve the problems in large enterprises but it does help you understand where your weaknesses exist.

SUMMARY . . . .

It is not possible to state that you have a secure environment unless you test that environment. Vulnerability scanners perform the most basic level of testing. Every organization that uses computers and is connected to the Internet should have a scanning process.

Organizations with an experienced technical staff and limited scanning requirements may find that free scanners are sufficient. However, the typically difficult user interface of those products may create an unwitting dependence on a technical staff member who could resign tomorrow.

Usage of network versus host scanners is a more complex decision. Ideally, because of the different classes of information they may discover, both should be used.

7 Virus Detection and Content Filters

In this chapter . . .

- The Virus Threat

- Virus Detection

- Content Filters—Keeping Malicious Code Off of Your Systems

$\mathbf{Y}$our machines have malicious software on them that you don't want there. Commonly known as *viruses*, malicious code is basically anything on your computer that does things you don't want, including deleting data, attacking other computers, and sending infected mail to a million of your closest friends. It's a fact and the problem gets worse as the number of servers and workstations you have increases. There is little you can do to eradicate these threats completely but you can control them using virus detection and content filters. These are classes of software that scan your machines and network traffic for viruses, malicious code, and threatening content.

VIRUSES . . . .

Viruses are one of the few clear and present dangers to enterprise security that has an effective countermeasure. Virus detection is one of the "Big Three" enterprise security solutions that most experts will tell you are "must haves." Almost every enterprise does virus detection first, then firewalls, and finally intrusion detection. Some of the more ambitious enterprises also have PKI and authentication initiatives but, without a doubt, if you have computers, you need virus detection.

The Virus Threat

A virus is malicious code that "infects" files on your computers. The virus replicates itself and moves from machine to machine. By malicious code we mean that a virus does things to your computer you don't want, such as reformatting your hard drive or locking up your computer so you can't log in. The replication aspect of viruses is where they get their name. Biological viruses replicate until they have completely overwhelmed the organism they infect. The same can be said of computer viruses. They infect your computer, then spread to all your computers until your enterprise is overwhelmed. Then they start in on your partners and everyone else connected to your network.

Viruses cost you time and money on multiple fronts. It costs money to put protection in place. It costs money to recover when they strike. However, the most expensive aspect of viruses is the loss of time and opportunity as your people sit idle while their infected machines are recovered. Viruses are a real threat and require serious proactive action.

The Wild List

Viruses have been around almost as long as computers. Some famous viruses have included "Melissa," " I LOVE YOU," "Michelangelo," and the "Morris worm." A virus is said to be in "the wild" if it has been verified by two or more of the roughly 50 recognized virus reporting agencies as being out there, spreading, and causing real problems for users. Virus expert Joe Wells started the official "Wild List." It is available at *www.wildlist.org*.

The wild list usually reports between 200 and 300 viruses in the wild each month. Remember that these are the viruses that are spreading. Estimates on the total number of viruses in existence are between 15,000 and 50,000.

How Viruses Work

To fight a virus infection fully, you need to know how viruses work—how they infect other files. There are three ways of writing viruses. The first method consists of overwriting the beginning of the file they are infecting with the virus's own code (see Figure 7–1). This method isn't too effective, because 99 percent of the time the infected

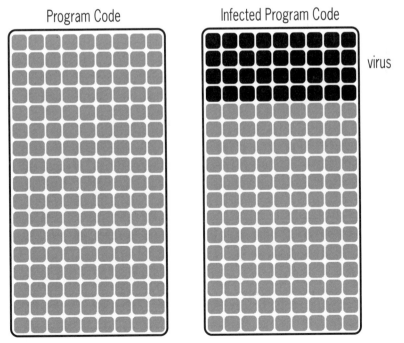

Figure 7–1
Virus infection by overwriting the beginning of a file.

file will not run properly. When the computer reaches the end of the virus code, it will continue with the code that is left from before, if it doesn't exit back to the system.

However, this method can create many errors because the beginning of the program code will be missing. You will usually realize very quickly that something is wrong when a virus spreads in this manner. Also, this type of virus usually causes the computer to crash because the rest of the code is not working. However, if the virus exits with an error message fooling you into thinking your infected application had some other type of error, you may not realize that you are infected until it is too late.

The second type of virus works by adding a jump to the end of the program, where its code appends itself, then continues with a jump back to the beginning where it left off. This is depicted in Figure 7–2. If this is well written, the program shouldn't crash, and your infected application should work as advertised (except, of course, you now have a virus in memory). Usually the only thing that you can detect is a subtle increase in memory utilization by the computer. It can also be detected through

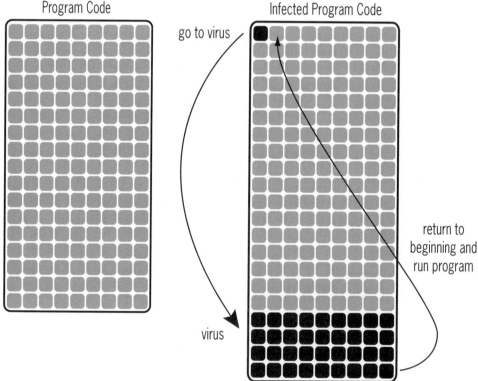

Figure 7–2
Virus infection by jumping to the end of a program.

a change in the size of the program file because it is appended to the end of the program.

The third type of virus works by inserting itself into the data section of the program without making changes to the original, as shown in Figure 7–3. This means that, in some cases, the original works as it used to but in other cases, it doesn't. It depends on how well the virus is written. This type of infection is hard to detect because it does not result in a change to the size of the file, which is usually used as a pretty good indication that a file has been infected.

How Viruses Spread

Viruses are pervasive because they infect multiple files and multiple computers. Viruses have two primary methods of spreading. The first is by infecting every file on the computer that matches their target profiles. Depending on the virus type, the target

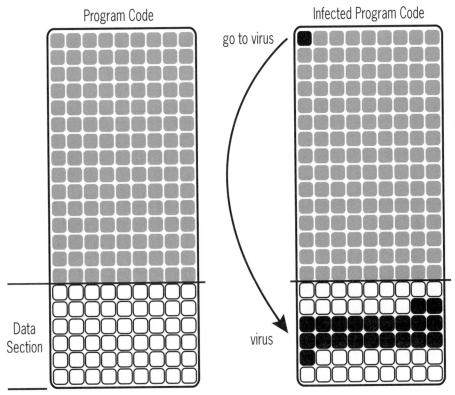

Figure 7–3
Virus infection by writing over data portions of the file.

profile could be data files, applications, emails, or system files. When a virus executes, one of the tasks it performs is a search of your disks for other files to infect. When it finds an appropriate victim file, it inserts (infects) virus code, using one of the methods described above. Depending on the virus, this could literally be hundreds or thousands of files on each computer.

The second way that viruses spread is across the network. Again, this is dependent on the type of virus, but the virus will find a way to scan your network to see whether it can move from computer to computer. The methods for spreading across the network can be as technically advanced as exploiting known vulnerabilities in your network or as simple as sending an email to your buddies asking them to click on the picture of Anna Kournikova. Go ahead, click on Anna. This virus has now moved from one computer to another.

The Virus Calendar

Many viruses have the added threat of spreading quietly, then striking at a predetermined time. "Striking" can range from something as innocent as putting a message up on your screen to something considerably more sinister, such as making you a drone for a distributed DoS attack or reformatting your hard drive.

The Michelangelo virus is an excellent example of the virus calendar. Michelangelo is a boot sector virus that lies quietly in waiting and will then delete your hard drive on March 6th, Michelangelo's birthday. Ironically, one of the Michelangelo virus's most famous traits is the fact that it was the virus disaster that never was.

Discovered in 1991 when a small computer manufacturer publicized the fact that it accidentally delivered 500 copies of the virus on new computers, the press went wild, and predictions of mass destruction on March 6th reigned. In 1992, about 20,000 computers were damaged, which is a relatively low number compared with the 5,000,000 connected computers at the time. The number of infected computers has significantly decreased each year, but every year in the weeks preceding March 6th, numerous press organizations revive the legend of the Michelangelo virus.

Virus Mutation

Computer viruses have many parallels to their biological equivalents. One of the more significant is their ability to mutate and adapt. Biological viruses are pervasive, not only for their ability to spread, but also for their ability to adapt to adverse conditions. Within the context of Darwin's survival-of-the-fittest concept, after the current conditions have killed off most of a virus, its remaining brethren adapt and continue to survive as a new "strain." The same is true in the computer virus world, although through slightly different mechanisms.

There is a dedicated, yet relatively small, segment of the programming population dedicated to the creation of viruses. These are the geniuses behind computer virus mutation. As a virus spreads and becomes "popular" and publicized, its developer will sometimes post the code to hacker and virus writer bulletin boards. Here, where virus writers exchange ideas and code, other virus writers will pick up the code and "improve" it. This is how new strains of computer viruses are born.

These improvements include such gems as taking a relatively innocent virus and adding code to reformat a drive or to insert a DDOS zombie. Sometimes, flaws in the original code are uncovered that allow the virus to spread faster or hide more effectively. Ultimately, the virus is adapting and mutating into multiple strains that have to be tracked and handled.

Common Virus Types

There are several common virus types that you should be aware of in case your organization is attacked. Each type of virus will require different protection measures and a slightly different response if you are hit. These basic types include traditional viruses, worms, malicious applets, Trojans, macro viruses, and email viruses.

Traditional Parasitic Viruses

A traditional parasitic virus is a virus that infects files on your computers and executes unwanted code on your systems. Traditional viruses, such as the previously mentioned Michelangelo virus, are an always-present threat but the virus tools on the market effectively deal with them.

Worms

Worms are a special type of traditional virus that spreads through the exploitation of known network vulnerabilities. The net effect of a worm is uncontrolled growth driven by the pervasiveness of the vulnerabilities exploited by the virus. One of the first and best examples of a worm is the Morris worm, which turned the fledgling Internet into a nightmare of sleepless nights and frustration in 1988.

At 6 p.m. on November 2, 1988, a small program written by Robert Tappan Morris, who was then a 23-year-old doctoral student at Cornell University, was released onto the Internet. It spread to over 60,000 computers in less than 12 hours. Ironically, the Morris worm was never intended to do harm. It did not alter files, destroy computers, transmit cracked passwords, or place versions of itself on the computer to execute at a later time. Its only purpose was to get on as many Sun 3 and

VAX computers as it could, using common security holes at the time. Unfortunately, the program had bugs and crashed the computers that it infected.

This disaster was caused by the fact that the vulnerabilities the program exploited were present in most computers, and the program was not smart enough to know that a machine was infected so it just infected every computer again and again. The program made so many copies of itself on each infected computer that the computer was "brought to its knees" and eventually crashed. When the worm was eradicated and the computer rebooted, the neighboring machines reinfected it immediately. The only way to prevent reinfection was to disconnect systems from the Internet.

It took several weeks to eradicate the worm and patch all the infected computers. The U.S. General Accounting Office has estimated damages to be between $100,000 and $10,000,000 at some hosts during the attack. The Morris worm stands today as the definitive example of a worm and single-handedly put an international emphasis on information security that did not exist before 1988.

Malicious Internet Applets

Malicious Internet applets refer to anything you can catch through your Web browser. An applet is a small application that is downloaded from the Internet by a browser and executed on a computer on your users' behalf to "help" them. Friendly applets perform useful tasks, such as playing music, displaying animation, or calculating your 401(k). Of course, this code can also be malicious and do things you don't want, including plant viruses.

These applets are usually written in Java, Visual Basic (VBS), or JavaScript and can be automatically executed by your computer by just clicking links in a Web page. Malicious applets usually show up on your system in benign forms such as "click on the dancing pigs to see something cool!" Remember this. Unwitting users always, *always*, click on the dancing pigs. The pigs dance, and you have a virus. Then the virus begins to spread...

There are several ways to protect yourself from malicious applets, including configuring your browser to be secure, using content filtering, and removing the ability for your computer to execute certain scripting languages, such as Visual Basic. The end of this chapter deals with filtering.

Trojans

Trojans are named for the Trojan horse of ancient Greek mythology. A Trojan is a quiet sort of virus with the sole purpose of capturing your user credentials and sending them back to its author. Once a Trojan has infected your computer, every connection you make to a computer or application will be captured. Every password you type in will be passed back to the hacker who wrote the Trojan. Every credit card number you type in will be copied. The only sign you will see of a Trojan is a few extra lights blinking on your modem. Then, of course, there will be the call from your credit card company or your corporate security office.

Macro Viruses

Macro viruses show up where you would least expect them—in your documents. This is uniquely a Microsoft problem. Microsoft, in its admirable quest to provide the most productive, flexible, and powerful desktop software in the world, added a very useful capability to its Office suite of products that led to this new class of threat. It added a small, executable language so that when you accessed a specific place in your document or a specific cell in your spreadsheet, context-sensitive decisions could be made with respect to formatting or presentation. To make it even more powerful, Microsoft made it possible to execute an application with all of the authority and control of the operating system.

This powerful capability is the perfect entrée for viruses. Now all you have to do is open a document with an embedded macro virus, and it will infect you. Macro viruses spread the same ways that all viruses spread but one key is that they infect documents, not applications.

There is one basic defense against macro viruses. Turn off macros in your Microsoft applications. When macros were first introduced into the Office suite, they were turned on by default. Today, when a document is opened with embedded macros (good or bad), a dialog box appears, asking whether you would like macros enabled. Unless you are *very* familiar with the document, its origin, and the requirement for macros, you should always respond "no" to this question. In fact, if you know that the author of the document is not advanced enough to be using embedded macros (they are a pretty advanced feature), you should immediately suspect that you have been sent a macro virus. This avoidance technique should be publicized widely within your security policies and security awareness program.

Boot-Sector Viruses

The boot sector is the place on your computer disk that executes first when you boot your computer. A boot sector virus replaces the code that is used to load your operating system with virus code. Boot sector viruses usually spread through infected disks that are in your disk drive when the computer boots. The best way to protect yourself from this type of virus is to configure your computer to boot from a local hard drive, as opposed to the diskette drive (A) that is usually the default.

Email Viruses

In an effort to make mail more powerful, Microsoft provided the capability for mail messages to execute code as an embedded part of the email document. Sometimes, the code you execute does things you may not want, including emailing your friends with the virus you just contracted. Luckily, configuring your mail program not to execute scripts embedded in email can control this type of virus.

Even if you have your mail program configured properly, you can still be a victim. Another form of email virus is exploited through malicious attachments that you are fooled into opening through simple misdirection. These emails are harmless when opened until the attachments are clicked on and opened. It is easy to fool an unwitting public into clicking on anything if they are offered a reward such as dancing pigs or singing fish. Hey, they're cool. And now you have a virus.

Virus Hoaxes

Not all viruses are viruses. One of the core reasons that people create viruses is to create mischief. Another group of individuals, who certainly overlap the group that creates real viruses, noticed that whenever a virus really hit its stride, it made the national news, got people worked up, mobilized work forces, and had many other "desirable" effects. All these effects were usually preceded by a rash of emails warning of a specific set of circumstances, such as an email or application to avoid. Somebody figured out that the precursor (the warning email) could bring about the same anarchistic effect as the real thing. So was born the virus hoax—threats and warnings of real viruses that mobilize work forces and significantly affect people's behavior. Some famous email hoaxes include:

Good Times. This is one of the original hoaxes that was a simple message sent by email, warning users that opening an email with the subject "Good Times" would result in a virus infection that would delete their hard drives. No such Good Times virus existed, but numerous people started sending messages with that subject line, just to be "funny." This hoax started in 1994 and is still circulating today.

Elf Bowling and Frog in a Blender. Nstorm (*www.nstorm.com*) is a creator of entertaining (if slightly off-color) animations. The popularity of these little applications led eventually to an email circulated claiming that these programs were infected with dangerous viruses. Nstorm has had one of the major antivirus vendors certify that the programs on its Web site are virus free and that there has been no major outbreak of infections based on these programs. However, people interested in sharing these programs with their friends should send them a link to the Web site, rather than the program itself.

Mobile Phone Infection. The creators of these hoaxes have become particularly inventive as they sow fear and doubt through all the technological "gizmos" in popular culture. This hoax claimed that when the caller ID on your mobile phone claimed the calling number was "Unavailable" and you answered the phone, you would be infected with a virus that would erase critical information in your phone, requiring that you buy a new phone. So the email warned "DO NOT ANSWER YOUR PHONE!"

It is easy to see how these hoaxes, with even a little credibility, can cause an impact on society. However, there is a number of sites that track these hoaxes, so it is relatively easy to keep up on legitimate threats and fake ones. Example hoax tracking sites are:

- *www.stiller.com/hoaxes.htm*
- *www.icsalabs.com/html/communities/antivirus/hoaxes.shtml*

VIRUS DETECTION . . . .

Viruses are a clear and present danger but they can also be dealt with very effectively using protection techniques in conjunction with detection and eradication software.

 KEY POINT

> Viruses are a clear and present danger but they can also be dealt with very effectively, using protection techniques in conjunction with detection and eradication software.

Tips to Protect Against Viruses

The following are basic virus protection steps. These steps should be part of both your security policy and procedures. Security awareness for your employees is a vital component of virus protection because many of these tips require actions on the part of your users.

1. Use virus protection software. This software scans your drives for malicious code and disinfects your computer, in most cases. There are several credible vendors. The most popular are Symantec, McAfee, and Trend Micro. And be sure your virus definitions are kept up to date.

2. Disable ActiveX in your browser.

3. Change the CMOS boot-up sequence to boot from a local hard drive. This completely eliminates the danger from pure boot sector viruses.

4. Keep backups of your critical data.

5. Scan email attachments for viruses. Your virus detection program should be able to do this automatically on both desktops and servers that handle email.

6. Disable Windows Scripting Host (WSH). This will prevent email viruses written in Visual Basic (.*VBS* extensions), such as Anna Kournikova and I LOVE YOU.

7. Enable macro protection in Microsoft Office to prevent macro viruses.

8. Block executable attachments from entering through your firewall. Educate your users never to execute a program they receive in an email from the Internet.

Enterprise Virus Protection

Detecting and eliminating viruses in your enterprise is a requirement. Viruses are pervasive and unavoidable. Virus detection software has been around for many years. It is a mature capability that should be deployed on every single computer in your enterprise. A good virus product should include central control, infected file repair, quarantine capabilities, and an Internet update capability, backed up by a qualified virus research team.

Central Control

Central control and administration are required to manage virus detection in enterprises of any size because the virus programs are enabled on each computer. It is unreasonable to expect each of your users individually to manage virus protection software, so central control allows security professionals to manage it securely and keep systems up to date.

Infected File Repair

Infected files should be repaired as soon as possible to prevent further spreading. File repair is a standard feature on most virus detection software.

Quarantine

Quarantine is a secure location on disk where infected files are placed for further study or recovery in cases where file repair was not possible. The end user and/or your virus response/security teams may access these quarantined files.

Research Team

The quality of the team that creates virus signatures for your tool is an important characteristic of your virus protection software. When making a purchase decision, you should look closely at the qualifications of this team, including history, number of viruses discovered (are they leaders or followers?), and time to create fixes after viruses are discovered.

Internet Integration

Internet integration allows the virus protection software to download the latest fixes directly from the Internet, providing the quickest protection. Viruses today are a very active field, and it is necessary to have immediate updates and easy distribution if you are going to keep up. Very large organizations may want to look for the ability to download updates from the Internet to a central control point and from there to various desktop and server systems.

CONTENT FILTERS . . . .

One of the significant ways that viruses and other malicious code spreads is over the Internet. This fact has led to the creation of "content" filters that work to prevent malicious code from entering your network. Content filters are network-based security mechanisms that scan network traffic for "suspicious" information. All content filters work on the same basic premise: to track Internet traffic going in and out of your network, looking for things that should not be going in and out of your firewall. This technology is in contrast to virus scanners that check objects on your disks for infection.

There are three separate categories of content filters: URL filtering, email filtering, and malicious code detection. URL filtering checks the Universal Resource Locator name (*www....com*) against a database of known sites to determine whether people are going places they aren't supposed to. Email filtering determines whether people are sending or receiving information through email that is suspicious. Finally, malicious code detection attempts to detect when a special class of Web-based viruses are attempting to infect your systems. We consider all three types to be "content" filters because they are detecting based on data content of network messages.

How Content Filtering Works

There are two basic ways to filter network message contents: pass-through and pass-by. Pass-through mechanisms intercept messages and make a policy decision before passing the message on to the recipient. Pass-by mechanisms "sniff" a copy of the message off the network and break the connection if the message violates policy. The method best for you will depend on your requirements.

Pass-Through Content Filters

A pass-through solution is server-based. Traffic passing through the firewall is stopped, and a query is made to a filter server for confirmation before the information is passed on. The filter server has a list of rules, configured by the user, as to whether the traffic is allowed. If it is, a message is sent back to the firewall to allow the traffic through. If it is not allowed, a response can be executed, such as a disconnect message sent to both sides of the connection. Software from Websense is an example of a pass-through solution.

Figure 7–4 shows a pass-through architecture. On the left side of the diagram is a user sitting at a desktop computer, using a Web browser. On the right side are two Web sites, of which one is allowed (business-related) and the other is not (*www.espn.com*). When the user selects the business-related site, a message is sent to the firewall, where the traffic is intercepted and compared with the rule-list on the filter server. It is on the allowed list, so the message is sent to the business-related Web site, and a connection is made. When the user selects *www.espn.com*, the message is sent to the firewall where the traffic is intercepted and compared with the rule-list on the filter server. It is on the not allowed list, so a disconnect message is sent to both sides of the connection.

Pass-By Content Filters

A pass-by solution is completely network-based. The network traffic flows freely but it is analyzed in real-time by the content filter to decide whether it is legitimate. Suspicious traffic is blocked. Surf-control is an example of a pass-by solution.

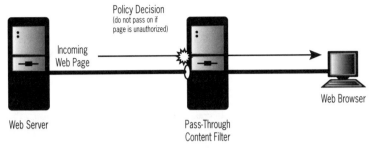

Figure 7–4
A "pass-through" content filter.

Figure 7–5 shows a pass-by architecture. Traffic is read in real time as it passes the monitor point. A rule set decides whether the connection should be allowed to continue. Using the example of connecting to a business-related site versus *www.espn.com*, the traffic is allowed through until the content-filter rule set decides that the connection to *www.espn.com* should be disconnected (which should take only seconds).

There are advantages and disadvantages to both approaches. The pass-through mechanisms have the advantage that no traffic will ever be allowed through that is properly identified in the rule set of the filter server, whereas the pass-by solution will let a small number of packets through. Most malicious code filters are pass-through

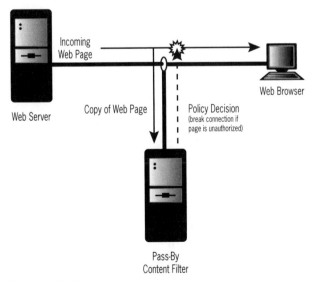

Figure 7–5
A "pass-by" content filter.

mechanisms because they are intended to stop the spread of viruses. The pass-by mechanisms have the advantage of not holding up traffic waiting for a go/no go decision from the filter server, as is done with the pass-through mechanism.

Email Content Tracking

An email filter can indicate how employees are using email. Email content filtering is valuable in determining whether insiders are passing information through email with security relevance. They have the additional benefit of being able to strip out large attachments to reduce network bandwidth usage and halting the proliferation of MPEG files. They can also be used to stop "VBA" script attachments that can spread worms.

Email filtering can also trigger from keywords to indicate unapproved email usage or other behavior. These types of mechanisms are usually triggered from keywords such as the following:

- Sending proprietary information home where it is less secure. Keywords: <Project Code words>, "FOR INTERNAL USE ONLY," "PROPRIETARY," and "TOP SECRET."
- Sending threatening information. Keywords: "KILL" and "BOMB."
- Sending inappropriate and potentially libelous messages. Keywords: Any swear word.
- Using email for unapproved purposes. Keywords: "ESPN," "SEX," and "STOCK."
- Email viruses. Keywords: "I LOVE YOU."

Malicious Code Filters

Malicious code is a special problem for enterprises. Malicious code is any program that executes things you don't want, such as planting a virus, sending information outside the firewall to a hacker, or formatting your hard drive. This undesirable code is often embedded in a program you do want to execute, as discussed above. Many times, these gems are included in those cute programs that you download from the Internet or that your friends send you in email.

You know that cute, animated cartoon with the frog in the blender? Okay, maybe *you* don't think it's cute but a lot of your employees do. There are hacker tools available on the Internet to embed any program a hacker wants into that cartoon. When any employee executes it, he or she also executes the hacker's code. When an administrator executes it with administrative privileges, the administrator is effectively giving the hacker administrative privilege.

For this reason, many malicious code filters are designed to keep executable programs from the Internet out of your system.

URL Filters

A URL filter is one of the most common types of content filter. These systems are designed to track, block, and control where your employees go on the Internet. These are very popular to track inappropriate use of the Internet. There are commercial tools specifically designed to do this type of filtering. URL filters are one of the fastest-growing segments of content filtering.

Benefits to URL filters include productivity gains (less time spent on sites not associated with work), bandwidth savings (less non-work-related traffic), and reduced liability (pornography). URL filters should be integrated with your acceptable use policy for the Internet. Some vendors, for example, allow users to spend 30 minutes surfing personal Web sites, after which they are cut off for the day. This balances company protection while retaining certain personal freedoms for the employee.

Incident Response for Content Filtering

It is important to have an appropriate and human resource-approved response for each of these incidents. Many of the examples above can be used for tracking purposes only, but many of them (for example, a bomb threat) require a measured and well-thought-out response that may include a phone call, a notation in a personnel file, or dismissal. Sometimes, the authorities will need to be brought in.

SUMMARY . . . .

The control of computer viruses is a well-understood problem. The tools to solve this problem are more than 90 percent effective. Although a virus will eventually get through, a well-configured and -managed virus control program will dramatically reduce the impact of viruses on both IT staff and end users.

Although virus control is critical, it is not sufficient. Viruses that replicate through vulnerabilities will continue to get through unless vulnerability scanning and configuration control and patching are also well managed.

Content filtering is a way to control the data that enters and leaves your network. Content filtering can track and control the Web sites that your employees visit and the emails that come and go from the company, as well as keep out certain types of worms and viruses attached to Web pages and email attachments.

8 Intrusion Detection

In this chapter . . .

- Why You Need Intrusion Detection

- What Network and Host Intrusion Detection Systems Do

- The Components of an Intrusion Detection System

- How Intrusion Detection Systems Are Used

- Some of the Common Misunderstandings About Intrusion Detection

A complete security process involves protection, detection, and response. Intrusion detection is the core process for monitoring your systems to detect security breaches, hacking, and internal misuse. Many intrusion detection systems also include response mechanisms to limit losses. A wise man once said that the only secure computer is one that is turned off. In a world where our computers have to be on and open to sharing information, intrusion detection is a vital component to protect businesses.

THE CASE FOR INTRUSION DETECTION . . . .

Why does a convenience store have locks on its doors when it never closes? This rhetorical question sheds light on one of the paradoxes that businesses face with respect to security. A convenience store stays open so that customers may access and buy products. In short, they provide access so that they can conduct business. Every now and then, a customer has been granted access who shoplifts or waves a gun and takes all the money in the register. The threat of these occurrences is one of the reasons that owners put locks on the doors. The paradox with security is now obvious: lock the doors and stay safe or open the doors and conduct business.

 Key Point

> The paradox with security: You can lock the doors and stay safe or you can open the doors and conduct business.

There are inherent risks in allowing access to computers, but the exchange of information has become more critical to business than almost any other factor. Even in the black world of intelligence gathering and national security, the free flow of data between authorized individuals is paramount to mission success.

The traditional response to security risks is access control, involving a series of preventative measures designed to keep unauthorized people out. To demonstrate access control, we'll use a metaphor from the physical world of protecting a warehouse full of some boxes of important information (see Figure 8–1).

As we peel back the layers of the security "onion," we can see many examples of preventive measures. On the outside of our metaphoric real world, we have physical security represented by streetlights that are comparable to any of a number of theft prevention devices in the computer world, including tagging devices, hardware locks,

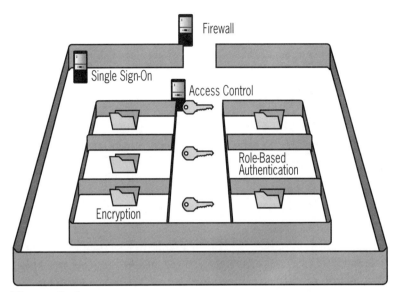

Figure 8–1
Access control mechanisms.

drive locks, and alarms. Moving inward, we find a wall around our warehouses that is comparable to firewalls in the computer world.

At the front gate, we pick up a set of keys from a sentry, permitting entrance into select warehouses, very much like our credentials that we pick up from a single sign-on authority on our computers. Then we get to the warehouse, and we have to use our key or password for access control to log in. After we're inside, there are rooms, each requiring a key, like role-based authentication, which allows access into only selected files and folders in the computer. Finally, in the physical world, we can encode the files so that theft will not result in unauthorized disclosure, just the way encryption does in computers.

Preventive controls are a vital part of information security and much of the focus of this book, but this paradigm has its limitations.

Unfortunately, preventive security measures tend to stand in the way of free information exchange. Managing access controls effectively is difficult, at best, and almost always comes at the expense of slowing down business. Firewalls, for example, place restrictions on who may enter a network, resulting in delays, such as procedures to allow access to a new business partner, which may take days.

Another problem with perimeter defenses is that most of the losses are attributable to insiders. Insiders are so effective because they already have all the keys. Access controls are almost worthless against the insider threat.

The key to success is balancing access and access controls with the need for free flow of information and connectivity. If 7–Eleven could invent a lock that allows paying customers in and keeps armed robbers out, it would have the perfect prevention mechanism. Instead, it uses video cameras.

Video cameras are not prevention devices, but they provide significant value. They are an excellent deterrent and, in case of loss, they provide a way to identify criminals, assess the extent of the damage, and assist in prosecution. Video cameras have been in use for years. They are a standard part of physical security with which most people are familiar and comfortable. The parallel capability in the computer world is known as *intrusion detection* (see Figure 8–2). Intrusion detection tools are not prevention devices, but they are an excellent deterrent. They also provide damage assessment and threat identification capabilities, just like their counterparts, the video cameras, in the physical world.

Returning briefly to our metaphor, in Figure 8–2, intrusion detection is represented by the video cameras inside and outside the buildings. The cameras inside the warehouse watching what files people open and what applications they run represent host-based intrusion detection. The cameras outside the warehouses watching people going in and out of the building and seeing what they're carrying represent network intrusion detection.

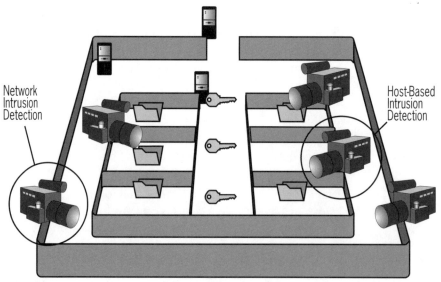

Figure 8–2
Video cameras are intrusion detection.

WHAT IS INTRUSION DETECTION? . . . .

Intrusion detection is the process of detecting and responding to computer misuse. The benefits include deterrence, detection, response, damage assessment, attack anticipation, and prosecution support. Different intrusion detection techniques provide different types of benefits for a variety of environments, so one of the keys to an effective deployment of intrusion detection is getting the right tool for your environment. The key to selecting the right intrusion detection system is defining your environment-specific requirements and cutting through the industry hype to determine the best system to meet those needs.

The Most Common Intrusion Detection

In the author's experience, most organizations are already doing some kind of intrusion detection. Usually, it is a simple application that does pattern matching against *syslog*, manual analysis of firewall logs, or a shareware packet sniffer to look at network traffic. The most common type of intrusion detection is manual analysis of router and firewall logs and the use of a package called *Snort*, developed by Martin Roesch.

 SNORT

> Snort is a libpcap-based packet sniffer/logger that can be used as a lightweight network intrusion detection system. It features rules-based logging and can perform protocol analysis and content searching/matching, and it can be used to detect a variety of attacks and probes, such as buffer overflows, stealth port scans, CGI attacks, SMB probes, OS fingerprinting attempts, and much more. Snort has a real-time alerting capability, with alerts being sent to syslog, a separate "alert" file, or as a WinPopup message via Samba's smbclient. It is available for download at *www.clark.net/~roesch/security.html*.

Thousands of detections are made with homegrown intrusion detection every year. Using commercial network and host-based intrusion detection products and a well-thought-out process, the number of detections can be increased, and the amount of effort required to detect can be significantly reduced.

NETWORK VERSUS HOST-BASED
INTRUSION DETECTION . . . .

There are two fundamental types of intrusion detection, known as *host-based* and *network-based*. Their roots are similar but their operational use is radically different. The root of all intrusion detection is based in analyzing a set of discrete, time-sequenced events for patterns of misuse. All intrusion detection sources, network or host, are sequential records that directly reflect specific actions and indirectly reflect behavior. Host-based technologies examine events such as what files were accessed and what applications were executed. Network-based technologies examine events such as packets of information exchanged between computers (network traffic).

There are two types of network-based intrusion detection technologies. Promiscuous-mode network intrusion detection is the traditional technology that "sniffs" all the packets on a network segment for analysis. A single sensor on each segment characterizes promiscuous-mode systems. Network node intrusion detection systems sniff just the packets bound for a single destination computer. Network node systems are characterized by a set of distributed agents on mission-critical machines.

Both host and network technologies are necessary for comprehensive detection but each has advantages and disadvantages that should be measured against the requirements for the target environment. The best intrusion detection systems are known as "hybrids." Hybrid systems include both network and host-based technologies under a single management console.

 ## AUDITING PRIMER

Any computer can only be known to be secure if we can tell what is happening inside of it. Even if we could see the work taking place inside a computer right now, we could not watch every computer all of the time. So we need a way to capture information about the activities taking place inside all of our computers, store it, and analyze that information later.

All computers designed for business have the ability to capture information showing the details of the work being performed by the computer. The computer component that does this is referred to as the *audit system*. Each computer operating system has its own way of turning auditing on and off, tailoring the data that is collected, and storing the data. Most computers installed by an IT department have the auditing functions turned off.

If we can't know that a computer is secure without seeing the auditing records, why would IT departments turn auditing off? The audit systems in most computers are very difficult to manage. Trying to manage the audit systems and the resulting audit records from dozens or hundreds of computers (much less the thousands in large companies) would be a disaster for the typical understaffed IT group. There are two related problems that cause this. First, most audit systems are difficult to tailor. Second, if the IT department members turn auditing on without defining exactly what activities it wants to capture (tailoring), the amount of data captured is tremendous, and the computer spends nearly as much effort capturing audit data as it does doing real work. This can severely impact the work the computer was bought to do.

Automated tools to manage the audit systems, as well as the audit records they create, are relatively new inventions. Tools that manage hundreds of computers, even though those computers are from various companies and running a mix of operating systems, are rare. But they do exist.

More limited knowledge of the work being done inside the computer can be obtained from less reliable sources. The audit system, because it is an integral part of the operating system in the computer, is tightly controlled. It is extremely difficult for someone to tamper with audit records. Under some circumstances, this allows for audit records to be used as evidence when prosecuting people who have damaged computer data. Also, the level of detail that can be captured by the audit system can provide a unique ability to diagnose security failures and to identify perpetrators. But if the audit system cannot be used, some information about the computer can be determined from the computer logging facility.

Why Can't I Just Use Computer Logs?

Computer logs are simply continuous recordings of the messages produced by the various systems and programs running in the computer, much as you might keep a logbook of activities or events. Most programs emit a message when they are started and when they complete. Most operating system components emit messages whenever a significant event occurs. All of those messages are stored in logs.

Logs are not as secure as audit records. If the computer is compromised, log entries can be modified easily. A program installed on a computer as part of a compromise can generate false log entries that indicate nothing is wrong. And the log entries, even if they are not compromised, have much less information in them than an audit system would capture.

ANATOMY OF AN INTRUSION
DETECTION SYSTEM . . . .

An intrusion detection system is a conglomeration of capabilities to detect and respond to threats. The intrusion detection industry supplies tools with capabilities and
features that may do more than detect intruders from the outside, as the intrusion
detection name implies. Today, intrusion detection encompasses the following
capabilities:

- Event log analysis for insider threat detection
- Network traffic analysis for perimeter threat detection
- Security configuration management
- File integrity checking

Many products provide only one of these capabilities. Tools or suites that provide several of these capabilities are commonly known as *hybrid intrusion detection
systems*. Figure 8–3 shows a hybrid system block diagram with a component breakdown. The left side of the diagram is a command console where the alarms are centralized and the system is controlled. The network intrusion detection capability is
provided through sensors distributed throughout the network at strategic locations.
Agents distributed around the enterprise inside mission-critical systems provide the
host-based capabilities.

Command Console

The command console is the central command authority for controlling the entire system. A good command console can be accessed remotely so the system may be controlled from any location.

The command console is the nerve center of an intrusion detection system. It is
typically a dedicated machine with a set of tools for setting policy and processing collected alarms. The command console usually maintains contact with monitored targets and/or network sensors over an encrypted link. Although most vendors provide
their own consoles with their products, there is an industry shift toward integrating
command console capabilities with network management systems, such as Hewlett-
Packard's OpenView, and other enterprise management systems, such as Tivoli.

On the console in Figure 8–3, you'll see an assessment manager, a target manager, and an alert manager. Different systems divide these functions into different
components. Fundamentally, the assessment manager controls the collection of static
configuration information, the target manager maintains connections with components on the target side, and the alert manager collects and maintains the alert data.

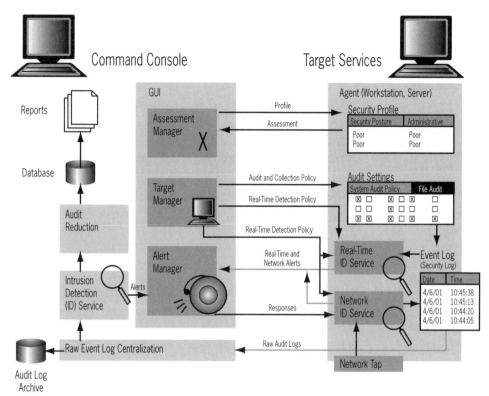

Figure 8–3
A command console used in a hybrid intrusion detection system.

For scheduled operations and data mining, the console has its own detection engine and database of detected alerts.

The right-hand side of Figure 8–3 represents a target. Targets can be monitored computers (either servers or end-user workstations), in the case of host-based intrusion detection, or they can be dedicated computers with network-based sensors that sniff network traffic, in the case of network intrusion detection.

Network Sensor

Network sensors are computer programs that run on dedicated machines or network devices on mission-critical network segments. They may also be implemented as agents on mission-critical destination machines in a network. Promiscuous mode network sensors typically reside on dedicated machines. Network node sensors run on the machines they monitor.

The network tap is the device that gathers data from the network. It can be a software agent running on the sensor or hardware, such as a router. The tap is important because it is a critical component for preventing packet loss in high-bandwidth networks. Certain types of taps may have limitations in selected environments, such as switched networks.

One of the challenges to host-based and network node intrusion detection is that there can be 10,000 or more targets to monitor in a good-sized enterprise. The largest enterprises have more than 100,000. Larger enterprises have deployment and management issues because of the distributed nature of the systems.

One of the challenges to deploying promiscuous-mode network intrusion detection is sensor placement. Typically, there are fewer than 30 sensors in an enterprise, although there can be as many as 100 in some of the largest enterprises.

Alert Notification

The alert notification subsystem contacts the security officer responsible for handling incidents. Standard capabilities include on-screen alerts, audible alerts, paging, and email. Most systems also provide Simple Network Management Protocol (SNMP), so that the Network Operations Center (NOC) can be notified. Newer systems will have the ability to interface with helpdesk software, such as Remedy, to generate a trouble ticket.

Response Subsystem

The response subsystem provides the capabilities to take action based on threats to the target systems. These responses can be automatically generated or initiated by the system operator. Common responses include reconfiguring a router or firewall and shutting down a connection.

Database

The database is the knowledge repository for all that the intrusion detection system has observed. This can include both misuse and behavioral statistics. The statistics are necessary to model historical behavior that can be very useful during damage assessment or other investigative tasks. Useful information may not necessarily be indicative of misuse.

Target Agents

The target agent is a software agent that performs a task on behalf of the intrusion detection system, such as sniffing TCP/IP packets, processing event log data, centralizing data, checking file integrity, verifying system configuration, or executing responses. Agents typically run in the background as daemons in UNIX or services in Windows NT/2000. There may be many of these agents on a single target, each performing a different task. One of the keys to a well-behaved agent is that it not degrade end-user performance.

ANATOMY OF AN INTRUSION
DETECTION PROCESS ....

Using an intrusion detection system effectively requires a good security policy. Security policy does not have to be extensive to be effective. Considering that most organizations either don't have a policy or have a large policy book sitting on a shelf gathering dust, you could be a real hero in your company by creating a simple, effective policy. There is an old axiom that there is very little difference between a little and a lot but there is a huge gulf of difference between nothing and a little. In other words, there is a world of difference in effective protection between no policy and a simple, effective policy. All you have to do is define mission-critical data, threats, and escalation procedures. In fact, this is required if you want to derive any value from your intrusion detection system.

 KEY POINT

> There is a world of difference in effective protection between no security policy and a simple, effective security policy.

Security policy defines acceptable activity. Not everything that can potentially go wrong with your system necessarily warrants your attention. Start by defining the perimeter threats that your organization is concerned about. For example, most organizations have ping sweeps on a daily basis and do not consider them threats. However, they can light up your intrusion detection system like a pinball machine. On the other hand, a fragmented packet coming in from outside the firewall with a source address from inside your network is probably worthy of your attention.

These policies are codified into rules and other configurations for your intrusion detection system. Each system has its own way of codifying policy, including expert system rules, event sequences with various degrees of granularity, operations scheduling, audit policies, and many others. In many cases, you have to use a text editor to define these policies, although most of the commercial systems provide graphical editors that are relatively easy to use.

After you have configured your system, you can begin to detect and respond to threats. Data is gathered and processed in real time or at scheduled times. When patterns of misuse are identified, the data can be centralized to the command console or, depending on the system, the alert data can be sent to your network operations center. This is a critical stage in the operation of an intrusion detection system. It has detected something. Now you have to do something, based on your escalation policies.

Don't Detect Every "Threat"

There are certain "threats" that you just don't need to do anything about, except, perhaps, make a note that an event occurred. These are sometimes referred to as *false positives*. Many threats need be addressed only when an aggregate of activity indicates sufficient threat to warrant a response. For example, a user who is authorized to access any server in the company is not interesting when one or two servers are accessed periodically. However, a pattern of routine downloads from each mission-critical system on the network may warrant attention. Aggregating lower level actions to detect real threats is an area where intrusion detection systems excel.

Escalation policies are as important as security policies because you need an operational plan that functions end-to-end to deal with threats effectively. This is where most organizations drop the ball. Do you call the offender's supervisor? Do you trace back the doorknocker? Do you launch an offensive attack over the Internet? Do you gather more information? If it's the CFO ignoring security policy, have you sufficiently protected the security officer from retaliation so that he might actually report it to someone? As you can see, escalation policy has many issues that need to be addressed.

Once an alarm is detected that requires a response, the intrusion detection system may send out a series of notifications. Notifications are intended to alert the security staff to security-relevant activities on the network. The standard set of notifications available in commercial products include:

- Email
- Page
- SNMP trap
- On-screen

The system may perform automated responses or be directed manually to execute a response. In most cases, automated responses are not recommended because they can be used as a DoS mechanism. Manually executed responses through the intrusion detection system are much more common. Responses can be elaborate, such as modifying access control policy based on user behavior, or very simple, such as logging off a user. Response mechanisms commonly available in commercial products include:

- Shut down a connection
- Shut down a computer
- Log off a user
- Disable an account
- Reconfigure a router/firewall
- Increase auditing

Many intrusion detection systems also include data forensics tools that provide trending and analysis capabilities. The tools are used to mine the database of historical activity maintained by the intrusion detection system for damage assessment, attack anticipation, and prosecution support. Damage assessment is determining the extent of damage after an attack. Attack anticipation is detecting patterns of misuse that may precede more significant threats. Prosecution support includes case preparation, data interpretation, and event log integrity for evidentiary use.

However, there is an important difference between traditional audit tools and intrusion detection. Intrusion detection systems look for differences in patterns of *behavior*, as opposed to the state of a control. For example, a configuration scanner will confirm that password policies are set properly on a target machine, whereas an intrusion detection system looks for three failed logins, indicating that someone has, in fact, *acted* suspiciously.

What Is Misuse?

> To detect misuse effectively, you have to understand it in its many forms. An infinite number of things can go wrong with your information systems. However, as security officers, we can't get our brains around "infinite" possibilities, so it helps if we can break it down into manageable categories that we believe we can protect and monitor. Conceptually, all misuse will *always* involve at least one of the following activities:
>
> - An unauthorized individual accesses or reads data.
> - An unauthorized individual modifies data.
> - Denial of service occurs.
>
> Misuse detection and policy should be grounded in identifying the data that is sensitive and should be protected from unauthorized disclosure, or data that is considered mission–critical, and should be protected from unauthorized modification, and operational components that must be available for the business to function.

INTRUSION DETECTION MYTHS . . . .

There are many common misconceptions about intrusion detection systems and the intrusion detection process. Monitoring can, at times, be more of an art than a science, leaving many aspects of the process open to interpretation. Add to this marketing people at commercial vendors, and misinformation can be rampant. Following are some of the more common myths and a little discussion to help you navigate the minefield of "facts" about intrusion detection.

Myth #1: The Network Intrusion Detection Myth

"Network-based intrusion detection is the only requirement for monitoring."

There is a myth that network intrusion detection is the sole requirement for monitoring in an enterprise. This follows the press penchant for chasing hackers, foreign governments, and cyberterrorists as the most significant threat to your information assets. Network intrusion detection is more appropriate to detect outside threats. As a result, network intrusion detection is what most people think of when they think of intrusion detection.

In reality, network intrusion detection is popular because of the press focus on external threats and the fact that most people put in charge of intrusion detection projects come from a network background. However, network intrusion detection focuses on outsider threats that represent less than 20 percent of actual losses attributable to computer misuse. Network intrusion detection is a valuable component of comprehensive monitoring but it is not the panacea that it is perceived to be.

Myth #2: The False-Positive Myth

"Intrusion detection systems have too many false alarms."

The myth is that the most significant problem with intrusion detection today is false positives. False positives occur when the system alarms ultimately turn out to be authorized activity or just plain wrong. False positives are tremendous time wasters and drive up operational labor costs. They also create so much noise that they drown out security-critical events that truly require attention.

The reality is that false positives are alarms that turn out not to be serious threats, leaving a security officer wondering why they were alarmed in the first place. False positives in an operational environment are matters of perspective. There is no such thing as a false positive in an operational environment because, unless caused by a poorly written signature, every alarm has value. It's just that not every alarm requires your full attention. Poorly written signatures are not false positives; they are system failures and should be treated as such.

Myth #3: The Automated Anomaly Detection Myth

"Anomaly detection can automatically distinguish good behavior from bad behavior."

The myth is that anomaly detection mechanisms can use behavioral models to provide automated intrusion detection. This powerful capability can distinguish one user from another, identify masqueraders and miscreants before they do damage, and alert the security officer automatically when a user changes his or her behavior pattern sufficiently to warrant attention. However, these systems can be trained over time, so they must be used conservatively.

In reality, anomaly detection works well in a decision support context but fails as an automated detection mechanism. The current models are not able to distinguish users reliably in most operational environments, and they can cause significant false positives. One of the primary reasons is that most user behavior is too random and too influenced by outside influences to be modeled reliably for automated detection.

What's the Difference Between Network- and Host-Based?

All intrusion detection systems process sequential event data. The primary difference is that network intrusion detection processes TCP/IP records, whereas host-based intrusion detection analyzes event log records from computer resident sources, such as the operating systems, databases, and applications. The architectures and techniques are different, as well. Data sources for host-based intrusion detection are distributed, whereas network data is more centralized as it is sniffed off the wire. The nature of the data is different.

Data quality goes up significantly as the source of the data progresses from the perimeter to the inside of the network. An operating system event can take the place of hundreds of network traffic packets. A single, well-placed application event can replace thousands of operating system events. For example, determining that a user has opened a document with Microsoft Word on Windows NT would require vastly different numbers of events, given different audit sources (see Figure 8–4). This phenomenon is one of the many reasons that network intrusion detection is insufficient to provide effective intrusion detection.

Conversely, implementation difficulty increases as the data sources move to the inside of the network. This is mostly because each audit source is unique and requires its own parser, policy management, detection policy, and audit policy. There is, at most, a handful of protocols that must be parsed for network intrusion detection of which TCP/IP is so dominant that most network intrusion detection systems process only that one protocol. There are as many as five operating systems in most large enterprises and closer to 20 when you include the different flavors of UNIX. Finally, there are thousands of applications, most of which aren't even instrumented with audit sources (as in the Microsoft Word example, above).

Even though application data is the best source for intrusion detection, it is exponentially difficult to manage and operate, compared with a network data source. This is another one of the reasons that most organizations choose to monitor networks first, then progress to monitoring the operating system (the traditional host-based audit source), then to the middleware infrastructure-enabling software, such as relational databases, and enterprise administration products, such as Tivoli, and finally to end-user applications.

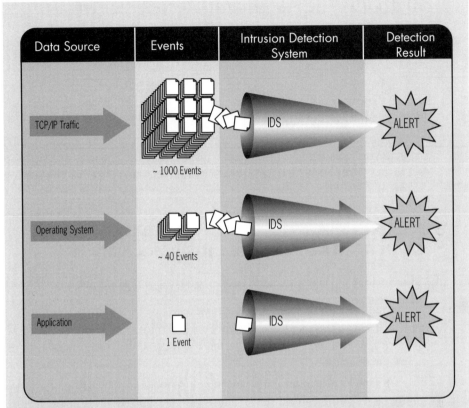

Data Source	Events	Intrusion Detection System	Detection Result
TCP/IP Traffic	~ 1000 Events	IDS	ALERT
Operating System	~ 40 Events	IDS	ALERT
Application	1 Event	IDS	ALERT

Figure 8–4
Number of events necessary to detect opening a document with Microsoft Word.

Myth #4: The Real-Time Requirement Myth

"Enterprise-wide real-time detection is a critical requirement."

There is a myth that enterprise-wide real-time detection and response is an absolute requirement to justify the expense of an intrusion detection system; if the system can't stop intruders within seconds of a breach (or microseconds, depending on your own definition of real time), the system provides little value.

In reality, most network-based systems operate in real time. Host-based real-time detection is a useful capability for a select set of misuse but many significant benefits of intrusion detection do not require real-time processing. In fact, enterprise-wide real-time detection has some significant disadvantages, even if a company is willing to front the resources necessary to accomplish it.

Myth #5: The Automated Response Myth

"Automated response can be used effectively to stop intruders before misuse occurs."

The myth is that automated response is a key feature necessary to stop intruders before they can do damage and that, without automated response, an intrusion detection system is worthless.

In reality, attackers can use automated responses as an excellent DoS mechanism to your own network. Automated responses should be used sparingly for a small set of positively identified misuses. Intrusion detection systems provide a wealth of capabilities to detect, deter, assess, and prosecute misuse that are unrelated to automated response.

Myth #6: The Artificial Intelligence Myth

"Artificial intelligence systems can identify new types of misuse."

There is a myth that researchers are working on artificially intelligent (AI) systems that will significantly increase the capabilities of intrusion detection systems in the next few years and that these systems will detect heretofore unknown threats and notify the operator.

In reality, researchers are working on AI systems that will probably not significantly increase the capabilities of intrusion detection systems in the next few years. Detecting "new" attacks is a misunderstood requirement that is routinely tied to AI techniques. Improved AI techniques will not improve a system's ability to detect attacks that have never been observed.

SUMMARY . . . .

Your computers are not secure unless you can know that they are secure. You cannot know that without being able to observe the activity within and between the computers. There is too much activity to observe directly, and host and network intrusion detection capabilities have been devised to provide notification of significant security events. These tools, when combined with appropriate staffing resources, policies, and processes, become the core of a security program.

9 Public Key Infrastructure and Encryption

In this chapter . . .

- Encryption Basics
- Public Keys as Infrastructure
- The Benefits of PKI
- The Problems with PKI

Public key infrastructure is a broad attempt to solve many of the problems faced by anyone trying to create a secure computing environment. In this context, *broad* means aggressive, complicated, and risky. PKI is being created as a set of standards bodies, in concert with a number of security hardware and software vendors. Before we attempt to explain what PKI is, we need to explain some basic concepts related to cryptography. If you do not need or want to understand what lies beneath the surface, feel free to skip ahead to the section entitled "Public Keys as Infrastructure."

ENCRYPTION BASICS . . . .

Encryption is the process of scrambling data so that it cannot be read by anyone who does not have the means of decrypting it. Encryption has three components:

1. An encryption algorithm
2. One or more keys that need to be passed to the algorithm to hide or un-hide the data
3. The data being protected

 DEFINITIONS

> **Algorithm**
>
> A finite sequence of steps for solving a logical or mathematical problem. In computer parlance, typically a piece of a computer program that is reused without change.
>
> **Key**
>
> A sequence of bits, usually shown as a set of characters. May be a number, word, or phrase.

There are two major classes of encryption algorithms: secret key and public key. Public key encryption does more than simply hide data. It also provides the ability to support two advanced capabilities: authentication and nonrepudiation. These are defined and described later in this chapter.

In this section, we describe secret key and public key encryption algorithms and how they are used. Although the most obvious use is to hide your valuable business data, there are other critical uses of encryption. Each security component must itself be secure. If a criminal can take over the security system, nothing can be relied on. To ensure the security of the security system, extensive use of encryption is required. All communications involving security components must be encrypted. The information that the security system uses to configure itself and operate must be stored in an encrypted form, and the identity credentials of the people authorized to change the security system must be encrypted. Most of the chapters in the second section of this book describe security technologies that implicitly rely on these encryption methods.

Secret Key Encryption

Secret key encryption has been in use for centuries, but became orders of magnitude more sophisticated during World Wars I and II. To support wartime communications, all sides of the conflicts worked hard to create unbreakable methods of hiding the content of radio transmissions. The techniques they invented are now called *secret key* because they all use algorithms that require both the sender and the receiver (or the encrypter and the decrypter) to know the same key. Anyone who knows the key can encrypt or decrypt the data, so the success of the encryption depends on keeping the key secret.

During World War II, each submarine and ship captain carried a book of encryption keys. A different key was used each day. If any copy of the book was captured or even suspected of being captured, every book needed to be replaced urgently. Until the new book of keys was distributed, the enemy might be able to decrypt every wartime communication and determine the location and plans for every vessel in the fleet. The war could be lost because a copy of the encryption keys was lost without that loss being detected. One of the reasons that the Nazis lost the war was that the Western powers successfully compromised the Nazi Enigma encryption system without the Nazis knowledge.

Secret key encryption is easy to understand. The key and data are transferred as follows:

1. The key and the data are passed to the algorithm.
2. The algorithm processes them and passes back the data in encrypted form.
3. That encrypted data can then be sent to another person or stored in the computer. In either case, only someone who knows which algorithm to use and knows the secret key can decrypt the data so that it can be read or used.
4. To decrypt the data, we pass the same key and the encrypted data to the same algorithm, which processes them and returns the same usable, decrypted data we sent during the encryption cycle.

Secret key encryption is relatively easy for the computer to perform. The computer processing power needed to do encryption and decryption of data depends on both the algorithm and the length of the key. Secret key algorithms with moderate key lengths can encrypt or decrypt data with minimal impact on the other work being done by the computer. The impact of key length on the level of security is discussed at the end of this chapter.

The major shortcoming of secret key encryption is the need to keep the key secret. Key management is the distribution and creation of secret keys. It can become a problem, even in small departments. It is almost impossible to manage shared-secret key encryption in large organizations with lots of data.

Think of a group of people who might need to share information. Perhaps your department at work has a common set of work files that your competitors would like to see. If you store those files in encrypted form, every member of your department needs to know the key in order to use the files. If one of your co-workers quits, an unauthorized person now knows the key, so the key needs to be changed (see Figure 9–1). Changing the key inside one computer is not too difficult, although it may take some time to decrypt and re-encrypt a large set of files with the new key. But now, every member of the department needs to be told the new key before they can get any work done. They need to receive that key in a secure manner. You could encrypt it before you send it to them, but what key would you use? Some organizations that rely on secret key encryption pass the keys on little pieces of paper. (Do you suppose they make you eat the paper after memorizing the new key?)

For another example of key management problems, consider email. If you want to send and receive emails confidentially within your department, you need to encrypt the email before sending it and decrypt the email you receive from others. If you do not want everyone in the department to be able to decrypt every message you send out, you need a different encryption key for each person to whom you might send an email. You would encrypt a message to Bob using the secret key that only you and Bob know. Bob would send a confidential email to Mary using the secret encryption key that only Bob and Mary know.

A key needs to exist for every pair of communicating employees. Of course, in this scheme, the only time you need to change a key is if one is compromised. If someone quits, you just retire all of the keys that person knew. Unfortunately, keys can be compromised fairly easily because people write them down and leave them in predictable places. If you needed to remember a key for every person for whom you might ever send an email, you would write the keys down, too. If a single key were compromised, you would need to let only two people know the replacement key. But each employee might need to keep track of hundreds or thousands of unique keys.

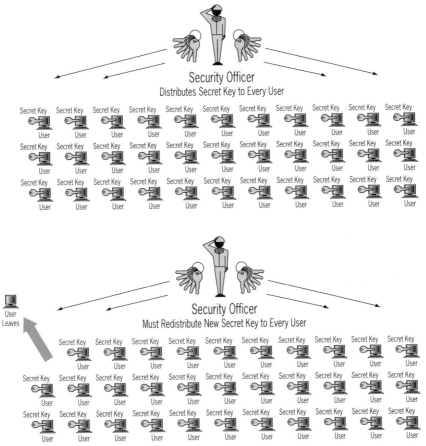

Figure 9–1
A new shared secret key must be distributed every time a user is removed from the system.

Public Key Encryption

Public key encryption uses an entirely different set of algorithms. Each person who wants to encrypt or decrypt data is given two keys—a public key and a private key. Everyone can know the public key. Only the person issued the private key can know it. To make the public key truly public, we normally store it in a directory service that everyone can read. The private key must be hidden away. When possible, private keys should be stored in smart cards, a credit-card-sized computer that can effectively protect the private key from misuse. A smart card can be inserted into a reader on a computer, but the owner must type in a password to unlock the card and make the private key usable.

Using the example from the previous section, if a co-worker quits, then the security officer need only revoke the public key in a central database rather than distribute new private keys to every user (see Figure 9–2). This saves significant effort in key management.

DEFINITIONS

A key is a protected value used to encrypt data. There are three different types of keys:

Secret—same key known to both sender and receiver.
Public—everyone knows my public key.
Private—no one but me can ever know my private key.

In some public key implementations, multiple pairs of private and public keys will be distributed to an individual. All of the public keys go into the directory service, and they are identified as being used for different purposes. All of the private keys get stored into the same smart card. The benefits of this approach are described later in this chapter.

Public key algorithms use the public and private keys to hide and unhide data in a way very different from the secret key system previously described. I can find your public key in a directory service, and you can find mine. If I want to send you a confidential message, I encrypt it, using your public key. I send you the message. You are the only person who can read it because only your private key can decrypt a message that has been encrypted by your public key.

If you want to send me a confidential message, you will look up my public key on the directory service. You encrypt the message to me, using my public key, and no one can read it except me, using my private key.

But public key algorithms have another use that is unique. If I encrypt a message using my own private key, anyone can decrypt it with my public key from the directory. The keys work both ways. If I use one of my keys (either public or private) to encrypt a message, only the other one (private or public) can decrypt it. If I have encrypted a message using my private key and no one else knows my private key, then only my public key can decrypt it. If my public key successfully decrypted the message, I am the only person who could possibly have encrypted it. This is the capability that allows us to create digital signatures, which are further described later in this chapter.

There is nothing wrong with encrypting data multiple times. If I encrypt a message using my private key, you'll know that I sent it because my public key can de-

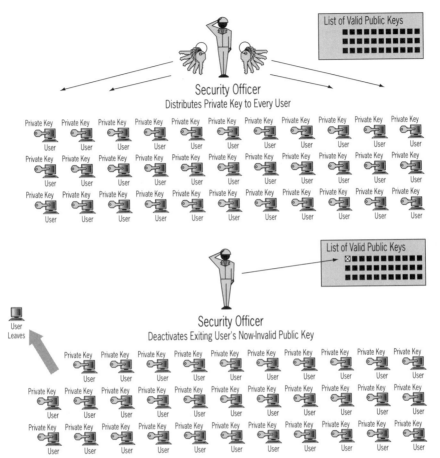

Figure 9–2
There is no need to redistribute keys when a user is removed from a public key system.

crypt it. If I encrypt a message with your public key, only you can open it because only you have your private key. If I encrypt the message twice—first with my private key, then with your public key—you will be the only person who can open it, and you will know for a fact that it came from me. That is why public key encryption is so important.

Because all of the private keys can be stored in highly secure ways, such as smart cards, and because all of the public keys can be published in a directory, key management is a much smaller problem than in secret key encryption. But directory services are still maturing, and smart cards and smart card readers are still somewhat expensive. So public key encryption has been slow to take off. Almost every organization has a PKI initiative in pilot but very few of them have gone to wide deployment.

Another problem is that public key encryption algorithms use a *lot* of computer cycles. Any attempt to do a lot public key encryption processing will have a major impact on the ability of any computer to get its work done. To reduce this problem, most public key encryption implementations use a combination of secret and public key algorithms to encrypt and decrypt data.

PKI sounds complicated, and it is. But as a computer user, you would see none of this. You might click on a button labeled *decrypt*, or you might not have to do anything. The message would simply appear on your screen after a brief processing delay.

A server trying to handle encryption and decryption for many users can quickly become overloaded. This is the most significant problem with public key encryption, and many software and hardware vendors try to reduce its impact with their products.

Key Lengths and Security Strength

You will frequently hear encryption described by its "bit length." For encryption, length does matter. We said that some types of keys are normally seen as a series of characters, perhaps a word or phrase. The length of the key has a lot to do with both how strong the security is and how much computer power it takes to encrypt and decrypt the data. The other major factor in both security strength and processing power is the selection of the encryption algorithms.

Security strength is usually measured as the number of tries it would take to guess the key. Of course, each guess needs to be used to attempt decryption. After each guess has failed, another guess is made. By using longer keys, you increase the number of possible keys and the time it would take (on average) to guess the right one. Longer keys also take more computer power to process. But that increased investment in computer power also dramatically increases the complexity of the scrambling being applied to the data. The result is that ways of compromising the data other than by guessing the key become much, much harder.

Well-designed (and well-implemented) encryption algorithms, using long key lengths, are unbreakable with the computing power currently available. Unfortunately, most computers are significantly weaker than that, due to poor implementation by the computer programmers.

So, how long is a long key? It depends on the algorithm being used. Key lengths are specified in bits (binary digits). Typically, eight bits equal one character if the key is represented in print. The most common secret key algorithms use key lengths of 56, 64, or 128 bits. A short key would be seven characters long (56 bits), such as the word *filbert*. Because the key is sent to the encryption and decryption algorithm as a series of bits, capitalization matters. A medium-length key would be eight characters long

(64 bits), such as the word *FILBERTS*. Note that this key and the 56-bit key used above, as an example, have no characters in common because capitalization matters.

A long key, used for maximum security, would be 128 bits or 16 characters long. Every character counts, including spaces, so a good key might be *gbLkZ102 880hJkm*. But no one could ever remember it. In a well-designed secret key encryption system, a computer program generates keys. Then keys are more likely to look like the last example. Most computer programs hide the actual keys being used and prompt the user for a password that is used to unlock the actual key.

Public key algorithms are very different. A computer program always builds public keys because the public and private keys must have a mathematical relationship. After all, what one does, the other needs to undo. Key length still matters; it still impacts the degree of security, and it still is directly related to the amount of computer power required. The two most common public key algorithms are called *RSA* and *ECC*, and they use very different key lengths to achieve the same security levels. RSA keys are typically 512 bits, 1,024 bits, or 2,048 bits long. That would equate to 64 characters, 128 characters, or 256 characters. But public and private keys are never seen as characters. They really are long binary numbers, and it is not possible to print them out as a series of letters and numbers, other than by interpreting them the way programmers do—in arcane hexadecimal notation (you don't want to know).

The ECC algorithm gets the same level of security and uses about as much computer power, with much shorter keys. Typically, ECC keys are 106, 132, or 185 bits long. In all other ways, they are like RSA keys.

PUBLIC KEYS AS INFRASTRUCTURE . . . .

Private keys are best hidden away inside smart cards, so no one ever needs to see the keys. The expense of smart card readers has led some vendors to support private keys stored in a computer instead of in a smart card. Many people may have access to a computer, so even password protection of the private key in that environment could cause a significant reduction in overall security. In addition, support of private keys in the computer has proven to be expensive. Seemingly simple changes to the computer software may cause the private key to become unavailable. The resulting help-desk call may take hours and require a lot of technical expertise.

When you are issued a smart card containing your private key, it becomes the tool you use to prove who you are. Using your private key, you can sign contracts and make other commitments that are legally enforceable. A lawyer would advise you that this has not yet been proven in court.

Public keys are stored on directory services. To put public keys in a standard format to create a cryptographic information binding, the computer program that generates the key creates a special computer record known as the *X.509v3 certificate*, commonly referred to as a *cert*. The cert contains a copy of your public key, as well as your name and some other identifying information. From the day your cert is published to a directory, the cert becomes your public identity.

The theory behind PKI is that, once everyone has a private key and a public cert and all computer systems and applications have been adapted to use them, all computer usage will be fully secured. The acts of inserting your smart card into a reader and typing in your password (or PIN) to unlock it will prove your identity and cause all communications to be securely encrypted and identifiable as being yours. Of course, if all of the people and computers in your company meet these criteria, your company accrues the benefit. If all of the companies in your supply chain conform, the most serious impediment to supply-chain automation evaporates. Before we look at the benefits and difficulties of PKI, let us walk through a typical user experience.

Our example user is named Jon. Jon arrives at work early Monday morning. He parks his car and unlocks the employee entrance door by waving his corporate identity card at a panel next to the door. At his desk, he inserts the same card into a slot on the side of his computer keyboard. The computer displays two lines for data to be entered. The first line contains Jon's normal account name.

Because Jon is a supervisor, he has a second account available for those times that he needs to override some of the rules. The second line on the screen is for Jon's password. Once he has typed it in, the computer accepts his identity, and every other computer he uses accepts the fact that he has proven who he is. Jon got married last week, and he needs to update his personnel and benefits records. The computer application that stores that data is open to him because his smart card and password have proven his identity, and the matching corporate authorization records show that he is an employee. Jon updates his records without typing in another password. Later that day, in the course of his job, Jon needs to commit his company to a major supply purchase. To complete the transaction, Jon needs to type in a different password. This one unlocks his special digital signature cert.

Another example of PKI usage is the establishment of a VPN session, using public and private keys that represent the computers at each end of a communications link instead of a person and a computer. This type of PKI usage is discussed in Chapter 10, "Encrypted Communications."

To implement PKI in the real world, a number of needs must be met. An organization must be created to issue and manage certificates and keys. The policies that define how certs and keys will be issued and revoked must be decided. All of the enabling technologies must be installed, configured, and integrated into the computing environment.

The benefits of PKI will not be realized until a significant portion of the computing environment has been connected to PKI. But what are those benefits?

The Benefits of PKI

A cert pair (public and private) identifies each person and each computer in a full implementation of PKI. All communications are encrypted. All data is stored in the computer system in encrypted form. Critical transactions (such as placing a large order) are recorded, along with the digital signatures of the person making the transaction, to show a record of how the data change was made. The only way a hacker or unauthorized person can break into the system is by stealing a smart card with an authorized private key in it and learning or guessing the user password that unlocks it.

In effect, PKI hacker-proofs the computer systems at the application level. That still leaves some dangers as a result of weaknesses in the operating systems, firewalls, and routers, but it eliminates some of the risk factors that typically result in compromises with very high dollar-value losses. Imagine that a hacker bypasses the operating system controls and steals a file containing all of the credit card numbers of your company's customers. If that file is strongly encrypted, the hacker has no way to read the information in the file. The hacker may have a copy, but it is useless to him or her.

In a large public environment such as the Internet, PKI can have other benefits. If I want to send you an email or a file, and I want to ensure that only you can read it, I can locate your public key on a public directory. Using your public key, I can encrypt my email or file and send it to you. Only you can read it. If I want to ensure that you know the file came from me, I can use PKI to sign the email before I send it. That uses my private key. You can get my public key from a directory and validate my signature. That proves that I issued the signature. If I want to do both things—make sure that only you can read it and ensure that you know I sent it—I can use my private key and your public key to encrypt the data. Once that is done, you will need to use both your private key and my public key to see what I have sent you. Lawyers love this stuff for communicating with their clients.

In effect, the broad use of PKI transforms the Internet into a reasonable medium for doing business.

The Problems of PKI

In order for you to have a private key and a public certificate that are useful, many things have to happen. Some group or person must issue your key pair. To do that, they must ensure that you are who you claim to be, and they must ensure that you are the person who receives it when they issue the private key in a smart card. Credit card companies have developed processes for ensuring that the correct person is activating their cards. They typically use your home telephone number and one other piece of information, such as your social security number or mother's maiden name, to ensure your identity before activating a new card. An organization that issues your keys and activates your smart card after you have received it is called a *registration authority* (RA).

The facility that actually builds and guarantees your keys and certificates is called the *certificate authority* (CA). A company using PKI technology will frequently have multiple RAs but only a single CA. A number of commercial companies provide similar services for multiple companies and for individual users on the Internet. The best known company providing these services is VeriSign. The first problem in establishing the use of PKI in an organization is creating the CA and RA functions and writing the policies and procedures that govern their operation.

Cost-effective use of PKI requires that smart card readers be installed on every computer used by a person who needs the applications that understand how to use PKI. If an organization uses PKI for most or all of its applications, the smart card reader cost is reasonable. Getting started with PKI typically involves a single application. In that case, the reader cost is frequently seen as a major impediment to deployment. Infrastructure is the second problem in the establishment of PKI.

Encrypting and decrypting data each time it is read or written between a computer and disk storage takes a lot of computer power. Doing the same each time the data is transmitted over a communications line takes a lot more. Any given hardware investment will do less real business work with PKI than it will without PKI because of this encryption and decryption overhead. Additional cost of computer server hardware is the third PKI problem.

In order for all of those smart cards, smart card readers, private keys, and public keys to be useful, some computer operating system or application program must be ready to use them. All of the other issues recede if many applications are prepared to use the costly infrastructure that underlies PKI. But most companies need to justify expenditures based on a single application that will be used to pilot the technology. Adapting the entire computing environment to use PKI, thereby spreading the cost of upgrading the infrastructure across all of the applications in use, requires a great deal of vision on the part of corporations. This is the roadblock that has delayed PKI for the last few years.

SUMMARY . . . .

PKI is a broad attempt to solve many problems with identification and authentication in large, distributed, open systems, such as the Internet. Ostensibly, when every user has public cert and a private key and all applications are adapted to use them, computers will be fully secured.

PKI has many benefits. It is superior to shared secret key encryption because there is no need for the two parties exchanging information to have ever met or exchanged keys. Shared secret keys are also very difficult to manage and to keep secret. Good security should never be based on secrecy.

PKI is challenged at this stage of its development. Many organizations have PKI pilot initiatives but very few have gone into wide deployment, due to these challenges. PKI should be a globally deployed infrastructure for maximum effectiveness, and it will take a few years before it reaches that level with cost-effective, interoperable solutions from multiple vendors.

10 Encrypted Communications

In this chapter . . .

- Virtual Private Networks
- Secure Sockets Layer
- Secure Shell

Securing confidential communications was important long before the birth of computers and the Internet. In the past, communicating parties used seals, special identifiers, and codes to ensure the integrity of messages sent from one to another. Today, confidentiality (third parties can't read a message in transit) and integrity (third parties can't change a message in transit) are still key issues in the modern world of messaging and transactions. VPN, SSL, and SSH are used to transmit various types of data securely from one entity to another.

WHAT IS A VIRTUAL PRIVATE NETWORK? . . . .

A VPN may consist of one or many computers connected to a single computer or network of computers. A private network is a dedicated line and set of equipment with the sole purpose of allowing two or more devices to communicate securely. A "virtual" private network is an encrypted link that allows parties to communicate securely over a public network such as the Internet. It is virtual because it does not exist in the physical world as dedicated hardware and lines.

The term *private* refers to the use of encryption or some other method to hide or mask the content of the communications. This is used to ensure that data traffic cannot be used or interpreted in the event it is intercepted. In addition to encryption, many systems require authentication to verify whether a user or device is allowed to communicate with the rest of the entities in a VPN.

VPNs may also be referred to as *secure tunnels*. Imagine the Internet as a large space with many threats between two parties who wish to communicate. A VPN sets up an encrypted, secure tunnel (see Figure 10–1) between the two parties so that they can communicate through the wilderness of the Internet in relative safety.

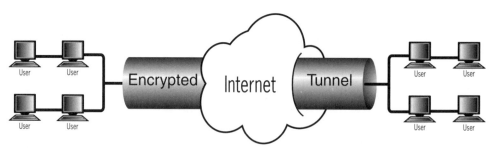

Figure 10–1
VPNs are secure tunnels, frequently used across the Internet.

A Brief History of VPNs

Before VPNs, an organization was required to construct dedicated or private networks between entities in order to conduct secure communications. Depending on the size and nature of an organization, this can be cost-prohibitive, as well as administratively difficult to manage. Another pitfall is the relative insecurity of data transmissions. Simple network access was all that was required to capture and use data traveling from one point to another.

In the late 1970s, organizations began using virtual networks. Also known as *virtual circuits*, this type of network builds a logical connection between two points over a number of gateways or routers. The points in between are referred to as *hops*. Although an organization can experience a cost savings utilizing this technology over a private network, it is also insecure.

As encryption technology matured, it was added to the virtual circuit model. In this case, data traversing a virtual circuit is sent via an encrypted tunnel that is built between the start and end points. With further advancements, authentication and encryption systems were added until information could be sent securely over public networks or the Internet.

 IPSec

Almost all VPNs are based on the IPSec standard. IPSec is an extension of the IP protocol family that provides confidentiality, integrity, authenticity, and replay protection through encryption. It works at the network layer, so it is completely transparent to your applications. You can use any IP protocol over IPSec.

IPSec extends regular IP with two new protocols called *Authentication Header* (AH) and *Encapsulated Security Payload* (ESP). AH is primarily responsible for providing authentication and integrity by establishing an encrypted header for the packet. ESP handles the encryption of the packet data. Both ESP and AH have a number of options for implementation within the standard, resulting in a fair amount of flexibility.

IPSec has a central Internet Key Exchange registry, so ostensibly, every machine on the Internet could talk to every other machine over an encrypted tunnel.

VPN Technology in Business

The use of VPN technology has become popular in business for a variety of reasons. VPNs allow organizations to create environments of privacy. This is important when considering the number of transactions that occur directly with clients, business partners, vendors, and even employees.

In a practical sense, businesses want to conduct commerce over the Internet. To ensure secure gathering of information, organizations add encryption to their Web sites. This is done to provide a secure means by which potential customers can register for, purchase, and check the status of products and services.

The same can be said for business partners who wish to access information resources on one another's networks. Often, this information is sensitive and can be detrimental to the business if given or leaked to the wrong parties. VPNs, coupled with authentication systems, are a good way for companies to ensure the integrity of information being transferred from one site to another.

VPNs allow organizations to order and pay for products and services from vendors securely. This is beneficial when the nature of discount rates, accounting information, and product or service descriptions must be kept in confidence. Also of note is the general ease by which these transactions can take place. Put more simply, transactions can occur electronically, with little or no human intervention.

Many organizations are seeing the value and cost savings of employing remote access VPNs, for example, remote users access the Internet through a local ISP. Once connectivity has been established, remote users can securely connect to an organization's internal information resources via a VPN. An example of this arrangement would be business travelers who dial in to a local ISP and connect to their company's email server or internal file systems. This is often accomplished using VPN technology to enable secure communication between the remote user's computer and the organization's network.

Finally, organizations are using VPNs because it is a requirement of recent legislation. The Health Insurance Portability and Accountability Act of 1996 (HIPAA) and Gramm-Leach-Bliley (GLB) are legislation governing health care and financial organizations, respectively. These laws are concerned with patient and customer privacy. To transfer an individual's personal health care information from one system or entity to another, health plans, health care clearinghouses, and health care providers must utilize security controls to guarantee integrity and confidentiality. The same holds true for the banking industry. Financial transactions must be held in confidence to ensure no disclosure of personal financial information. You can read more about HIPAA and GLB in Chapter 19, "Legal Issues."

VPN Technology

VPNs operate in a number of different fashions. There are point-to-point (P-to-P), client-to-server and even client-to-client VPNs. In addition, there are various technologies and protocols by which the different VPNs can be deployed. It's important to understand how these technologies work and their application in enabling business.

Point-to-Point VPNs

A P-to-P VPN refers to two devices that make a connection and communicate securely using encryption. These can be hardware- or software-based. In a hardware-based P-to-P VPN, a device such as a network router is deployed for the sole purpose of creating an encrypted tunnel to an end device of the same purpose. In this configuration, a device acting as the encryption mechanism would service an entire network, as depicted in Figure 10–2.

When two networks need to communicate with one another, such as a vendor and a supplier, the least expensive way to do this is over the Internet. To provide a secure means of data transfer, a VPN is used. In this case, there is a VPN device at the head of each network. When data originating from Network A is destined for Network B, the VPN Device A creates an encrypted tunnel between itself and VPN Device B.

The purpose for this configuration is to allow two geographically separated networks the ability to communicate securely with one another. The following real-world example provides further clarity to the use of this configuration and how an organization can take advantage of a VPN.

Your company has decided to outsource the monitoring, management, and administration of its mainframe computer systems. Because your company is located in Chicago and the outsourcer is located in San Diego, secure, private communications between the two companies is essential. To reduce costs, all parties involved have decided it's best to utilize VPN technology, as opposed to provisioning a dedicated connection between the sites.

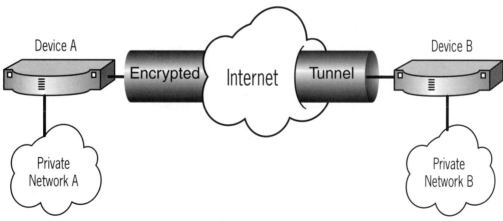

Figure 10–2
Hardware-based P-to-P VPN.

Because there is a number of mainframes, your company has decided to implement a VPN device that can serve the entire network where the mainframes reside. In addition, the outsourcing company has decided to act similarly, because it has a large number of analysts on various shifts caring for your systems.

The VPN devices at both the outsourcing company and your company are configured to construct and maintain an encrypted tunnel between the two organizations. This allows management and monitoring systems at the outsourcer's location periodically to poll your company's mainframes securely, without manually authenticating every time. In addition, any remote access to your systems initiated by analysts from the outsourcing company will be encrypted.

Client-to-Server VPNs

Client-to-server VPNs are functionally the same as P-to-P VPNs. Data traveling from point A to point B is encrypted to prevent prying eyes from intercepting and using the information. The method requires client software in addition to a VPN device. There are other scenarios requiring software on both ends of the VPN.

In this configuration, an encrypted tunnel is constructed from a remote workstation. The termination point is a VPN device that services the destination network, as shown in Figure 10–3.

Functionally, a remote workstation needs to access information resources on a private network, such as a remote user who needs to retrieve mail from the private

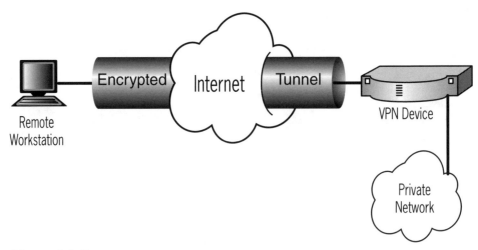

Figure 10–3
Client-to-server VPN.

company network. In this case, it is more cost-effective to do this over a public network than to support a dial-up infrastructure. In addition, it would be too difficult and too expensive to construct dedicated networks for this type of communication.

Technically, this configuration works much the same way as the P-to-P VPN; however, the initiating VPN device has moved to a remote PC instead of a device that services an entire network. In effect, the job or function of encryption and decryption has merely moved from one device to another.

This is accomplished by installing a software package whose sole purpose is to create and maintain an encrypted tunnel with a defined end point. This requires configuring the software package based on the attributes of the VPN device that is to be accessed. Unlike a P-to-P VPN, the client-to-server VPN has more individual flexibility, in that the client can be configured to communicate in a number of VPN configurations. Although this can be done in a P-to-P VPN configuration, the ramifications pertain to the networks that are being served, as opposed to individual needs.

Organizations with remote employees are excellent candidates for using client-to-server VPN technology. For example, suppose you are employed by XYZ Company as a regional sales manager. Although the company is headquartered in Boston, you work from your home in Boise. To perform your duties effectively, it is important to stay in touch with the headquarters and access information resources that reside there. A telephone and fax machine are essential tools, but you also need access to email and sales and marketing collateral, in addition to the company's sales forecasting and lead tracking system.

To ensure the confidentiality of XYZ Company's operating information, all the systems are contained on private networks and not accessible over the Internet, where clear text could disclose trade secrets and customer information. To access this information, you need a private connection to the company. And, because you are the only person working from home, it isn't cost-effective to maintain this sort of connection. A VPN makes sense.

Your company has provided you with a dial-up and/or broadband connection to your local ISP, in addition to a laptop computer. The corporate IT department has installed VPN client software on your machine. This software is configured to create and maintain an encrypted tunnel between your machine and a VPN termination point servicing the entire corporate internal network. By running the software and providing proper authentication, you can now access needed information resources via a secure channel over the Internet.

As an added benefit, this software can be used any time you are connected to the Internet. If you are out of town on business, you can dial up to the Internet from your hotel room and access company resources, even when you are on vacation. This is accomplished because the VPN client software requires only Internet connectivity. Your actual IP address information is arbitrary, providing that you issue the proper authentication. This occurs by design and because of the specific configuration of the VPN client software.

Another variation of the client-to-server VPN parallels the client/server computing model. In this example, a remote workstation needs to communicate or transmit data securely to a server. VPN software also runs on the end device, in addition to performing other functions, as shown in Figure 10–4.

This configuration is most often used in applications requiring secure transfer of information from a remote station to a centralized station. In the first scenario, VPN technology is native within the software application requiring secure communications. These applications often use shared key encryption, meaning that a shared secret key used for encryption must be present on both the sending and receiving devices. Whereas other techniques use tunneling to achieve a VPN, this scenario employs application-level encryption. Simply put, the datagram contained in the IP packet is encrypted, as opposed to encapsulating the entire packet.

The sending device must first contact the receiving device and verify keys. Then the sending device enciphers the datagrams being sent. The receiving end, in turn, deciphers the datagram.

Application-Level VPNs

Client-to-client or server-to-server VPNs are usually accomplished with software only. When an encrypted tunnel is required between only two computers (clients or servers), it is possible to have the two computers establish an encrypted link without any outside devices. This software can be either between two applications that can establish an encrypted link (application-level VPN) or software embedded in the operating system to create a network-level VPN, using IPSec for all traffic between the two computers. Some operating systems have this software embedded, such as Windows XP, or it may be purchased separately.

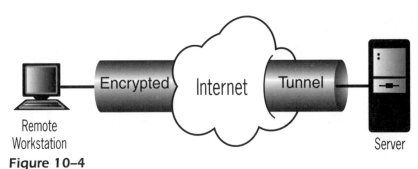

Figure 10–4
Software-based client-to-server VPN.

Suppose that your organization has deployed a large number of host-based intrusion detection agents to monitor and audit critical information resources in one of its server farms. Because the server farm and the management network reside on geographically separated networks, the IT department wants to ensure that the information sent between the host agents and the central management console has not been altered en route.

The host agents were installed and configured with the same secret key that resides on the central management console. Any time the management console communicates with the agent, or vice versa, the information is encrypted at the application level. This ensures safe passage from one point to another.

SECURE SOCKETS LAYER . . . .

SSL creates an encrypted link between Web servers and the end user's Web browser. Digital certificates are used to enable SSL on a Web server. The certificate itself can be used to verify the identity of the remote Web server. This gives your browser and the server the ability to communicate securely. SSL is, by far, the most common form of secure communication for Web servers. Any Internet communication based on Web servers and transferring even minimally sensitive information should be using SSL.

SSL is available for applications other than browser-to-Web-server communication. However, the more generic PKI (as described in Chapter 9, "Public Key Infrastructure and Encryption") should be used for non-Web applications. SSL, as it is applied to Web servers, uses a variation of the normal HTTP Web protocol. The SSL-enabled version of HTTP is called HTTPS. Because SSL has become a Web standard, it has been formally adopted by the IETF, which has renamed SSL to TLS (transport level security). The new name has not yet caught on.

SSL is used in conjunction with Web servers to allow Web site hosts the ability to conduct secure exchanges of sensitive data with site visitors. This is done to ensure the safe passage of information, so that users' data cannot be intercepted and used.

Browsers initiating a connection to a secure Web server first go through an SSL handshake process. In lay terms, this process defines the cryptographic parameters for the session. Initially, the client sends a hello message to the server. Upon receipt, the server returns a hello message, followed by its certificate. Most Web pages labeled as requiring security need only this server-side certificate. This is called *SSL2*. Depending on the security level chosen, the server may go one step further and request a certificate from the client. This is referred to as *SSL3*. If the Web page being accessed has been labeled as requiring SSL3 but the browser has no end-user identification certificate to send, access is denied.

Once certificate and/or key exchanges are complete, the client chooses a data encryption algorithm, such as triple-DES. It completes and transmits its message to the server, using the new cryptographic parameters. Finally the server transmits a similar message. Upon completion of this handshake, the client and server can begin communicating securely.

While SSL is active, all communications between the browser and the Web server are encrypted. That means that both the server and the browser must remember the encryption key and which communication path it is associated with, and both must know when the key is no longer valid. In fact, this is a session, and the use of SSL provides a level of session control that is not otherwise available for Web-based applications. In doing so, it places a significant burden on a Web server that needs to remember session status for perhaps thousands of concurrent end users.

Just as with PKI, and for many of the same reasons, SSL places burdens on the servers that use it. A Web server that successfully handles high workloads without SSL may find itself seriously short of both computer memory and processor cycles if SSL is turned on for even a few Web pages.

SSL Example

Your company wants to offer online banking, through an existing Web site, to its customers. Due to the sensitive nature of personal banking information and legislation (such as GLB, mentioned previously), your company needs to take appropriate steps in securing the transfer of banking information via its Web site.

The Web site is, in effect, a query engine for a backend database that stores customers' banking information. To accomplish this within GLB constraints, SSL has been enabled on the Web site, in addition to the construction of the normal HTML, CGI, and SQL code. Once everything is working, the Web site is opened to customers. They are required to authenticate. The customer's login information is tied to a profile. This profile instructs the database and associated Web pages with the proper information to present. Once the end user has completed the sign-in process, all of the Web pages displayed are transferred as HTTPS instead of the standard HTTP. This instructs the Web server to maintain an SSL-encrypted tunnel for that end user until he or she either signs off or times out (typically after five minutes without requesting a new page).

This secure session creates an environment of privacy, so that all information requests are encrypted to the Web server. Additionally, all data sent back to the browser is encrypted. This provides your customers with a secure way of managing accounts, paying bills online, verifying balances, and so on.

SECURE SHELL . . . .

SSH is a software-based solution and acts as a secure replacement for traditional UNIX commands, such as Telnet, FTP, rsh, rlogin, and so on. It can also be used in conjunction with Microsoft Windows NT/2000 servers. This is a software-based solution. To use SSH, the software must be installed on both the sending and receiving devices.

The use of SSH is not unusual and can be used to create other types of secure connections between devices. As with the other technologies and their corresponding examples, the goal is secure communication between two devices.

In using SSH, all communications are encrypted, using industry-standard algorithms. Encryption keys are exchanged using RSA (a public key exchange method), and data used in the key exchange is destroyed every hour. Keys are not saved anywhere. Every host has an RSA key, which is used for authentication.

SSH Example

It's 6:00 p.m., and you need to generate a number of financial reports for Tuesday's big meeting. It's impossible for you to enter the server room where the UNIX-based reporting system is located, because you are not permitted access. However, the IT department has given you access to the server via SSH.

You launch the software and type in the attributes of the device you want to access. Because you will be using the X Window System—a graphical interface for UNIX and very insecure, due to its clear text nature—you also enable the client to tunnel the X Window System data securely. The client software initiates the connection. You are prompted to authenticate, and the two devices exchange key information. Now you have a secure connection to the financial reporting server.

You quickly bring up the reporting software, configure the reports, and run them. Because of SSH, all communications taking place between your machine and the server are secure. If anyone is eavesdropping on the network, he or she will be unable to decipher and use the commands you issued or the information you requested.

SUMMARY . . . .

Encrypted communications are vital in today's environment. VPNs, SSL, and SSH allow two or more parties to communicate securely with one another, in a fashion that mitigates the damage done by electronic eavesdropping.

VPNs encrypt communications between two points or between two applications. VPNs may be implemented in hardware, software, or a combination of both.

SSL provides an encrypted link between Web servers and end-user browsers. SSL is vital in electronic commerce for Web-based businesses.

SSH is a simple application-level encryption option to encrypt sessions with remote computers.

There are many reasons for businesses to use encrypted communications, but the foremost are privacy, confidentiality, and integrity. These are important in maintaining competitive advantage and strength of brand. In addition, recent legislation requires it of industry segments dealing with patient health care and financial records.

11 Mobile Workers and Wireless LANs

In this chapter . . .

- Mobile Users' Security Concerns

- The Emergence of Wireless Standards

- Bluetooth (A Wireless Standard)

- Security in a Wireless World

167

Most companies suffer from limited space, due to the high cost of corporate real estate. In the modern office, there are also a lot of mobile workers—people who move from office to office, city to city, or across continents as a normal part of their jobs—and wherever they land, they need to be able to hook into the corporate network. These people face the same problems in the office and at home: "Where can I sit with both power and access to the network?" The increase of mobile users and the emergence of wireless networks have created new security concerns.

MOBILE USERS AND SECURITY . . . .

In the early days of laptops, mobile users would put their work on a floppy disk to transfer data from their corporate network to their laptop so that they could work on the road. When they returned to the office, they would copy their data onto the network, again using a floppy disk. This quickly evolved to the ability for mobile users to connect to the corporate network and synchronize their laptops when they were in the office. On the road, they could use a phone line to connect and synchronize work. Today, mobile users are becoming more common, and they're requiring high-speed connections to connect to backend systems—virtually at any time and from anywhere, including branch offices, customer sites, airports, and even airplanes.

Mobile users have a unique set of security requirements for a variety of reasons. First, they can't rely on any physical protections for their machines. Second, they need to access mission-critical data outside the protected networks. Third, they use a multitude of (questionably secure) methods, from dialing up to the Internet to wireless networks, to access that data. These stresses manifest in security policy and practices as methods to identify, authenticate, and secure communications for mobile users.

Chapter 4, "Authentication, Authorization, Access Control," covers identification and authentication, and Chapter 9, "Public Key Infrastructure and Encryption," and Chapter 10, "Encrypted Communications," provide detail concerning some forms of communications security. Bear in mind that mobile users will require your organization's chosen methods and products to work on laptops and through a variety of connection methods. The emergence of new connection devices, including Internet-connected mobile phones, pagers, and PDAs (personal digital assistants), adds an additional dimension of complexity to the issue.

A Glossary of Wireless Terms

Cellular

GSM—Global System for Mobile Communications. It is the basic technology for cellular telephones in much of the world. In the United States, GSM competes with systems such as CDMA, TDMA, and PCS. All of these represent "second-generation" (2G) cellular systems. In these systems, data communications use standard, low-speed modem signaling or slight variations, such as CDPD (cellular packet data protocol).

GPRS—General Packet Radio Services. An attempt to add faster data transfer capabilities to 2G cellular networks.

2.5 G—Another name for GPRS, indicating that it makes second generation closer to third-generation capabilities.

3G—A generic name for all proposed third-generation cellular communications systems. High-speed data transfer is designed into the technology for the first time.

WAP—Wireless Access Protocol. This is the data communications protocol used in most cellular data transfers. A competitor is DoCoMo, which is popular in Japan. WAP and DoCoMo are supposed to converge in the next few years. WAP is a subset of HTTP, the WWW protocol.

WTLS—Wireless Transport Level Security. This is the security mechanism for WAP. It is a subset of SSL, the Web security protocol.

Wireless LAN

WLAN—Wireless LAN. A generic name for inbuilding communications equivalent to a wired LAN, using one of the standards listed below.

802.11b—Currently the most popular WLAN standard.

802.11a—The next-generation wireless LAN standard. Faster but not more secure.

HiperLAN—A proposed European wireless LAN standard that, at the time of this writing, appears to be losing support.

Radiospace—An invented word describing the radio wave spectrum being used for many competing technologies.

Personal Area Network

Bluetooth—A new standard for very local communications, typically within a 30-foot radius, but frequently even smaller. Designed for all of the devices you carry around and anything those devices may want to communicate with. The possibilities are endless but few people are able to find one that makes enough sense to create the first Bluetooth market.

Physical Security Issues in Mobile Computing

Physical security is a significant issue when dealing with mobile devices because they leave your security perimeter. What happens if you lose your laptop, PDA, or cell phone? Depending on what your concerns are, you may be faced with losing intellectual property, such as the sales contact database, quarterly figures, due diligence reports, design specifications, and so on. You may also face the loss of expensive hardware and software and experience inconvenience, at the least. In most cases, the loss is due purely to theft of the device and could be written off. But if you want to make sure that your competitors haven't tried to gain advantage, you need to consider ways of keeping the data safe and possibly tracking the device itself.

 Key Point

Physical security is a significant issue when dealing with mobile devices because they leave your security perimeter.

Today, there are many options open to you but basically it comes down to either passive or active methods. The differences are simple: If the technology is active, the protected device effectively alerts you. If the solution is passive, you can verify that it's yours only when it's returned to your possession. We will consider only active methods. There are basically four approaches:

1. **Protect access to the device.** There is a plethora of methods to accomplish this, including BIOS protection passwords, operating system passwords (not recommended), radio tokens, infrared tokens, smart cards, USB tokens, software smart cards, and remote authentication (you need to access a server on the Internet to authenticate the local device). Some of these can be built into a corporate PKI, if required, or can stand alone.

2. **Protect the data.** Deny the thief access to the data, whatever the circumstances. These methods include encrypting the data from individual files to encrypting the entire hard disk. There is a problem with this is if the device suffers a hardware failure, which can be very inconvenient. For instance, if valuable data is on a corrupted hard drive, it is possible to have a company specializing in data forensics recover most if not all the information—but not if the hard drive was encrypted. It can also be very difficult for the system administrator if a user loses a password or PKI certificate needed to access the encrypted data. Usually, there is little that can be done until the user returns to the office. Most of these issues can be addressed. Solutions must be flexible, must support IT administration and management needs, and must be designed for use by mobile workers.

3. **Track the stolen device.** Another method is to track the stolen laptop, using location devices or software. The options for this solution range from using a radio location technology to alerting the owner whenever the device connects to the Internet. Obviously, these need some sort of stealth property so that they can't easily be detected or removed. They also need a form of administration or management tool—you don't want ex-corporate laptops reporting their whereabouts years after they were sold off!

4. **Combine the first two methods and protect the device and the data.** There are companies offering solutions based on the computer's BIOS—the piece of embedded software that helps a computer start and run before the operating system becomes active. So, even if the computer is stolen, the thief needs to crack the BIOS-level authentication before the system will start; then the operating system, or possibly the applications, refer to encrypted parts of the BIOS before they will operate. Failure to meet the security requirements means that the system might not start or that it will try to "phone home" whenever it sees an opportunity.

WIRELESS NETWORKS . . . .

One of the more important and emerging connection methods is wireless networks, providing convenience and power on an entirely new scale because they require no physical connection. Over the past 10 years, "wired" LANs have grown in speed from 10 Mbps to 100 Mbps. Now, if you have enough money in the corporate IT budget, you can have speeds of 1 gigabit per second (Gbps) to each desktop over a physical connection.

The idea of wireless networking is that your computer or PDA is attached to a computer network using a radio transmitter/receiver that is normally built into laptops and even some PDAs. Older technology laptops can be converted to use these technologies using PCMCIA (Personal Computer Memory Card International Association) cards. It means, that no matter where you sit—be it a conference room, someone else's desk, or even out in a hallway—you can gain access to all the network resources. However, instead of connecting with a piece of wire, you can use a radio interface. There are three basic types of wireless technology: wireless over long distances (hundreds of miles), within a single building or campus (wireless LANs), and personal LANs (less than 50 feet).

Wireless over Long Distances (Miles)

Wireless over long distances is usually accomplished using cellular technology or satellite communications. Satellite communications are still in their infancy but will likely use the same security as cellular communications. The GSM system, which was first developed in Europe but later adapted for use in the United States, sits alongside existing cell phone systems. The emerging 3G (see Figure 11–1) cell phone systems in some ways are derived from GSM, although there will still be some differences between American and European implementations.

GSM is mentioned simply because it is one of the few truly mobile systems that works across the globe, crossing national, political, and ideological boundaries. It exists in the Middle East, the Pacific Rim (including Japan and China, among others), and Australia, and it is ubiquitous over Europe. There are even a few cellular networks within the United States that use GSM.

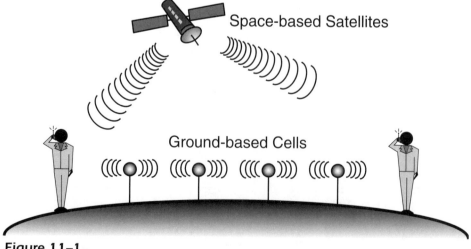

Figure 11–1
Wireless networks over miles are cellular or satellite communications.

Cell phone systems, such as GSM, provide not only voice communications but also the ability to transfer data across the entire world. But it has some serious shortcomings. For example, data is transferred at 9,600 bps, which is the same data rate as you can expect from a standard modem built in 1985.

The data communication was used in the same way as a fixed-line modem. Typically, you would connect a laptop to the mobile phone, then you'd make a dial-up call to a service provider and, thus, to the Internet. Alternatively, you could connect directly to your corporate network via a remote access technology service.

The data rate was limited to about 14.4 Kbps. That isn't a lot if you are trying to exchange a 4-Mb file. So service providers and others in the mobile communications space looked for a way to improve data communications using existing technologies.

In 1992, a committee of the United Nations, the International Telecommunications Union (ITU), proposed a new global vision for radio-based communications, called *IMT2000* (International Mobile Telecommunications in year 2000). The UMTS (Universal Mobile Telecommunications System) project was set up to realize this. UMTS was supposed to bring together all types of public radio communications.

Part of this overall vision was 3G (third-generation wireless or mobile communications). This nirvana proposed that the ordinary man in the street could enjoy something like a 2-Mbps "always-on" connection that would carry voice, video, and any other kind of data traffic, would permit instant access to the Internet, and would use the existing Internet protocols (TCP/IP). It may seem unlikely that mobile devices will be capable of 2 Mbps but, judging by the way technology is moving and with a current timescale that sees 3G introduced in 2003–2004, it is entirely possible that this technology will be touching our lives within a few years.

 KEY POINT

The term *always-on* refers to the ability of a device to use the Internet without forcing the end user to go through a connection or sign-in process more than once.

However, nirvana wasn't going to come as quickly or as easily as people had hoped; 3G has experienced delays in rollout. So, in an effort to bring a sampling of advanced data communications services to the market, manufacturers and service providers suggested General Packet Radio Services (GPRS). GPRS is truly a halfway house and, indeed, it is sometimes referred to as *2.5 G*. It uses the existing GSM radio technology and, behind the scenes, turns this into TCP/IP.

GPRS should reach speeds of up to 56 Kbps, which is roughly equivalent to the modern modem. It has one other advantage, which is that it's an "always-on" technology.

This means that you don't need to dial, so if you have one of these connected to your PDA, all you need to do is point and click to go straight onto the Internet.

GPRS is very common in Europe and less so in the United States and elsewhere. What's exciting about GPRS is that the technology doesn't have to be inside your mobile phone—it comes in various forms. Smart phones use it in their tiny little screens; PDAs, such as the Compaq iPac, Psion, and Palm devices, have cradles or attachments. It wouldn't be unreasonable to assume that there are PCMCIA cards for laptops.

Wireless LANs (in the Same Building)

A WLAN, usually used in a campus of buildings (see Figure 11–2) isn't quite the same as the wired LAN network. The major differences lie in the speed and the standards. The initial American standard 802.11 gave us 8 Mbps. This was quickly followed by 802.11b, which gave us 11 Mbps, and now we have 802.11a, which promises 54 Mbps but is more likely to work at 12 or 24 Mbps. There are already additional suffixes that promise to take us up to the letter z and cover all sorts of things. Standard 802.11 is a product of the Institute of Electrical and Electronics Engineers (IEEE). In Europe, the European Telecom Standards Institute (ETSI) produced HyperLAN and HyperLAN/2, which offer 25 and 54 Mbps, respectively.

The WLAN standard is likely to come to the fore in the corporate environment, especially with demands for hot-desking and limited real estate. Originally, hot-desking allowed multiple (mobile) workers to share deliberately limited office resources (chairs and desks, for example) on the basis that not everyone is expected to be in the office at the same time. It accommodates staff who have to travel between offices (and would otherwise need a desk in every office) or are usually on the road

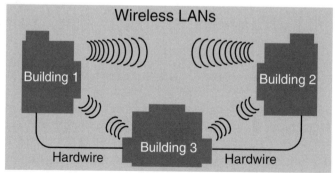

Figure 11–2
WLANs are usually used in a campus of buildings.

(so-called road warriors). Some staff would end up working in free conference rooms, corridors, and rest areas, where IT hadn't installed the network. Using wireless LAN technology meant that staff could work anywhere they wanted, and now the term is synonymous with the convenience of working how and where you want. There are also solutions for the home office that can be used in conjunction with cable modems and DSL.

Competition is rife in this arena, with manufacturers working on applications for this new radio technology, including use in airports, hotels, and other places where people are likely to want to check email, download information, or connect to their corporate LAN without having to find a phone to make the connection.

Personal LANs (Within 10 Meters)

Bluetooth, an emerging standard for the personal LAN, is another radio technology designed simply to replace the need for wires. It really shouldn't become a replacement for wireless LANs and cannot, in itself, be a long-distance medium like GPRS or 3G. Having said that, it does have its place and is a very useful technology for personal area networks. Bluetooth is not really designed to go beyond 10 m in distance (see Figure 11–3); although 200 m may be a possibility, it will drain your battery very quickly.

The speed with Bluetooth is never likely to go beyond 1 Mbps—fine for a little bit of Web surfing but not for serious corporate data traffic. Imagine trying to print your 7 Mb Microsoft PowerPoint presentation when it takes three minutes just to load it up to the printer.

Bluetooth has interesting uses, such as wiring all the appliances in your house so that they can talk. These "piconets," as they are known, have several very useful

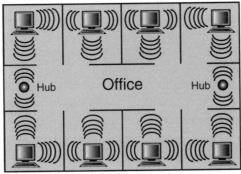

Figure 11–3
Personal LANs are wireless networks over very small distances.

possibilities and some frivolous uses. Why your toaster and your refrigerator need to talk is something the marketing department is working on very hard . . .

Bluetooth can be used to help achieve seamless connectivity so that an executive stuck in traffic can start the meeting and simply verbally instruct the car to send the presentation to another person. Voice recognition translates the command to instructions from the car to the laptop to access the named file (a voice verification biometric identifies the user). The laptop then looks into the Bluetooth environment for a GSM, GPRS, or similar service. Using that connection, it calls the other party and transfers the presentation to his or her computer. Applications will be built around this to ensure that the necessary levels of security and positive identification are employed to avoid mishaps.

SECURITY IN THE WIRELESS WORLD . . . .

Huge strides have been made in terms of increasing telecommunication bandwidth in recent years. But building security specifications into communications standards was almost an afterthought until the last couple of years.

When these various technologies converge, security becomes a primary concern. For example, Bluetooth technology could be added to a large range of devices, such as mobile phones, PDAs, laptops, desktops, door access controls, access passes, and fixed telephones. When merged with WLAN, GSM, and GPRS, it opens the way to total connectivity. It also becomes a far greater security risk.

Wide-area wireless over the cellular telephone network most often uses a communications protocol called *WAP* (wireless access protocol). Security for WAP is modeled on that used in Web sites, which is known as SSL or TLS (see Chapter 10). The WAP subset of TLS is called *wireless TLS* (WTLS). WTLS provides protection of selected content, not overall channel protection.

Your hand-held device establishes a call (through an always-on connection) to a WAP server, typically installed at a telecommunications carrier. An encrypted channel using WTLS is established between your device and the WAP server. When information is transferred from your device to the server, it is decrypted at the server, then usually re-encrypted before being sent through to your corporate network, frequently via another TLS tunnel.

Some WAP servers do not support WTLS. That would force all communications to be in clear text, a serious security threat. If WTLS is used, the decryption at the WAP server represents a serious weakness. Newer WAP servers with true TLS support and direct pass-through of encrypted data should be on the market by the middle of 2002. This will significantly improve the security of WAP.

Security in Radiospace

WLAN has another set of security issues. *Radiospace* is probably a term you haven't heard before but it is likely a concept with which you're all too familiar. It's the universe, as seen from the point of view of a radio wave. There are no walls, doors, or windows. The radio wave can't get through metal but it can travel *along* metal. And it can't go deep underground but it can get there via pipes and conduits. In the modern world, nearly every person wants a free and unrestricted radiospace. It's the way we get our TV signals and radio programs, and when it doesn't work, we don't get our mobile phone signal.

Traditionally, anyone who wants to gain access to your corporate network surfs the Internet, travels through cyberspace, and eventually bumps against your firewall. But now, you put in a WLAN, and they can sit comfortably in a nearby hotel and hack the network, all because the radiospace for your network goes outside your own four walls and extends to other nearby buildings.

There is no such thing as a radio firewall, and until there is, networks that are accessible by radio will leak beyond the physical limits of the building. Of course, traditional wired networks don't leak outside buildings. From this point of view, the network could extend tens of meters outside the buildings in which they are sited.

With the WLAN, the security concern arises because of the air interface. This is defined as the communication and security protocols between transmitter and receiver—it is, in effect, the way that radios speak to each other. This opens up the unpleasant possibility that a corporate network employing WLAN could be hacked into from outside the office, for example, from a nearby hotel. This means that a determined hacker could conceivably spend weeks unnoticeably trying to crack the encryption on the WLAN air interface without going anywhere near corporate offices.

Securing Your WLAN

WLAN transmissions should be protected by encryption. Every WLAN device has the ability to encrypt the data being sent and to decrypt it on receipt. There are two gaps between this protection and reality. First, most organizations do not turn on the built-in encryption. Researchers driving through many major U.S. cities with WLAN sensors have determined that over 90 percent of installed WLANs are not encrypted, allowing complete access to anyone passing by with any generic WLAN device. Second, the encryption built into all 802.11b devices is weak. Although it may stop an untutored hacker and slow down the highly skilled and motivated ones, it will not prevent a determined hacker from breaking in to your network. Encryption is being improved in 802.11b, so this may or may not be an issue when you implement.

Ideally, WLAN infrastructures should be kept separate from the fixed LAN infrastructure in terms of their wiring and routing. The two infrastructures should be separated by a well-configured firewall with at least network-level intrusion detection. In addition, everyone using the WLAN should, to all intents and purposes, be treated as a remote worker and be required to use a VPN and strong authentication.

A great deal depends on the sensitivity of the information being secured. Valuable information could be protected by the use of VPNs. A useful security policy could be to enforce the use of a VPN over air interfaces. This doesn't prevent someone from stealing the laptop but it does protect data in transit. This, then, begs the question of securing the laptop or the data on it. So do we need biometric-based access control for the laptop and/or file or hard disk encryption? Somewhere along the line, there is usually the need for a PIN or password, and most security professionals understand that users will, like hackers, take the line of least resistance when it comes to passwords.

Security and Bluetooth

When Bluetooth was developed, security was a consideration, and a certain amount was built into the model. However, security of Bluetooth needs to be more seriously addressed: There is a potential for someone promiscuously attempting to interface any other Bluetooth device, and currently, there appear to be no applications that will monitor and defend a network from Bluetooth-based attacks. Expect manufacturers to provide products that can defend against Bluetooth attacks and provide a solution for PDAs and other devices connected to laptops. This is such a contentious issue that many corporations ban the use of PDAs within the corporate network.

Bluetooth-enabled devices could promote a new physical security paradigm—the dynamic security environment. Bluetooth devices always remain on standby. If someone breaks into a home and starts moving Bluetooth-enabled hardware (a computer, a refrigerator, a stereo), it would send an alert to warn that someone has gained unauthorized entry to the property and is trying to make off with specific equipment. The user might also employ specific security layers. For example, if a request is made for a logout when your PC needs only a login, the piconet (the network that connects one Bluetooth device to another) can alert the user to this unusual request.

Cellular Security

In a cell phone environment that uses GPRS, users do not necessarily even need to keep logging in. The reason for this is that GPRS is an always-on technology—much like a leased line (such as the office connection to the Internet) or DSL or cable modem connection. In the kind of world offered by GPRS (and the similar always-on connections), there is an increased importance on encryption and authentication layers being built into systems. It is entirely feasible (although probably not preferable) to be permanently logged in to the corporate network via the GPRS connection. This could provide a challenge and an opportunity: The challenge is for network managers to control this type of access; the opportunity is for application developers to come up with continuous authentication systems for the mobile world.

There are many ways to bypass security frameworks that have not been thoroughly assessed using formal methods. Think of this like the suit of armor that a medieval knight would wear into battle. These were heavy, clumsy, expensive, and difficult to manage (sounds like a secure network!) but they saved the knight's life *if* they were properly designed and fitted. Sometimes, if the armor was ill fitting, there would be "chinks"—small gaps between pieces of the armor—and an astute enemy could take advantage of these. It is the same with security. Just because your GPRS or 3G service provider seems to have (network) security in place does not mean that there is no way to circumvent it. For example, just how does a telephone company sufficiently investigate the backgrounds of all its employees and ensure that vital codes are not given away?

The same concerns apply to any device capable of supporting GPRS or 3G interfaces, and there are many PDAs today that have optional GPRS cradles. Some now even have them built in.

WIRELESS AND MOBILE
COMPUTING IN THE FUTURE . . . .

Wireless networks and mobile users are becoming the normal paradigm. You need to address these subjects in your policies and procedures. It is important not to make assumptions about network security and corporate security policies, and the procedures that enshrine them need to be flexible and not, in themselves, tied to a particular technology or view of how the world works. Otherwise, as time passes, it becomes more and more difficult to build on top of the old policy. It is also time-consuming and wasteful of resources to keep rewriting the policy. For example, if the procedures require that the corporate network perimeter be defined by firewalls, how does that translate to staff working from home, where there is no firewall? Or, how does this policy translate to staff members who can access dial-up phone lines in the office or maybe can simply use a cell phone attached to the laptop to dial up the Internet?

It may seem simple but how often have people blamed a government for having a policy that disregards advances made before the policy is turned into law. The government gets blamed for being shortsighted, narrow-minded, or making the policy for purely political reasons. These pitfalls must be kept in mind. If not, the corporate policy becomes a bulky tome that is full of exceptions to the rule and, therefore, is unworkable in practice.

It is important to keep in mind what is being protected. Is it the network, the laptop, the cell phone, the servers? Or is it the information that these devices store, transmit, and process?

SUMMARY . . . .

Mobile computing requires special consideration when implementing security. Mobile users leave your security perimeter, both physically and logically. Therefore, you need secure methods for mobile users to access mission-critical data, and you need to protect the physical devices and data in the event of theft or compromise beyond your sphere of control.

Wireless networking enables mobile computing, both inside and outside your security perimeter. Wireless networks are gaining in popularity, with standards and implementations for spanning miles, going between offices, or connecting devices within a few feet. Each of these technologies has its own advantages and security challenges.

GPRS and other long-range wireless data transmission standards that use always-on technology can be risky because it is not necessary to authenticate with each connection. Wireless LAN transmissions should be encrypted. Most organizations today do not do this, making it very easy for someone to tap into the organization's networks and do anything from sniff passwords to hijack sessions and take over computers. Bluetooth is an important emerging standard for devices within 10 meters of each other. However, a chain of Bluetooth devices can create a far-reaching network that can be hacked.

If your organization is planning to use any of these wireless technologies, it is important to address these issues in security policy, architecture, and implementation.

12 Single Signon

In this chapter . . .

- What Is SSO?

- Why SSO Is Important

- Why SSO Fails

- Should Your Organization Address SSO?

T he people who need to use computers in their daily work frequently think of information security as being in the way of getting that work done. One of the most visible and irritating issues imposed by security is the frequent need to type in a user account name and password (see Figure 12–1). In large organizations with poor control over the computing infrastructure, the account names and passwords are different for each computer application used. Getting control of user authentication in the form of account names and passwords across multiple computer systems is called *Single Signon* (SSO), and it is the mythical "white whale" of information security.

WHAT IS SSO? . . . .

SSO is an authentication process in which each user enters only one user name and password to access the multiple applications needed to perform a day's work (see Figure 12–2). At the first request to sign in, the user enters a valid user name and password and is immediately given rights to the server. The user is already authenticated, so when he or she switches applications, there is no need to enter yet another user name and/or password.

The SSO product that virtually every IT organization would like to purchase would provide a translation layer between each employee (or contractor or any end user) and the computer systems each needs to access. The translator would check against some central control mechanism for two things: Has the user proven who he

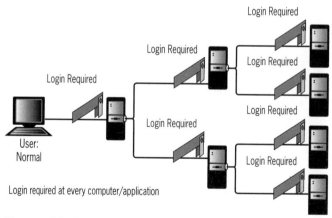

Figure 12–1
Without SSO, a login is required at every new computer and application.

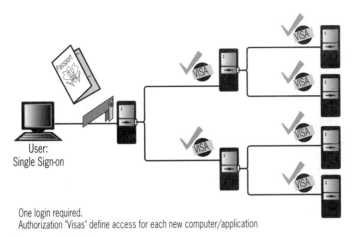

One login required.
Authorization "Visas" define access for each new computer/application

Figure 12–2
With SSO, one login provides a set of credentials (visas) to access multiple computers/applications without new logins.

or she is already, and what is the user authorized to do? Then the translation layer would retrieve the appropriate account name and password from a secure storage place and send it to the computer system that the end user wants to use. Because everyone wants one of these, there must be some reason they do not already have one. This chapter covers two topics: why most SSO implementations fail and what you should do instead, both tactically and strategically.

WHY SSO FAILS . . . .

Five hundred people may use three hundred computer applications. Each person uses a slightly different combination of applications. Each computer used to gain access is configured slightly differently. Each computer application was created using a different set of security assumptions. The applications run on many different types of computers and operating systems. The network path that connects users to the applications is different for each location from which the users may work.

In effect, given the number of variables in the preceding paragraph, each user has a unique set of connection requirements. The details of just how, when, and why a user submits an account name and password have a surprising degree of variability when the problem is analyzed closely. The result is that each user requires a customized set of SSO parameters, and it is generally impossible to predict what those parameters will be before an installer sits down to work directly with each end user.

The typical time to install an SSO product in a large organization is a half-day per user—and the 10,000th user will still require a half-day of customization.

That makes the installation of SSO expensive. But it would still be worthwhile for many organizations if not for one other factor. Many of the variables listed earlier change frequently. In an SSO-enabled environment, those changes can break the SSO capability and require recustomization. In an organization that is undergoing frequent change in its computer and network infrastructure, that can result in up to 20 percent of users being unable to use those applications each week. The staff to support recustomization increases costs. But more important, the money spent to ease end user inefficiency via SSO has been wasted! Lost productivity due to inoperable SSO has exceeded the improved productivity. And users are just as unhappy because of the impact of this new type of failure on their job. But the cost of maintaining the SSO system continues until someone admits that it was a disastrous investment.

This does not mean that SSO is wrong for everyone. In a relatively stable IT environment, the initial cost of customization may be acceptable and may provide real benefits in productivity and user satisfaction. But success stories are rare.

Computer users complain about three issues related to SSO: too many account names to remember; too many passwords to remember; and having to re-enter them both too often. When these three issues arise, there is generally a fourth issue that is seen only by IT—the helpdesk is spending too much time and money issuing password resets. Most organizations that have these problems also have one more—their user account management is out of control. This leads to security risks because many employees who left the organization years ago still have active computer accounts. Each of these problems should be addressed separately.

Too Many Account Names

An account name identifies the person authorized to use the computer. A case can be made that some people require more than one identity. Frequently, this is used to allow a person with supervisory or system administration authority to operate without those higher level rights whenever they are not needed. But for all other cases, each person should have one identifier (account name), and that should be used for all computer access.

Many organizations implemented computer systems over the past decades without any centrally dictated policy about user identifiers. The result has been a mess that will take some organizations a decade or more to fix. Many of the projects currently under development in this area focus on the establishment of a single, centralized directory, typically known as an *LDAP* (pronounced el-dap, for Lightweight Directory Access Protocol) directory, to contain the list of standard identifiers. The result of these projects will be that all newly developed applications will use a common account name for each user. Unluckily, adapting existing computers and applications to make use of this common identity will take years.

While the implementation of an LDAP directory to hold these common identifiers is absolutely the right thing to do, any impact on the list of user accounts that exist within your organization will be minimal unless significant investments are made in changing all of the existing systems and applications to use that LDAP directory. That is an investment that few organizations are prepared to make.

Gradually, new applications built using the LDAP directory will grow in number. Even small investments in upgrading older applications to use the directory will start to accumulate. Over time, the problem of having too many identifiers will become less irritating. This is clearly not the grand SSO solution. But it is one piece of solving a real problem at realistic expenditure levels.

Too Many Passwords

In the same way that account names are out of control in many organizations, passwords have taken a wide variety of forms and have been controlled by irritatingly inconsistent policies. System A requires six or more characters and must be changed every 30 days. System B requires eight characters that include at least one "special" character—such as a question mark or an exclamation point—and must be changed every two weeks. When the list of passwords that each person must maintain gets too long, security fails. People rebel and do everything possible to undermine security.

Password policy must be clear and consistent for all systems and applications in the organization. If one person needs to remember more than one password, there must be a clear business reason, such as the classification of the data being accessed or the role being performed, such as system administrator functions. Once the passwords are all formed and changed according to common rules, a solution to the user's complaints can be found. Password synchronization is an automated process that causes any password change activity to be passed to all of the other systems and applications to which a user has access.

If the rule says that all passwords must be eight characters long and that they will be changed every 45 days, the first application that a person signs into on day 46 will display a message requesting that the user assign a new password. When the user responds with a valid new password, that application and all of the other applications that know about that user will start using the new password. For this to work efficiently, you must first have solved the problem of too many identifiers. How else will the computer systems know how to relate an account on system A to an account owned by the same person on system B?

Frequent Re-Entry

Once the account identifiers and passwords are fixed, the next problem is that users must frequently re-enter their account names and passwords as they shift from one application to the next. There is no single thing that you can do that will significantly reduce this problem. Individual points of coordination among different systems are sometimes possible. Third-party software tools to connect the authentication systems of very popular computing environments are available for a few cases. But if the identifier and password problems are solved, the two major causes of SSO maintenance cost have been handled. At this point, an SSO product may become a viable option. Keep in mind that the first-year cost will continue to be high.

Password Resets

No matter how few passwords a user has, he or she will eventually forget one. Given the current problem of having, in some cases, dozens of passwords, forgetting is common. The resulting call to the IT help desk for a password reset generates a high workload in a department that must be responsive to user issues at all times. Automation of the password reset process should be a high priority in any company that desires SSO.

Password reset products store information about the user that should not be easily guessed. Normally, three or more items of data per user are stored. When a user requires a reset, the automated system prompts the user for a particular piece of that stored information, and if the user can produce the correct answer, the password is reset. If the user fails, the account is locked until the user makes contact with a human being at the help desk.

User Account Management

The creation of an identifier to represent a new user and the deletion of all identifiers when someone is no longer authorized represent critical tasks in any security program. In between these two actions, the rights and applications allocated to an employee, consultant, or temporary worker may change on an unpredictable schedule. These activities must take place using the LDAP directory when a user has access to the new applications built, using the common identifier. But account maintenance must be performed against each and every system and application that a user has ever had access to when someone changes roles within the company or leaves. The years of poor control in this area have left many companies in a severe quandary. Doing the work correctly would take a large staff constantly performing searches of every computer for unrecorded accounts. Doing the work poorly (or not at all) leaves significant openings in security.

Automation of user account management is possible. Although the initial investment is high, the benefits to a large organization with many legacy computer systems are significant. Clean account management contributes to the goals of SSO: better, faster user support and better quality of that support.

SHOULD YOUR ORGANIZATION ADDRESS SSO? . . . .

The problem of having multiple sign-ins was created by the computer manufacturers and magnified by internal conflict within the organizations that used the computers. Fixing the problem will require the cooperation of the computer manufacturers, but even if that were to occur, the problems caused by internal conflict would stop any benefits from resulting. For organizations that have addressed the tactical problems listed above, there is hope. Once those problems are solved, some foreseeable progress by the computer manufacturers may actually result in something like a real-world SSO.

Once the account identifiers and passwords are synchronized, a technical solution is possible. Microsoft may have created that solution by embedding the necessary technology in its operating system. For Windows 2000 and subsequent releases, Microsoft decided to make Kerberos the default authentication method. Most other computer manufacturers provide a version of Kerberos authentication with their operating systems, but few companies have turned it on because it was platform-specific. Despite a design capability of Kerberos to be used in multiplatform environments, most versions failed to be fully interoperable with competing computer systems or were simply too expensive to manage.

By making Kerberos its default authentication system, Microsoft established a de facto standard that computer manufacturers are likely to match. By amending their own versions of Kerberos to work with the Microsoft version, the vendors will make their computers more desirable. In effect, all of the computers that cooperate in a Kerberos environment become part of a SSO network. Eventually, you will be able to have SSO without buying and installing another product to offer the service. For this to work for you, you must have already cleaned up your account identifier problems. For this to be cost-efficient to manage, you will need user account management automation. You (and your co-workers) will also need a great deal of patience. It will take more than five years for this solution to become pervasive. In the interim, you should work on each of the problems listed above individually.

SUMMARY . . . .

SSO is a mission-critical capability designed to address the complexities and security issues associated with many users across many applications. For example, users with 20 passwords will tend to write them down, which compromises their security. When they forget their passwords, the organization has to reset them, which creates a management nightmare. SSO is a mixture of password management and authorization providing a single authentication that controls access to all applications and computers for each user.

SSO implementations have a number of problems, including the ability to scale to the number of users and passwords they must manage and the amount of management required to operate them. One of the key issues with implementing SSO is enabling your applications to work with your chosen SSO solution. The adoption of Kerberos authentication is an important first step in this process. An easy, integrated SSO solution is likely to be several years away.

13 Digital Signatures and Electronic Commerce

In this chapter . . .

- Electronic Commerce Security Issues
- Digital Signatures vs. Electronic Signatures
- Electronic Signature Legislation
- Transactional Security

The most significant issues affecting any type of transaction over the Internet are the positive identification of the parties involved, the integrity of the messages exchanged between the parties, and, in electronic commerce (e-commerce), the creation of legally binding contracts from button clicks. If you are an online retailer, you have special security needs and requirements.

E-COMMERCE ....

Both sides of a transaction over the Internet have special security requirements because there is no physical meeting, as when something is bought from a store. To explain this fully, we'll look at Internet transactions in terms of a sale where a merchant and consumer wish to exchange goods for money. There are many other examples of transactions, including:

- Confirming an identity
- Signing a contract
- Timestamping a transaction

In the case of a sales transaction, the merchant has certain requirements. He wants to be sure of the buyer's identity because it may help determine the buyer's ability to pay. The merchant needs to be able to confirm that the consumer did, in fact, authorize payment and that the user can't deny that authorization was made. The merchant may also require certification that the buyer meets certain requirements, such as being over the age of 18 or living in a country that is not restricted for export of the merchant's goods.

The consumer also has special requirements. The consumer wants to confirm the merchant's identity to prevent being swindled. The consumer requires a level of integrity in the transaction to prevent unauthorized payments. The consumer needs a receipt of the transaction and the ability to take action if the seller fails to perform or deliver. The buyer will also be concerned about privacy and anonymity in the transaction.

Authentication, authorization, integrity, privacy, anonymity, and nonrepudiation are all required for a good Internet transaction. Internet transactions are not a great deal different from face-to-face sales, except for the need of a trusted third party to authenticate the respective parties. This authentication is provided through the use of digital certificates and trusted third parties, known as *Certificate Authorities* (CAs).

A digital signature is a technology for appending a strong authentication/integrity proof to a message. A digital signature is an encrypted package appended to any transmitted or documented message that binds a user's identity to that particular message. As discussed in Chapter 9, "Public Key Infrastructure and Encryption," PKI provides the CA capability. CAs provide many services, including:

Identifying Certificates. This is a simple certificate that binds a name and identity to a public key. The CA can confirm for both buyer and seller that they are who they claim to be.

Authorizing Certificate. This certificate contains other information, such as age and location; or personal information, such as height and weight. Authorizing certificates can be used to provide information to online merchants, such as the requirement to be over the age of 21 in order to purchase alcohol.

Transactional Certificate. Rather than binding information to a public key, transactional certificates act as witness to a transactional event, providing nonrepudiation, such as a denial from either party that a transaction was consummated.

Timestamp Certificate. Like the transactional certificate, this certificate provides nonrepudiation that certain witnessed events happened at a certain time.

If your business requires transactions over the Internet, you will need to establish a relationship with one of the many certificate authorities to provide these services.

ELECTRONIC SIGNATURES . . . .

Digital signatures are different than electronic signatures. A digital signature is an encrypted hash that binds an identity to a document. An electronic signature is a legal term referring to an electronic version of your personal signature. Electronic signatures almost certainly include some form of digital signature, but not all digital signatures perform the function of an electronic signature. To add to the confusion, several organizations use the terms interchangeably.

According to an American Bar Association (ABA) document addressing the use of electronic signatures (available at *www.abanet.org/scitech/ec/isc/dsgfree.html*), a signature is not a substantive part of the transaction, but rather a representation of it that accomplishes four goals: evidence, ceremony, approval, and efficiency. The ABA contends that a good digital signature will serve these same four purposes.

1. **Evidence.** The evidentiary aspects of a signature tie the signer to the document.

2. **Ceremony.** Ceremony means that the signer, through the act of signing, is acknowledging the legal significance of the signer's act, preventing "inconsiderate engagements."

3. **Approval.** The signer is expressing approval or authorization in certain legal contexts with certain documents.

4. **Efficiency and logistics.** It is easier for a document to change hands with minimal interruption because the need to inquire about the document has been lessened by the presence of a signature.

E-SIGN

On June 30, 2000, then-President Bill Clinton signed the Electronic Signatures and National Commerce Act (E-SIGN) into law. E-SIGN essentially states that signatures in electronic form are now valid. To fully understand E-SIGN, you have to know what it doesn't cover, as well as what it does.

What E-SIGN Does Not Cover

Many things were not covered by the legislation and are left up to either individual states or the marketplace to fill in the gap. The following aspects of electronic signatures are not covered by E-SIGN:

Standards of use. The law does not set any standards for the use of electronic signatures. The law does not require digital signatures to accomplish the same goals as traditional "wet" ink signatures, except in the case of transferable records (loans secured by real property).

Unique signature. The law does not require that the signature be unique to the signer, except in the case of transferable records.

Demonstrably created signature. The law does not require that the signature be created demonstrably by the signer, except in the case of transferable records.

Integrity requirements. The law fails to require that a signature be tied to a document in such a manner as to detect changes in the document after signing, except in the case of transferable records.

Technology. The law does not address how signatures should work. Implementation is left to the marketplace. This was done on purpose to avoid favoring any one technology and to allow for advances in technology.

Protection against fraud. The law does not require businesses to use any protection mechanisms against fraud. Although it is true that most implementations of electronic signing mechanisms include some types of protection, many see it as a significant failure of the law not to require this.

What E-SIGN Does Cover

The law does cover terms and circumstances under which an electronic signature may be used.

Definitions. It does say that an electronic signature is defined as "an electronic sound, symbol, or process, attached to or logically associated with a contract or other record and executed or adopted by a person with the intent to sign the record." Some people have misinterpreted this to mean that any electronic sound symbol can be used to make an electronic signature. For example, E-SIGN excludes the use of recorded oral communication as an electronic record. Good news! Pressing a key on your telephone does not make a legally binding contract under E-SIGN.

Documents must be electronic. Consumers must have the correct equipment for accessing electronic versions of documents.

Consumer disclosure requirements. Consumers must explicitly consent to the use of electronic signatures, and they must have the right to withdraw this consent.

Specific exclusions. Electronic notifications are prohibited in the following areas:

- Cancellation of utilities (heat, water, power), life insurance, health insurance
- Product recalls
- Wills
- Divorce decrees
- Court orders
- Adoption
- Documents accompanying the transportation of hazardous materials

It should be obvious that E-SIGN does not meet all the requirements set forth by the ABA to meet or exceed traditional (wet) ink signatures. In effect, all E-SIGN does is remove the possibility of invalidating a signature that is electronic simply because it is electronic. More information about electronic signatures, including the full text of the law, can be obtained at *www.ecommerce.gov*.

TRANSACTIONAL SECURITY . . . .

Transactional security goes beyond electronic signatures. Secure e-commerce protocols address online debit and credit card fraud, identity theft, and transactional privacy concerns. Merchants benefit from reduced liability and cost savings from substantially reducing chargebacks and fraudulent denials of purchase (repudiation). Customers benefit from increased anonymity, privacy, identity protection, and the convenience of making secure online transactions.

We will describe here how an electronic transaction is usually conducted (see Figure 13–1). A consumer (you) makes a purchase, either in person or online. You present your credit card and personal information to the merchant. The merchant, in

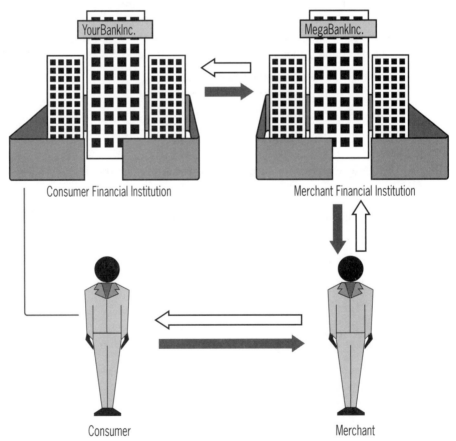

Figure 13–1
An electronic transaction.

turn, sends that information to their bank, the merchant's financial institution (MFI), who, in turn, sends the information to your bank, the consumer's financial institution (CFI). The CFI then approves the purchase by checking your account for available funds (or credit line) and sends an approval to the MFI, who then responds to the merchant by telling them your purchase is approved. Later that day, the accounts are settled up, and the funds are actually transferred (in the case of credit card transactions).

All this takes place in the 30–60 seconds you wait after your credit card is swiped, waiting for approval. It takes place on a set of networks run by the financial institutions. There are several security and privacy issues with this system. First, the consumer has to provide personal information, such as identity, to the merchant. This is a privacy concern because the merchant now knows who you are and what you bought, so your purchasing habits can be tracked. Second, the consumer has to give account information. This is a security problem because once that information is given up, it can be stolen, either over the financial network or out of the dumpster in the back.

The security of your credit card information and the privacy of your personal data, including who you are and what you purchased, are of primary concern in an electronic transaction. Transactional security deals primarily with keeping this information secure. Consumers are concerned about putting their credit card numbers on the Internet, and there are a number of technologies designed to provide security and privacy.

Identrus: A Transactional Security Infrastructure

A number of global financial institutions, such as Barclay's, Bank of Tokyo, Bank of America, Citigroup, and Deutsche Bank have created a company called *Identrus* to provide a PKI-based infrastructure for secure electronic transactions. Identrus uses industry partners that provide the technology to identify participants positively in a transaction, protect data in transit, create legally binding contracts, and provide non-repudiation.

The steps of an Identrus-enabled transaction are:

1. A merchant requests consumer identity verification from the MFI.
2. The MFI contacts the CFI.
3. The CFI confirms the identity of the consumer.
4. The MFI uses the Identrus infrastructure to confirm the identity of the CFI.
5. Identrus provides a warranty against any residual risk to the party relying on Identrus.

A B-to-B, B-to-C Primer

Many of the electronic transactional security elements described in this chapter are relevant only to selected types of transactions. There are two basic types of transactions, B-to-B and B-to-C.

B-to-B. B-to-B transactions are used between companies to sign contracts or sell mass goods, such as a manufacturer's order from a distributor that delivers to all the stores in a state. These are usually low in volume but high in value. Security for these transactions is mission-critical because of the high value, and due to the low volume, more resources can be spent for security.

B-to-C. B-to-C transactions are transactions for small orders to individuals. These are usually low in value but high in volume. The lower value of these transactions reduces the amount that is spent on security for each transaction but the high volume allows for the investment of security infrastructure.

For example, amazon.com, the online bookseller, will make a B-to-B transaction to order a supply of books from Prentice Hall, but will sell them to its customers in a B-to-C transaction. Due to the high value of the transaction with Prentice Hall, the security will be high, including auditing checks on the quantity of the order and the identity and ordering authority of the buyer. However, when a book is sold to a customer, the security is focused on nonrepudiation of the transaction by the buyer across thousands of small individual transactions each day. These are two very different security infrastructures.

It is important to note in the discussion regarding digital signatures that these are not yet an everyday part of electronic commerce because the infrastructure does not yet exist to employ them. Many of the topics in this chapter are security controls that are being implemented over the next few years, as opposed to a description of the current state of business.

According to Identrus, the following are some of the realized benefits:

Lower Transaction Costs. Ostensibly, by adding trust to the system, fewer resources will need to be spent investigating trading partners.

Real-Time Identity Assurance. This allows instant confirmation of trading partner identities and the management of residual risk.

Global Reach. Identrus is a global partnership spanning industries and national borders.

Consistent Application of Rules. Transactions flow freely with common technology standards, business rules, legal principles, and regulatory and privacy protections shared by all participants.

Audit Trail. Transactions are fully documented in the event of a dispute.

Increased Markets. Merchants may be able to move into new markets faster without lengthy reengineering of business process.

Relationship Development. Financial institutions can become single point global providers for merchants.

Brand Building. Financial institutions can provide cobranded certificates and smart cards to merchants.

Smart Cards in Electronic Commerce

Smart cards are credit-card-sized objects that have a "smart chip" in them. This chip can contain your identity and other facts about you, such as height, weight, age, and bank account information. Smart card use is on the rise in online transactions because it helps provide two-factor authentication.

Single-factor authentication is something you know, such as a password or PIN number. Two-factor authentication is something you know and something you possess, such as a smart card. For an individual to compromise a two-factor system, he or she would have to know your password *and* steal your smart card. In a three-factor system, authentication is based on something you know, something you possess, and something you are (such as a biometric fingerprint, retina scan, or palm print). For more information, see Chapter 4, "Authentication, Authorization, Access Control."

Smart cards use secure protocols to authenticate users and securely complete transactions. You may be familiar with credit cards that are also smart cards. These include brand names such as American Express Blue and the Smart VISA Card. One disappointment in these cards today is that they don't do much right now. These cards are more of a marketing gimmick because most merchants (or consumers, in the case of Internet purchases from home) don't have the hardware or software to use the embedded security features. This will change over time.

CERTIFICATELESS E-COMMERCE

Identrus is a PKI-based solution that assumes a third-party present in the transaction to confirm the identities of the two participants. These transactions (with the third-party verification) can be "heavy," meaning that they take significant resources to complete, due to the certificate processing. One of the original PKI-based financial standards was SET (Secure Electronic Transaction). SET has all but failed because the implementation did not scale, due to, among other things, heavy certificate processing.

Certificates are necessary in open systems where the two parties do not know each other, such as global online trading between consumers and merchants. However, there are many "closed" systems where the merchant and the consumer have a well-established relationship, such as a frequent flyer card, a fuel card, or a grocery store card. When the merchant and the consumer have an established relationship, it is not necessary to go through a third party to confirm identity for each transaction. Certificateless standards are being developed to address transactions in these environments.

AADS is one such standard. AADS is based on the use of a "digital signature" that is invoked when a PIN is entered to activate a smart card for both debit and credit transactions. When either an Internet or point of sale transaction is made using a smart card and PIN, a consumer's digital signature is created and encrypted prior to being issued to the merchant. The payment transaction and digital signature is then routed through the MFI to the CFI. The CFI uses a public key to verify the transaction, making repudiation a nonissue.

The X9.59 standard, "DSTU X9.59-2000, Electronic Commerce for the Financial Services Industry: Account-Based Secure Payment Objects," is the foundation for AADS. X9.59 defines electronic payment objects used in consumer-oriented, account-based transactions. These secure payment objects use standard cryptographic tools and techniques to offer authentication, integrity, and prevention of replay.

The standard specifies a collection of electronic payment objects and the digital signature techniques to secure their content. The objects are all defined in terms of how they need to be constructed, signed, and verified in computing machinery that is acting on behalf of a consumer or merchant. A concrete syntax is specified so that the signature can be constructed or verified at any location that has access to the consumer's public key and associated data.

Presentation of X9.15 payment objects by the merchant to the consumer must be provided through a template to the merchant for incorporation into the merchant storefront shopping cart at the time of merchandise selection and order aggregation "check-out" for payment. This allows the consumer to sign the payment object digitally, thereby creating an X9.59 digital signature that is encapsulated into the X9.15 payment object.

AADS, X9.59, and other such standards have not yet gained acceptance in the financial community and may not be common for several years.

VISA COMPLIANCE STANDARDS . . . .

Cost is one of the most significant factors in the deployment and widespread use of security and secure protocols between merchants, consumers, and financial institutions. Smart card readers and security practices cost money. Consider the little swipe boxes that merchants currently run your card through for a face-to-face transaction. Replacing all those little boxes (including the ones integrated with cash registers) with ones that accept smart cards is expensive for a major retail chain. There are also significant expenses associated with adding security processes and procedures. However, the rewards of enhanced security include reduced fraud and misuse.

VISA International has come up with a financial incentive using interchange fees for merchants to invest in becoming more secure. Interchange fees are how financial institutions make their money with VISA cards. Every transaction costs the merchant a small fee, usually 2–6 percent of the cost of the sale. VISA has instituted a program for increased security where merchants who are considered secure pay lower interchange fees and merchants considered insecure pay higher interchange fees. Retailers with millions of dollars each day in credit card transactions will be highly motivated by a one- to two-point difference in their interchange fees.

The VISA Account Information Security Standards (AISS) define practices that are acceptable to VISA for protecting account and transactional information. Here is a summary of the requirements covered by the AISS:

1. Establish a hiring policy for staff and contractors.
2. Restrict access to data on a "need-to-know" basis.

3. Assign each user a unique ID to be validated when accessing data.

4. Track access to data, including read access, by each person.

5. Install and maintain a network firewall if data can be accessed via the Internet.

6. Encrypt data maintained on databases or files accessible from the Internet.

7. Encrypt data sent across networks.

8. Protect systems and data from viruses.

9. Keep security patches for software up to date.

10. Don't use vendor-supplied defaults for system passwords and other security parameters.

11. Don't leave papers/diskettes/computers with data unsecured.

12. Securely destroy data when it's no longer needed for business reasons.

13. Regularly test security systems and procedures.

14. Immediately investigate and report any suspected loss.

15. Use only service providers that meet these security standards.

These are pretty good guidelines for any business. More information can be obtained from the following sources available at *https://www.visa.com/nt/gds/main.html*:

Account Information Security Best Practices Guide, Visa International

Account Information Security Standards Manual, Visa International

Quick Reference Self Assessment Questionnaire, Visa International

Comprehensive Self-Assessment Questionnaire, Visa International

Cardholder Information Security Program, Visa USA, Version 5.5

Visa CISP Self-Assessment Form, Visa USA

SUMMARY . . . .

Nonrepudiation is a key concept in all forms of commerce. A commitment, once recorded in some form, must be met. A commitment in writing is frequently referred to as a *contract*, and the signatures on it are used for nonrepudiation. Electronic contracts and transactions also need signatures. The legal form of those signatures is still evolving, but the E-SIGN law guarantees that some type of electronic signature will become acceptable.

The various participants in the credit industry govern many electronic transactions between unrelated parties. Credit-card-related organizations are trying to establish new standards to support nonrepudiation and, thus, lower transaction costs for e-commerce participants.

Digital signatures and certificate authorities are technologies in wide use today for meeting these requirements. Electronic signatures are the legal equivalent of your personal (wet) signature.

Electronic commerce transactions are complicated machinations between a consumer, a merchant, and their two respective financial institutions. The financial networks maintained by the banks handle most of these transactions. There are new protocols and methods in development to make these transactions more secure but they have an associated cost, delaying their acceptance and deployment.

Identrus is a PKI-based transaction infrastructure supported by many global financial institutions. Certificateless transaction systems work in closed systems where the consumer and merchant have a well-established relationship, but these standards have not yet gained market acceptance.

VISA has stated its intention of incentivizing merchants to become more secure by offering them lower interchange fees for increasing security.

Part 3

Implementation

14 Establishing a Security Program

In this chapter . . .

- Who Is Responsible for Your Security Program

- How to Establish Core Processes

- How to Determine Requirements

- The Importance of Communication

The information in this book provides the raw material for making intelligent decisions about investments in computer security. Policy and technology are two important issues in establishing a secure computing environment. There is, however, a third issue that also must be included—process. Security processes define how decisions are made and how actions are completed. Processes show how people interact in performing tasks, so they clarify responsibilities.

If an auditor were to review the computer security in your organization, he or she would view security as a series of business controls. Although this view has value, we propose that you take an alternative view. Security is a service provided to the business to make the management of computer-related risks explicit. In doing this, a security program will frequently lead to a reduction in risk. But the decision to reduce risk is a business decision, not an IT or a security department decision.

STEP ONE: DEFINE
RESPONSIBLE PERSONNEL . . . .

Someone has to be responsible for security. Under current audit principles, the board of directors holds fiduciary responsibility for supervising all aspects of security, including computer security. The board delegates that responsibility to the CEO. The CEO typically delegates the responsibility for computer security to either the CIO or a CSO. If the CIO has it, he or she establishes either a CSO position or one of a CISO. Whether these titles are used is irrelevant; someone has to hold this hot potato. For simplicity, we refer to the highest level manager who focuses largely or exclusively on computer security as the CSO. In larger organizations, there may be a person with CSO responsibilities in each business unit. In this case, a corporate CSO should be coordinating their actions.

The CSO is responsible for creating security policies, managing their implementation, and measuring their success. The CSO is also responsible for overseeing security processes. The one security issue that is not normally the responsibility of a well-defined CSO is the actual management of the security technology! That is more properly handled by the various technical service functions of IT.

The first task undertaken by a new CSO should be to define and get approval for a security charter. The charter is the formal delegation of responsibility. It is a brief document signed by the CEO, which identifies the responsibilities of the CSO and the approach to security the CSO must take. The security charter is a public document that is a part of the security communication programs described in step four, later in this chapter. Once the charter is in place, assuming that the CSO does the job well, there should be no further need for approvals by the CEO.

The second task of a new CSO should be to gather information about the existing security policies. This is referred to as *creating a baseline*. This information will be invaluable in understanding:

- What currently works and what does not
- How to communicate risks to upper management
- How to prioritize security projects and tasks
- How the existing security processes are structured (or not)

There may be many other roles and people either in a department run by the CSO or associated with security processes. In larger organizations, many of the responsibilities we list as belonging to the CSO will, in fact, be delegated to staff members. For our immediate purposes, there is one other role that needs to be defined—the resource owner (RO). ROs are involved in many of the core security processes.

An RO is not in IT. In fact, the RO never has *resource owner* as an actual job title. The role of an RO is to define business requirements for security. This is a management responsibility within any business operation that uses computers. The existence of RO responsibilities should be identified in the security charter, and department heads should be encouraged to identify resource ownership responsibilities formally within their organizations.

STEP TWO: ESTABLISH CORE PROCESSES . . . .

A few security processes are crucial to the success of a computer security program. These should be documented and formalized as soon as possible. The core processes of a security program are presented here in the sequence that we believe most organizations should address them.

We place these four core processes in step two to make it clear that the processes need to be defined early. As you will see in the descriptions, many of the steps intertwine during execution.

The Risk Assessment/ Data Classification Process

How much security is enough? We define this process first because it becomes the basis for gathering security requirements in step three. It is also a prerequisite to establishing a successful policy definition process, and success in defining the risk assessment process can help immeasurably in fixing a broken user administration process. The purpose of the risk assessment and data classification process is to have the CSO provide effective guidance to the ROs as they answer the question, How much security is enough?

The risk assessment/data classification (RA/DC) process consists of a series of formal, documented conversations between the CSO and the ROs. The first conversation involves data classification. In defining the RA/DC process, the CSO should establish a clear classification scheme that matches the needs of the entire organization. A typical classification scheme allows for three to five classes and general rules to guide the allocation of each major data store or application system into one of those classes. The classes relate to the value of the data to the business and generally take forms such as public, private, confidential, and restricted. At the end of the first conversation, all of the data stores owned by that RO should have been assigned to a class. The CSO documents the result, and the RO approves the document. Data that has been classified at low levels of value are not discussed in the later conversations.

The second conversation is about risk assessment. In preparation for this conversation, the CSO must research two areas for each of the high-value resources identified during the data classification step. The probable sources of threat must be identified, and the existing security measures that offset that threat must be documented. The conversation consists of the CSO and the RO coming to agreement on which threats are not currently fully covered by the security measures, then agreeing on whether additional security investment is appropriate.

Residual threats—those not offset by existing or planned security measures—must be documented. The RO must then make the decision to accept the residual risks into the business operation plan—and perhaps account for potential losses—or agree to invest additional money and time in security measures. It is the job of the CSO to propose an initial design for those measures. The information needed to create those designs is gathered in the requirements gathering of step three. The creation and refinement of those designs is described in the technical implementation planning and design process in this step.

The third conversation is about access rights. That is described in the next section, as a base for the user administration process definition.

The fourth conversation is about requirements. That is described in step three of the program, because it provides the information for resolving security issues in a manner that matches the needs of the business.

The User Administration Process

The third conversation between the CSO and the RO is about access rights (permissions). The CSO gathers information from the RO about who should have various types of access to the data. The process by which users are identified and granted access to the computing resources they need to do their job is the user administration (UA) process. This process should include a method for handling exceptions to the general rules established for these permissions.

Execution of the UA process can be handled either by a central administrative department or by groups within each of the business units. The process should be consistent, no matter by whom or how it is executed. The CSO should audit the performance of this process on a regular basis.

One of the ways to improve the scalability of the UA process is by moving to role-based permissions. In this approach, access rights are granted, based on various roles that may be assigned to an individual as a result of the job that he or she has within the organization. Figuring out what the appropriate roles are for an organization can be a lengthy process. The return on that investment becomes clearer for large organizations.

Some advanced security technologies place special requirements on the UA process. PKI is generally implemented using a certificate practice statement that defines the conditions for issuance, revocation, and use of the digital certificates upon which PKI is based. A typical certificate practice statement is 60–90 pages in length.

The Policy Definition Process

The RA/DC and UA processes are revisited continuously. Policy definition (PD) happens when some event or change in the business environment causes a re-evaluation or extension of security policy.

Security policies are defined in response to an identified business need. Policies may apply to only a portion of the organization if security domains are being used, as described in Chapter 3, "Security Policies." Policies result from negotiation between the CSO and the RO, with approval from the business executive above the RO, in most cases.

There are many sources of security policies in ready-to-use form. These can provide a starting point for the negotiation. Any change in a security policy may generate a requirement that becomes a security project to achieve compliance with the new policy.

Technical Implementation, Planning, and Design

The technical implementation, planning, and design (TIP) process is executed at the beginning of every security-related project. It is triggered by the acceptance of some set of requirements as a funded (or potentially funded) project.

Instead of working with the RO in this process, the CSO must work with a much more difficult audience—the IT department. Solving security problems can cause wide-ranging side effects. The CSO is responsible for policy and process but has only an oversight role in technology solutions. Understanding the organization of IT and knowing who to involve in each stage of solution planning for technology is critical to the success of security projects.

Other key factors for success include project scope and effective communications. Project scope can be constrained using the security domain model discussed in Chapter 3. By limiting all projects to a single domain, the CSO can limit the risk of project failure. Communications is discussed in step four.

STEP THREE: DEFINE REQUIREMENTS . . . .

The fourth conversation between the CSO and the RO is to define requirements for improving security. The CSO proposes solutions to the issues identified in the three earlier conversations. The resulting requirements become project definitions for the TIP process.

Requirements definition is typically overlooked but is vital. Every environment is different, so you can't just do what someone else has done. If you don't spend enough time in the requirements definition process, you could end up protecting non-critical data from nonexistent threats. This step also allows ROs and security personnel to agree on the steps that will be taken to protect assets.

STEP FOUR: COMMUNICATE! . . . .

Many security programs fail because of an unwillingness to communicate effectively and fully. Many new CSOs come from technical backgrounds and believe that technical solutions are sufficient to any problem. It is imperative that every security program has two communications components and that each program receives sufficient resources and attention to ensure success. The two essential components are the awareness program and the executive communication program. Without all this, the chances of program failure and elimination of the security department budget increase dramatically.

The Awareness Program

The employees, contractors, consultants, and business partners are using the computers in your company every day to perform their jobs. How many of them understand the impact that security policies are supposed to have on their behavior? The awareness program is the training that teaches them what is needed.

Awareness programs vary from classroom lectures to booklets to be read and signed by employees to establish that they have seen the information. Awareness programs are attempts to change the behavior of individuals. As such, basic marketing techniques are relevant in the design of an awareness program.

The Executive Communication Program

A formal program for maintaining executive buy-in to information security should be created. Security can be viewed as a cost center, rather than a business enabler—so it is vital that executives understand the benefits and processes of security. One of the most serious mistakes a CSO can make is to forget to highlight success. Success breeds success, but only if people know about it.

STEP FIVE: AUDIT AND MONITOR . . . .

The auditing and monitoring of your process is required to test your program continually. These processes will help the organization to prevent stagnation, update with the latest tools and techniques, and reassess the business periodically for relevant changes. Part of this process is scanning for actual threats and the response to those threats.

Configuration Control and Audit

It is not possible to have a secure computing environment without control over some of the configuration options of every computer. If a system administrator can turn off a security function without detection, all security is ineffective.

Security-related configuration information for most common computers and operating systems is widely available. The CSO should establish policies that define the appropriate security configurations. Frequent monitoring of compliance to those policies is necessary.

Intrusion Monitoring and Vulnerability Scanning

Networks and systems can be monitored for attempted intrusions. The tools to do this can provide critical information about unusual behavior or unauthorized access attempts. Vulnerability scanners run tests from outside of your network to identify at-risk systems before hackers can discover those vulnerabilities. Installing, configuring, and operating these tools requires the establishment of a security operations function. Because this is a cross-check on, among other things, the operations and system administration staff, it is appropriate for security operations to report to the CSO.

Intrusion Response and Forensics

If you monitor for intrusions, you had better have a plan for what to do when a serious one is discovered. Response is the process by which incidents are managed and escalated. Forensics is the process by which intrusion and security failure data is analyzed and the failure repaired.

Security Performance Reporting

Over time, metrics must be developed that reflect the performance of the security function. These metrics may include the number of incidents, the level they reached in the escalation process, and some kind of quantification of costs associated with the program and actual attacks. There are currently no widely accepted standards for security metrics, so they should be specific to your organization and measured against themselves from year to year.

SUMMARY . . . .

Establishing a security program is the process that brings security into your organization. It includes five steps:

1. Define responsible personnel.
2. Establish core processes, including risk assessment and data classification, user administration, policy definition, and implementation.
3. Define requirements.
4. Communicate through an employee awareness program and an executive communication program.
5. Audit and monitor for continued improvement.

The remaining chapters in this section address many of the processes discussed in this chapter, including risk assessment, managed security services, response, and recovery.

15 Security Assessments

In this chapter . . .

- The Definition of Assessment

- Penetration Testing

- Vulnerability Assessment

- Security Posture Review

- Security Audit

- Risk Assessment

T here are numerous reasons to have an assessment done. Thus, there are numerous assessment types. Unfortunately, many people make the decision to be assessed without understanding the range of options and so fall prey to unscrupulous (or just hungry) service providers.

WHAT IS ASSESSMENT? . . . .

Most projects involving information systems (as well as many other types of projects) are best planned by determining exactly what exists currently, comparing it with what you are trying to achieve, then designing the project around the difference, or gap. Many security projects follow this pattern. Because security starts with policy (a statement of the "desired state," or how you want the organization to be), our first step for most security projects is to learn the existing security policies. If policies have been documented, this is an easy step. If they have not, the step is nothing more than determining that no policies exist.

Whether or not policies exist, the next step is not so easy. We must understand the current security environment. That means analyzing both the behavior of people and the protections provided by current technology as it is actually used. Without the information provided by these first two steps, we are in the same situation as Alice in Lewis Carroll's *Alice's Adventures in Wonderland*, when the caterpillar tells her, "If you don't know where you are and you don't know where you are going, then any road will take you there." To know which way to move, we must know where we are. Thus, the current security situation must be assessed—but assessed by whom?

Any organization with a competent technical staff is likely to come to the conclusion that the easiest (and cheapest) way to assess its current security is simply to ask the people who installed the hardware and software. That does not work. A competent technical staff will always install technology in the best way they know how. An incompetent technical staff will do the same. In neither case will the people doing the work be able to assess their own work accurately. This simple observation is the basis for one of the most essential principles of security. No matter how competent, smart, or dedicated the individuals, the people who do work (whether it be selection, configuration, installation, operation, or use) must *never* be the same people who determine whether security is effective. This simple rule controls the organization of security teams in the world's largest companies, and it applies equally in the smallest office.

Although this principle may govern how you assign staff and who does what within your organization, it also leads to one inescapable conclusion: The best way to determine your current security level is to ask an outsider. Security service providers are prepared to analyze your current situation with dispassion and to report on strengths and weaknesses without any bias created by ownership or authorship of the current environment.

We said that there are numerous reasons for having an assessment done. Those reasons relate to your immediate objectives. The most common reasons for having a security assessment are:

1. Trying to justify security budgets and projects
2. Determining the priorities for hardening the organization perimeter
3. Creating a list of security issues around which to build projects
4. Reviewing the detailed security posture of the entire organization to meet specific requirements

In addition to reviewing these four objectives and how to achieve them through assessments, this chapter will also discuss an area that many people try to resolve through security assessments—risk assessment. Nothing we say about security assessment applies to risk assessment. It is another whole can of worms.

It is important to know that there is no generally accepted terminology to describe security assessment. The objectives, terms, and differentiations described in this chapter are useful and consistent. Most vendors will use the terms that we define concisely to mean whatever they believe you will buy at whatever price they believe you will pay. When you negotiate with a security service provider for these services, show them this chapter and make sure they are using the same terms to mean the same activities.

Selecting an outside firm to do any type of security assessment is a critical business decision. Most of the service providers vying for your business will be local firms—untested and with few documented credentials. Many of the tasks you will be asking of them require intense technical detail. Frequently, the people with that level of competence come from a background that may be questionable, in that they were part of the hacker community. The results of an assessment will be a report that lists your security vulnerabilities. If one vulnerability was discovered but not included in the report, the person performing the test will have the ability to take over your computer systems without your knowledge. What if they sell that access to your competitor? What if they have a social agenda antithetical to your company? You will not know about it until it is very much too late.

Choosing a business partner to do security assessments is not simple. As we describe in each section below, the service providers for each type of assessment vary. You will need to satisfy yourself that the providers you select are both competent and trustworthy for the type of assessment you are contracting. And, of course, price is always an issue.

PENETRATION TESTING . . . .

The simplest type of security assessment is a penetration test. As with each of the other categories of assessment, there is a range of options that equate to a range of prices. You will probably want a penetration test done if your objective is to establish the need for a security budget.

During a penetration test, the service provider will attempt to breach your security. This is typically done as a series of escalating efforts, using automated tools and then a single person or a small team. The first step is typically an automated scan, similar to the automated vulnerability assessment described in the next section. Step two involves a technical staff member (sometimes referred to an as *ethical hacker*) using the scan information to bypass your current security protections and log into your supposedly secure servers. Having accomplished this (typically within four to six hours), the tester leaves some evidence of his or her activity to prove that penetration has taken place.

If the automated scan does not point out a likely target for compromise, the tester may resort to either manual penetration attempts, such as those described below with manual vulnerability assessment, or social engineering. Social engineering describes the work of getting people to tell the tester everything needed to penetrate the computer systems. This is almost always the easiest way to break into a computer.

A typical social engineering effort goes like this:

1. Determine the main telephone number of the target company.
2. Make random calls to phone numbers just above the main number.
3. Identify yourself as a help-desk person.
4. State that a critical password file has been damaged. Ask for the users' passwords so that the file can be recreated.
5. Get the password and use it to sign into secured computer systems.
6. Use known system flaws to take complete control of the computer.
7. Leave evidence of the compromise and sign off.
8. Take a coffee break, because you have been working for almost an hour.

Almost all penetration tests are completed within two days. Many are completed within four hours. The objective of the test is to show how quickly and easily security can be breached. A well-secured system in a company that has effectively trained its staff in dealing with social engineering efforts (yes, it can be done) will resist penetration for as long as five days. It is important to understand that all penetration tests succeed. On the fifth day, the tester will typically visit the target company site and walk past reception. If that entrance is tightly controlled, the tester will use a back entrance that employees use to bypass reception. Once inside, the tester simply looks under mouse pads and keyboards to find password information. After collecting 10 or 12 passwords from unoccupied offices, the tester returns home and completes the penetration. Very few companies avoid penetration for all five days.

The skills needed to do an effective penetration test build on the vulnerability assessment processes described later in this chapter. We list penetration tests first because they are done to accomplish the most limited objective: Show me how easy it is to penetrate my computer systems. A normal penetration test will conclude with a report that shows the total amount of time spent and the top two or three openings used to compromise your computer systems.

This report is useful only to increase the attention and focus that an organization places on security. If the organization is already allocating significant resources to maintaining a secure environment, a penetration test is a waste of money. Penetration tests are priced by the hour, with typically a minimum one-day charge. Hourly charges can be extremely high, due to the technical nature of the work. Typical costs for a penetration test vary between $5,000 and $15,000 per day. The service provider should be bonded. Most are not.

Almost any security consultant will be willing to perform a penetration test on your computer network. This type of assessment takes little effort and has few costs to the consultant. The most difficult part of selecting a consultant to do a penetration test is deciding to trust someone.

VULNERABILITY ASSESSMENT ....

Although a penetration test tells you the easy access routes that a hacker may take, a vulnerability assessment tries to identify all of the possible entry points for the hacker. It is important that you recognize that no report created at a single point in time can actually catalog every vulnerability. New vulnerabilities are discovered daily. The hackers stay very up to date on those new discoveries. In addition, most vulnerabilities result from the selection of configuration options on your computer and network equipment. In the normal course of business, your technical staff will reconfigure the computer systems to meet new business needs. One common source of vulnerabilities is the inadvertent openings created through normal reconfiguration.

Because of these changing conditions, it is important to repeat vulnerability assessments on a regular basis. We stated at the beginning of this chapter that internal staff should not do security assessments. Therefore, it is clear that vulnerability assessments are best handled through an ongoing service contract.

Vulnerability assessments fall into two categories—automated scan and manual. An automated scan takes place without direct human intervention. A script running on a computer connected to the Internet contacts your computer network. As you contracted for the scan, you provided the Internet address list (IP addresses) that represents your company. The scanning service then attempts to identify each computer and network component in your network. For each address it can reach, it runs a series of tests similar to those that a hacker might attempt. The results of these tests show the computers that are most easily compromised from the Internet. Typical automated scans make use of three to four software products to ensure that all possible vulnerabilities are caught. These products are typically a mix of commercial and free software. Hackers use and build the free software, so its contribution is important. But commercial vendors are motivated to extend the free software tests and try to stay a bit ahead of the hackers. The more tools that are used, the better the results.

Some automated scan services will go a step further and search for other avenues of potential penetration. They may call every telephone number in the range of phone numbers used by your company. The calls will be made by a computer (typically late at night), and each time a phone is answered an attempt will be made to access a computer modem. If a computer modem is found, a series of tests will be run to determine potential vulnerabilities.

An automated scan will produce a lot of paper. The service provided by a vendor of automated scans must include some reduction of the resulting data. A 400-page listing of tests and results is not of use to you. Not all service providers understand this.

A manual scan builds on the results of the automated scan. A highly skilled technician (that "ethical hacker" again) uses the automated scan result as a starting point to create a more accurate report. He or she works the way a hacker would, using the scan information to attack your systems. The manual scan identifies suspected weaknesses. Some of those will not actually be useful to a hacker. Others will have protections that may not have been visible to the automated script. But in other cases, weaknesses may exist that are simply not detectable via a script. The automated scan may provide an indication of a potential weakness that only a skilled hacker could use. During the manual scan, the tester will eliminate the automated scan entries that were not significant and amplify on the areas that are less obvious but still significant risks.

The service providers that do vulnerability assessments generally can provide both automated and manual scan services. Small consultancies will frequently agree to take on vulnerability assessment contracts. Unfortunately, those groups tend to have access only to the free software tools. These are not sufficient. Also, these groups may or may not have the skills to use the automated information to do an appropriate job in the manual scan. The study effort needed to stay up to date on manual scan techniques requires the dedication of a hacker. Most security consultants simply do not have the time to keep up.

Because vulnerability assessment never requires on-site work, unlike a penetration test, which may require someone to walk through the door, service providers can perform the work with no office near your premises. National and multinational services have now been built that can provide both automated and manual scans at a reasonable price.

Any vulnerability assessment constitutes a simulated attack on your network. Your existing technical staff may have installed tools to detect attacks. Although it may seem like an interesting test of your internal staff to see whether they detect an unidentified attack, we advise against contracting for a vulnerability assessment without informing everyone who might be involved in responding to an attack. A strong response by your internal staff to the appearance of an attack will result in the test being terminated, and you will have wasted your money. A weak response can still cause significant interference in normal business processing while the attack is identified and controlled. If everyone knows that a simulated attack is under way, responses will be muted, and normal business will be allowed to proceed.

One question you should be asking yourself is, How often is enough? If your only connection to the Internet is for outgoing access to the Web through a firewall or proxy server, an annual automated scan is probably sufficient. If your organization is exposed to the Internet via an e-commerce application, at least a quarterly automated scan and an annual manual scan are recommended. Organizations that have integrated Internet access to their business processes should be doing weekly automated scans and monthly manual scans. An automated scan for a mid-sized network may cost as little as $750 when contracted as part of a scheduled series. Manual scans associated with an automated scan add approximately $7,500 to that cost.

SECURITY POSTURE REVIEW . . . .

Penetration tests and vulnerability assessments focus on threats from outsiders. Although hacker attacks make the headlines, the more serious threats to computer resources come from inside any organization. Employees, temporary workers, and contractors are constantly granted privileges to use sensitive computer applications in performing their work. An unhappy employee may decide to place his or her interests (or those of a competitor) ahead of an employer's interests. A competitor may have already offered him or her a job.

Also consider the result of a successful attack by a hacker. Once a hacker has penetrated your network, the hacker will operate within your computer systems as though he or she is an employee. Having captured one computer or one set of authorized credentials (maybe your password), the only way a hacker can be found is by internal controls. Thus, for all intents and purposes, the outside hacker has become an employee. We discuss many of the tools needed to find such a penetration in Chapter 8, "Intrusion Detection." Assessing the weaknesses of the company to internal attack is part of a security review.

The first chapters of this book focus heavily on the need for documented security policy. Phase 1 of a security review is a review of your security policies. Any service provider competent to do a security review has an existing model with which to compare your policies. If you have not established a reasonable policy base, the service provider's existing model should provide you with an effective starting point for deriving the policies relevant to your organization. Once the policy review is done and agreement has been reached on the appropriate set of policies to use for the remainder of the review, the service provider begins the second phase of the review, which compares your existing computer environment against those policies.

Security reviews are generally limited to technology issues—and not all of those. The set of policies selected for the second phase of a security review involves the configuration and use parameters of computer systems and network components. The reviewer will collect information about each computer and network device and compare it with your policies. A typical security review looks at things such as:

- The existence of default computer accounts provided as samples by the manufacturer
- The use of passwords that are easily guessed or engineered
- Operating system settings that are known to be weak
- Network router parameters that fail to protect networks from DoS attacks
- Firewall parameters that allow passage by hackers
- Computer accounts with administrative privileges that are not necessary
- Network configurations that are unintentionally exposed to the Internet
- And many, many more

The service provider you choose to perform a security review must meet much more difficult standards than needed to do a penetration test or vulnerability assessment. A security review requires inside access to critical information about how your internal systems operate. There is no way to protect you from a firm that acquires this level of information. One rogue employee at this service provider can destroy your company. Thus, the level of trust between your organization and the service provider must be exceptionally high.

The service provider must be competent to handle technical issues for all of your computer and network equipment. That implies a significant staff of technical specialists who have configured similar equipment. If you have three types of UNIX, three Microsoft operating systems, and a set of network routers and switches, the service provider must be able to demonstrate competence on all of those machines.

Much like the vulnerability assessment, there is a potential for the service provider to deliver its results in the form of a mountain of paper detailing every test and result produced from the second phase of the review. The report that results from a competent security review should:

- List the security policies that were reviewed and identify the ones needing revision
- List the security policies that were identified as being missing and suggest a starting point for their content
- List the policies that were used for the second phase—the detailed analysis
- Provide a prioritized list of policy violations found

The prioritized list of policy violations is critical. All organizations will have some policy violations. Most organizations that have not had previous security reviews will have hundreds of such violations. Bringing a complex network of computers into compliance with policy must be done carefully to avoid undue impact on the business. Many of the policy violations will exist because of business needs that were most easily met by varying from policy. In each such case, an evaluation will be needed to determine whether a valid exception to policy is possible or desirable. If local variation from policy does not increase the threat to the rest of the organization and the variation results in an improvement to revenue or costs, it is probably a good business decision to allow it.

Understanding the relative threat that results from each policy variation is the key to making those judgments. The service provider must provide you with that information by prioritizing the policy violations that are found. The high-risk violations should also be analyzed in the report from the service provider, so that you can fully understand the implications of the violation.

The service providers that are competent to perform a security review tend to be moderately sized organizations with multiple office locations, so that they can support on-site services and maintain the wide technical expertise needed. Phase one studies—the policy analysis—will typically be done remotely, using documentation you provide. The cost will depend on the set of existing policies and whether you request the service provider to provide updates and replacements for existing and missing policies. It will also depend on how fully you want those policies customized to your organization.

Phase two studies—the variance from policy—will be done to the standards of the service provider. They will have a list of functional assessments that they believe your policies should cover, and within the agreed-upon list of your policies, they will gather current configuration information and compare the results with the policies. The charge for this will typically be per device.

Other, more specialized, security reviews are also possible. Large organizations with existing security teams may request an organizational review. This typically consists of interviews with the "customers" of the security department (the business users) and a comparison of existing skills, priorities, roles, and responsibilities against some "best practice" benchmark.

Because of all of the variables, it is difficult to estimate the cost of a generic security review. A typical starting assumption is that a security review will cost in the range of $50,000–$500,000.

SECURITY AUDIT . . . .

A security audit may be predefined for your industry. Financial institutions are subject to multiple levels of security auditing as a result of government regulation. For other industries, a security audit is a customized review, at a detailed level, of any of a number of aspects of security. A typical security audit might include:

- Searching the wastepaper baskets of nontechnical and technical employees for discarded but unshredded sensitive computer printouts
- Reviewing the source code of computer application programs for weaknesses or "back-door" access capabilities
- Extensive social engineering attacks, such as those described in the section of this chapter regarding penetration testing
- A business continuity test to determine the readiness of your staff to continue operating after a successful hacker attack

Most organizations that request a security audit actually want a security review. They are quite shocked at some of the resulting bids. An unqualified request for bids on a security audit may result in service providers responding with project descriptions varying from small (actually a security review) to multiple millions of dollars.

If you still want a security audit, focus on those organizations that are actually competent to do one. This typically means one of the large accounting and audit firms. If your organization is audited annually, that auditor should be your starting point for information on a security audit. The board of directors of the company being audited contracts most security audits.

RISK ASSESSMENT . . . .

The last class of assessments we are going to describe is very different from any of the previous assessment types. Your organization needs to do risk assessments, and this is the one type of assessment that should *not* be done by outsiders. A risk assessment is the evaluation of threats and protections that exist for a set of applications or data files and the impact *on the business* of threats that are not protected against. This is a business impact assessment of threats against the computer systems. A risk assessment determines how much money to spend on securing your computers. We recommend a "qualitative" risk assessment process, where the ROs work with the security people, as opposed to a "quantitative" analysis that yields expected loss numbers.

Responsibility for a qualitative risk assessment is shared between business users and security professionals. Successful risk assessment requires that business organizations assign responsibility for data to a management person who is authorized to make decisions about how data is to be used. Protection is then an additional responsibility. The person with this assignment is typically referred to as the *data owner* or *resource owner*.

Identifying which data is owned by which manager is not always easy. Many data files are shared between business organizations. Ownership must be negotiated. IT plays a key role by determining the aggregation or granularity level, i.e., which files or tables in the computer constitute a set of resources with a single owner.

The security officer guides the RO in understanding three things:

1. The sensitivity of the data
2. The classes of risk (the threats) that exist
3. The current and potential protection mechanisms

Highly sensitive data with many threats and no protection should receive additional security investments. Insensitive data with low threat levels and reasonable existing protections should be ignored. Everything in between needs judgments made about possible threat offsets. In the end, it is up to the RO to decide what level of security investment is appropriate. Any residual threat left after that investment should be documented and absorbed into the business plan. Of course, if the threats constitute risks to a wider audience, other priorities may override a single RO.

Problems with Quantitative Risk Assessment

Quantitative calculations are made and traditionally represented as ALEs. The purpose of a risk assessment in this context is to make a case. The credibility of the author, presentation, and supporting material is the most critical characteristic for success. Consider the following issues with respect to quantitative risk assessment:

Completeness. Although it may be possible to enumerate all of your mission-critical assets, it's impossible to enumerate all threats and vulnerabilities to which your network is subject. The best you can do is to make the lists as comprehensive as possible, with credible supporting material.

Probabilities of Occurrence. For the most part, these are made up. The nature of threat events is such that standard probabilistic distributions do not apply, so we have to make "best guesses." This is where the credibility of the author is the most important. Try to use examples that have anecdotal evidence at a minimum to back up your claims.

Loss Calculations. The costs associated with an incident can vary wildly. If a server crashes, how do you calculate the lost time of each of the users? The number will vary, depending on the time of day and amount of time to recover. How many users will actually lose time? How do you calculate lost work if there is unrecoverable data? Good examples will lend credibility to your suppositions.

Risk Mitigation Calculations. It's hard enough to calculate the probabilities of occurrence for a less-than-perfect list of threats and vulnerabilities, so how do you know how much a security system will lower those probabilities?

Quantitative risk assessments are like software estimation—a black art. Risk assessments in general are a valuable tool to make a business case. Although it may not be possible for you to do a comprehensive risk assessment of your network (some have suggested it's not possible, anyway), do not discount the power of showing selected examples of risk mitigation with ALE calculations. It will show that you've done your homework and thought the problem through. Also, listing your risks is necessary for your requirements analysis, anyway.

Quantifying risk is one of the best ways to convince management to spend money on security. Unfortunately, protection against unseen adversaries does not make a great business case by itself. Money is redirected when a business case supports a return on investment. Using a qualitative risk assessment process where the security personnel work closely with the ROs, as described above, overcomes many of the problems associated with quantitative risk assessment.

SUMMARY . . . .

Assessment is the process of determining your current state so that you can identify gaps in your protection and apply resources appropriately. There are several types of assessments, including penetration, vulnerability, security posture, and risk assessment. Each one has a different focus and different benefits.

Penetration testing is a straightforward attack on your defenses to determine points of weakness. Its primary benefit is to make the point that you are not as secure as you think you are. Vulnerability assessment determines the state of your security, due to configuration and administration of your computers. Vulnerability assessments should be performed regularly.

A security posture review usually focuses on insider threats and demonstrates your readiness to handle a security breach. A security audit is a static review of your security posture usually based on industry standards.

Risk assessment is a paper study of specific risks against mission-critical assets. Risk assessments are great budget justification tools but it is far more effective to do a qualitative risk assessment working together with ROs than a quantitative risk assessment filled with potentially meaningless numbers.

16 Managed Security Services

In this chapter . . .

Trying to implement and manage security in-house can be a complicated and expensive process. Recruiting a staff of security professionals can be challenging, and maintaining them is even harder, given the demand and value of these skills in the market. Training costs are also high because of the depth of knowledge required by these individuals. Add to this the requirement to keep complex software and hardware up to date, and you will understand why many organizations are turning to MSSP as a way of meeting their security requirements.

WHAT IS MSS? . . . .

MSS is outsourced security. Most providers offer a suite of services for one monthly fee that involves some level of on-site installation, consulting, and 24/7 management so that, as the ads say, "you can focus on your business while we take care of security." These services are not a panacea, but they can certainly be used to lower your risk and address many basic security requirements. Often, these are basic security capabilities that many companies have tried and failed to provide adequately in-house.

The core services of most managed security offerings are centered on managed firewall services and provide the following capabilities:

- Firewall/router management
- Perimeter access control and authentication
- Virtual private networks
- Web content filtering
- Intrusion detection
- Virus scanning
- Vulnerability assessment/penetration testing
- Incident response

These capabilities are tied together through real-time, historical, on-demand reporting and analysis to protect both inbound and outbound network services. Collateral benefits, such as load balancing, are also available because all the network traffic passes through the managed service.

Most solutions involve hardware, including one or many security devices or appliances. Sometimes, these are custom devices developed by the provider but most often, they are an integration of off-the-shelf software and hardware. These appliances can be installed at your site or they can collocate your servers at their site to provide security and other network management services. The implementation can significantly affect scalability.

THE BUSINESS CASE FOR OUTSOURCING . . . .

Outsourcing can potentially make a lot of sense for your organization. There are many hard-core objective benefits to outsourcing that send savings directly to the bottom line. You can avoid the high costs of developing a security system yourself—including finding and hiring the necessary personnel to manage and administer your security policy internally. You can lower the total cost of ownership for maintaining a security infrastructure, including the expenses associated with monitoring and maintaining security on a 24/7 basis.

Managed service providers have the advantage of scale, making outsourcing less expensive and more efficient than doing it yourself. Using remote management tools, a provider can manage your firewalls without traveling to your site, thereby servicing multiple branch offices without incurring travel expenses.

Consider the following cost/benefit analysis of using a managed service provider over doing the work in-house. Assume that you are a company with a single T1 Internet connection and with a requirement to create a firewall and monitor this connection 24/7.

In-house. To create a firewall for this connection, you will need to buy firewall hardware and software at a cost of about $60,000. Next, you will need to hire staff to manage and monitor the firewall. If you want good people (and a firewall is only as good as the people who manage it), you should consider salaries in the range of $60,000–$80,000. Because you need 24/7 coverage, you need at least three people, at an annual cost of about $200,000. Next, you will need to train your people at a cost of about $30,000 annually (they need to stay up to date).

Software and hardware:	$60,000
Salaries:	200,000
Training:	30,000
Total in-house costs:	**$290,000**

MSSP. The hardware and software costs are still yours, in most cases—even if you buy from the MSSP—at about $60,000. You won't have to worry about salaries, but there are still monthly management costs that will equal around $80,000 a year. There is a one-time setup cost of about $20,000. There are no training costs.

Software and hardware:	$60,000
Monthly management fee:	80,000
One-time setup fee:	20,000
Total outsourced costs:	**$160,000**

The annual savings by using a managed service provider is about $130,000 in this example:

Annual in-house costs:	$290,000
Annual outsourced costs:	160,000
Annual savings:	**$130,000**

Sounds great. Where do I sign up? First, do these calculations for your organization. The MSSP has economies of scale. If your organization is much larger than the MSSP customer base, you probably have better economies than the MSSP. Smaller organizations get the most benefit from this type of outsourcing.

HOW MUCH SHOULD YOU OUTSOURCE? . . . .

There are many reasons to consider outsourcing, including lowering your risk by letting experts take care of something you know nothing about, as well as protecting against information security-related losses in revenue, shareholder equity, productivity, proprietary data, and customer confidence. However, you have to consider how much of a mission-critical process, such as security, you want to give to someone who is not an employee of the company.

Approach outsourcing carefully. No provider can completely assume responsibility for your security requirements, and you wouldn't want them to. You will still need staff members who understand your business and the policies that govern your security. Outsource simple, technical things first, leaving your mission-critical policies and mechanisms to internal people. This explains the list of services normally available from an MSSP. These firms do not take over responsibility for your security program. They accept contracts for specific security-related tasks and operational processes. Any MSSP that proposes to take over your entire security program should be avoided.

Think of these people as your security partner.

SECURITY ELEMENTS YOU CAN OUTSOURCE . . . . .

There is a variety of security elements that can be outsourced to a managed service provider. Some of these are continuous operational processes, and the MSSP has the advantage of being able to support 24/7 staff coverage. Other elements are more project- or task-oriented, and the MSSP advantage lies in its ability to train and keep a specialized, highly skilled staff that would be difficult for you to justify (or keep interested).

Perimeter Protection

A provider can build a perimeter defense around your business's private network. Using packet filtering and other security techniques, an MSSP can limit inbound and outbound access. This will usually include perimeter authentication packet filtering, application-level proxies, content filtering, and expert security consulting into one service package. Connections to your network are monitored 24/7.

If you have complicated Internet configurations to connect partners and customers to back-end systems, such as an extranet, you should pay special attention to perimeter security.

Firewalls

Small and midsize businesses are prime candidates for outsourcing their firewall management. There are multiple reasons to outsource your firewall management. As stated earlier, firewalls are only as good as their configuration, and their configuration is controlled by the people who manage the firewall and set its policy. Even a correctly configured firewall is constantly degenerating as new partners come on line and various departments make requests to open holes for new applications.

A managed service provider can provide the expertise to see that your firewall is always correctly configured. Usually, these services are remotely managed with electronically transmitted policy and network configuration updates. Usually, the providers set up and configure the firewall for you. The firewall may be located at your site or it can be collocated with your ISP.

Intrusion detection and VPN services can be provided in conjunction with the firewall. If you have multiple sites, with a firewall at each site connected with a VPN, your firewalls have to talk to each other. Some providers require that you use the same firewall at each site, and others are more vendor-neutral, allowing you to have any firewall equipment you want. If you have legacy hardware, check with your proposed service provider to determine whether it can work with your existing equipment. Also, make sure that your selected provider can add more firewalls easily if you need them to grow with your business.

Client-Side Firewalls

If you use personal firewalls (such as Zone Alarm or BlackICE Defender) on the end-user workstations in your enterprise, your provider may be able to manage the policies that govern these through an MSSP solution. This type of solution impacts systems inside your perimeter, so it can have more impact on your operations if it is mishandled. You should manage the outsourcing of this service carefully and work closely with the provider.

Virus Detection

You should use a centralized antivirus solution that can deploy virus file definitions for detection and eradication across the mobile perimeter. By maintaining a central antivirus server, you can make antivirus definitions available to your clients quickly and efficiently. Without it, you'll have to rely on your users or support staff to ensure that antivirus definitions are manually kept up to date.

Your managed service provider should be able to manage your central virus definition files and the scanning of servers that are managed or controlled by the provider.

VPNs

Client VPN services establish encrypted communication links between users, partners, vendors, and customers. Through a managed service provider, these services usually include consulting services for design, configuration, and implementation. The service may also include documenting rule set naming and change guidelines for future additions and other ongoing management tasks. These services may also include creation of end-user media and installation instructions to get remote clients up and running with the VPN.

Vulnerability Assessments/ Penetration Testing

Some providers offer proactive, periodic perimeter-penetration scans to uncover potential misconfigurations of firewalls and other holes in your perimeter security. This penetration testing can be extended to include vulnerability scans of mission-critical servers. There is a wide range of quality in these services. Some just run the scan and give you a large report; others interpret the report for you and recommend fixes applicable to your environment. A few have teams of expert technicians that attempt compromises well beyond the ability of any scanning software.

Web Filtering

Managed Web filtering services are used to monitor Internet resources and specific Web addresses to ensure appropriate usage. These services provide usage policies based on time, Web address, automated profile distribution, and usage reports. The real-time monitoring service generates immediate alerts for potential threats or issues. They also provide statistics about the managed Web filtering service and security configuration.

Intrusion Detection/Monitoring

Corporate firewalls, intrusion detection systems, and other security devices generate an immense volume of data that is virtually impossible to interpret without consuming significant in-house IT staff resources. There is an MSSP available that is capable of detecting, analyzing, and responding in real time to the security data your network produces.

A central platform is used that collects log data and alerts generated by the firewalls, intrusion detection systems, VPNs, and other security devices and applications. The data is processed and correlated from across the enterprise, and the central platform compares it against thousands of attack signatures to identify suspicious network activity. Engineers in a security operations center (SOC) at the MSSP investigate each event and initiate a response in accordance with customized escalation procedures. Security analysts take action to react to intrusions, based on an agreed plan.

Incident Response

A complete security program includes protection, detection, and response. MSS uses incident response to help organizations prepare for and respond to information security breaches. Expert staff members develop emergency response plans, respond to attacks in progress, perform after-the-fact forensic investigations, and help clients establish their own incident response capabilities. Incident response is usually available in a variety of subscription and single incident offerings designed to meet the unique needs of individual organizations.

SELECTING A MANAGED
SECURITY SERVICE PROVIDER . . . .

As your "security partner" the MSSP will need to integrate tightly to some of your IT and business processes. That indicates that some level of corporate culture alignment is beneficial. Here are a few of the criteria you should evaluate before signing an MSSP contract.

Service Offerings

Do the MSSP offerings match your requirements? There is a wide range of providers and services, so you should first compare their offerings with your needs. Can they scale to your needs? Do you need intrusion detection and firewall management? Does their incident response offering match up well with your internal processes? Try to project at least two years ahead in both your requirements and the services that the provider plans to offer. Ask what its business and technology strategies are.

Service Level Agreements

Service level agreements are the only definition of what you get for your monthly fees. Make sure that they are well defined; this includes processes and response time periods. This should be a legal document that covers deployment, configuration, and change processes. If the vendor fails to meet the agreed-upon service levels, there should be clear penalties. The contract should be comprehensive, detailed, and guaranteed.

SOCs

SOCs should meet your requirements. A poorly protected SOC represents a weak link in your protection for all the requirements you rely on. An SOC should have a se-cured, protected infrastructure, both physical and technological. Qualified personnel should staff it at all hours. You should also look for backup procedures and locations in the event of power failure or attacks on the primary SOC. You should visit the SOC. Vendors have been known to describe a server in a locked closet as "an ad-vanced, highly secured physical facility with rigid access control."

History

Does the MSSP understand your industry? Who are its customers? What is its history with customer satisfaction? You must aggressively check the references provided by the vendor.

THE GROWING MARKET . . . .

According to the Yankee Group (*www.yankeegroup.com*), MSSP is expected to be $1.5 billion in 2002.

The brief from Forrester Research (*www.forrester.com*) entitled "Exsourced Security Arrives" states:

> Personnel costs for a starter monitoring setup with problem resolution will run at least $60,000 per month. Equipment and software maintenance runs up the bill even more. For the same money, you can get 10 firewalls, virus protection, active threat management, and 24/7 support from an exsourcer [Forrester's term for an external IT contractor] with no capital or human resource investment.

SUMMARY . . . .

Outsourcing some of your security processes and tasks may be exactly right for your organization. Understand your needs and the advantages and weaknesses of any outsource security vendor you deal with. If a vendor can provide an effective service at a lower cost than you can and the service is not mission-critical to your organization, outsourcing is a reasonable strategy. This is a relatively new type of offering, and many vendors announce capabilities they cannot deliver on. If you are careful, you can succeed.

17 Response and Recovery

In this chapter . . .

- Incident Response and Escalation
- What Is Business Continuity?
- Functions of a CERT

Information security is more than barrier defenses; it also includes monitoring, incident response, escalation, and recovery in the event of compromise. The two functions required to meet these objectives are a computer emergency response team (also known as a *CERT*) and a business continuity plan.

INCIDENT RESPONSE . . . .

After information security processes, procedures, and technology have been deployed to protect the enterprise from insider and outsider threats, what do you do when a problem is detected? Monitoring systems, such as network intrusion detection, in the case of external attack, and host-based intrusion detection, in the case of internal compromise, are usually at the heart of driving incident response.

Initiating incident response procedures means that you have caught someone misusing your computers and you need to do something about it. Incident response procedures may involve a number of different departments, including information services, legal, and audit. They may involve all levels of management and groups from the outside, including law enforcement, depending on the severity of the incident.

KEY POINT

> Initiating incident response procedures means that you have caught someone misusing your computers and you need to do something about it.

Incident response may be necessary only at the end of a potentially lengthy investigative process. *Lengthy* is a relative term. It may be minutes, hours, days, or weeks before an investigation goes from one stage to the next during an incident response. Rarely will you get a single, clear indication to kick off a full-blown incident response. Monitoring systems provides many indications of misuse that may lead to a single incident requiring incident response. Also, many incidents are not single acts that can be addressed in a simple manner.

Sorting through the flood of information and indications is the investigation process. The correct actions for positively identified misuse are governed by your escalation procedures. The pinnacle of escalation procedures is incident response.

Escalation Procedures

Increasing the severity of an incident during the investigation process is done through escalation procedures that are critical to effective operation. You can't send out the cavalry every time a mission-critical system is accessed in a manner deemed to be suspicious. Many of these activities ultimately turn out to be legitimate, so good escalation procedures will help you manage your limited resources to point them at positively identified misuse.

Most organizations have established some kind of escalation procedures. However, in many cases, existing procedures are designed for nonsecurity-related issues. Frequently there are escalation procedures tied to the help desk and designed to handle administration issues.

For example, most organizations know how to handle a locked-out account but most would fail spectacularly at dealing with suspected embezzlement. Failure would be very hard to define, however, because most organizations would not have an established policy for something so severe. Unfortunately, in the absence of good escalation procedures, they may tip the perpetrator during the investigation before they can stop the perpetrator from covering his or her tracks.

Existing procedures usually cannot handle a detection rate commensurate with operating an automated monitoring system. This book offers the following advice regarding escalation procedures: When you first start operating an intrusion detection system, you *will* find many things you do not expect. Be prepared.

The bottom line is that escalation procedures developed in the absence of a monitoring system will probably not be sufficient to handle both the volume and nature of the misuse detected. Updates will have to be made to handle issues, such as incident triage, involving extremes of severity and incident volume.

Incident Triage

Incident triage is the process that ensures that an incident is handled properly. Keep in mind that some of the misuse you detect will raise liability issues, so proper incident handling is about more than efficiency. Triage needs to be built into your escalation and incident handling procedures. As incidents progress through the process, there needs to be constant status reevaluation when new information comes available.

What starts as a simple investigation into suspicious access to mission-critical data could turn into collusion between multiple parties to defraud the company. What starts as a simple denied access attempt from a trusted partner over the network could actually be a spoofed IP address from one of many online terrorist groups attempting to infiltrate your business.

The point is that the lion's share of your incident procedures will involve relatively junior people, and there will come a point in some of your investigations where senior people will need to take over. Constant triage and clearing procedures to identify when an incident should be elevated to proper channels will protect the company and increase the efficiency and overall effectiveness of the intrusion detection process.

BUSINESS CONTINUITY . . . .

Disaster recovery, business continuity, or business resumption—call it whatever you wish but realize that the ability to recover from a compromise, intentional or otherwise, is an important aspect of information security. Many organizations separate information security and business continuity, so they may not be tied together organizationally but they are certainly logically connected. Remember that one of the tenets of good information security is availability. Business continuity ensures availability.

Elements of Business Continuity

Business continuity is usually associated with natural disasters, fires, or power loss. However, the elements of business continuity also prepare you for significant information security compromise or attack, such as a distributed DoS. Existing business continuity plans, in many cases, need be extended only to account for information security incidents.

According to Disaster Recovery International (DRI), one of the premier organizations for the certification of professionals in the field, the elements of a good disaster recovery plan include the following steps:

Project Initiation and Management. Proper project management is necessary for success, including establishing the need, getting buy-in from the proper management levels, and agreeing on time frames and budget levels.

Risk Evaluation and Control. Traditionally, this is the phase where natural disasters and their likelihood are assessed. Using the risk assessment concepts derived in Chapter 15, "Security Assessments," you can identify information security breaches that would impact availability.

Business Impact Analysis. Again, using the steps from Chapter 15, you would associate risks with business impact. For example, if you are an online retailer with two data centers, you would determine the impact of a DoS attack on one or both of your data centers.

Developing Business Continuity Strategies. Having determined the threats you are subject to and the business impact of those threats, this step is where you develop responses so that you can continue to operate. In the case of the online retailer, you may choose to fail over to a third, hidden data center if attacked.

Emergency Response and Operations. Here you decide what steps you will take and how you will manage the different types of incidents. This would include coordination elements with the CERT capability.

Developing and Implementing Business Continuity Plans. These are the processes and procedures that will be followed in the case of significant incident.

Awareness and Training. Security awareness is important, as described earlier. Awareness and training for these special extreme circumstances will reduce their impact.

Maintaining and Exercising Business Continuity Plans. Practice will ensure smooth execution and periodic checks on the continued efficacy of your plans.

Public Relations and Crisis Coordination. Never underestimate the power of a coordinated message to shareholders and the press in controlling the damage caused by a significant computer security incident.

Coordination with Public Authorities. In the case of information security breach, make sure that you call the proper authorities and coordinate the preservation of evidence for future prosecution.

Business continuity is a big subject, well beyond the scope of this book. However, realize that you can—and should—extend existing processes to account for information security incidents. A good coordination point for these processes is your internal CERT.

CERT . . . .

A CERT usually handles incident response. A CERT is an incident response team inside your organization that coordinates activities and information before, during, and after an attack. CERTs fulfill a variety of requirements, depending on your organization's needs. There are also national CERTs in most countries to coordinate information regarding multiorganizational, nationwide, or worldwide attacks, such as the "Code Red" worm in the summer of 2001.

National Coordination CERTs

The CERT name is actually a registered trademark of Carnegie Mellon University, who started the first CERT in response to the Morris Internet worm in 1988 (see Chapter 7, "Virus Detection and Content Filters," for more information on worms). After the entire budding Internet was brought down worldwide, it was decided that a central coordination center was necessary to help battle future threats. The U.S. Defense Advanced Research Projects Agency (DARPA) funded the University's Software Engineering Institute to create the CERT Coordination Center (CERT/CC), a central location for handling Internet-related incident response.

Today, the CERT/CC at Carnegie Mellon performs incident response, publishes security advisories, conducts research, responds to requests for information, and develops and maintains a vulnerability database. Since the creation of the original CERT, many CERT-like organizations have formed, each with its own specific geographical or organizational focus. There are somewhere between 50 and 100 active CERTs in the world. Table 17–1 lists a few major CERTs:

Table 17–1   National CERTs

CERTS		
United States	CERT/CC	www.cert.org
Asia and Pacific Rim	APSIRC	www.singcert.org.sg
Australia	AUSCERT	www.auscert.org.au
Europe	EuroCERT	www.eurocert.org
United States (DOE[1])	CIAC	www.caic.org
United States (GSA[2])	FedCIRC	www.fedcirc.gov

[1]Department of Energy.
[2]General Services Administration.

These regional and industry-focused CERTs can help you gather information and coordinate information in the case of an attack that extends beyond your own organization. For a comprehensive list of national CERTs from Albania to Switzerland, see *www.ti.terena.nl/teams/index.html*.

The CERT Inside Your Company

National CERTs are great resources for worldwide threats and threats beyond your own network, but an internal CERT is necessary to deal with all the other incidents that relate only to your company. An internal CERT capability should accomplish several tasks:

- Maintain an information base of relevant current threats
- Maintain and execute the incident response plans
- Act as the coordination point during incident response
- Conduct investigations

An internal CERT capability is very organization-specific. This is primarily because your CERT capability should be designed to coordinate and track, as well as fill holes in your response policies not covered by other groups in the company. For example, you may have an excellent disaster recovery team with all the training and infrastructure to handle fires and floods but no ability to handle a computer breakin. In this case, the CERT can use the public relations process and personnel of the other team while providing the expertise to understand and respond effectively to computer threats.

Training courses can be found for both establishing a CERT and training the people who will work in your CERT.

SUMMARY . . . .

Incident response and recovery are as important as the aspects of security you use to protect yourself. Well-documented escalation procedures will walk you effectively through the steps from first indication through investigation, incident response, and recovery. Incident triage will help you sort the "wheat from the chaff" when distinguishing real threats from false indications.

Business continuity (also known as *disaster recovery*) is usually associated with natural disasters but is a vital part of information security. Information security is concerned with availability, and availability is one of the primary goals of business continuity, so the two processes should work together.

National CERTs are valuable centers for information dissemination and coordination during attacks that span multiple organizations. You should also have an internal CERT, and your internal CERT should coordinate with and complement your business continuity procedures and organization.

18 Implementing Web and Internet Security

In this chapter . . .

- Writing the Security Policies That Govern Your Internet Connection

- Designing a Web Application That Will Be Secure

- Designing the Infrastructure on Which Your Web Site Will Run

- Maintaining Security Through Good Security Operations While Connected to the Internet

Connecting your organization to the Internet is both good and bad. Access to Internet resources can improve your business efficiency. But the risks inherent in such a connection must be addressed. In this chapter, we show how to bring together the information from earlier chapters to address Internet insecurity.

ESTABLISHING THE POLICY BASE . . . .

Policies set the rules that application developers, infrastructure designers, and users of the computer systems must follow. Some of the policy issues will be in the later sections of this chapter. But before making the first steps toward Internet connection, you should have a few basic policies established. The most important of these are:

- Appropriate use
- Privacy
- Data location and protection

Appropriate Use

Your first connection to the Internet is likely to provide internal staff with the ability to make use of Internet resources. It is imperative that the use of that connection be explicitly controlled via policy. Once such a connection is made without an existing policy, employees will strongly resist the controls represented by a reasonable use policy. Allowing Internet access without having established a policy for its use can create a very high liability for your organization.

For example, complaints of sexual harassment may result from employee use of the Internet to gather pornography. The complaint will be against your organization, not the guilty individual. If you have no published policy that forbids such use, you have no effective defense.

Your appropriate use policy should state the reason that Internet access has been granted and the uses that are allowed. Illegal activities should be identified as cause for termination. Many organizations allow personal use of Internet resources for nonoffending activities during breaks or outside of work hours. This can be construed as a benefit.

Privacy

Read Chapter 19, "Legal Issues." Even if your company is not covered by legislation that mandates a privacy policy (and implementation), you will need to establish such a policy before creating Web applications that give your organization a home on the Internet via the World Wide Web.

A privacy policy should cover each of the six privacy principles described in the legal issues chapter. You must tell people what you are collecting about them and how you will use it. For the simplest class of data, such as name and address, you must give people the option to be removed from your proposed uses (opt out). For more sensitive classes of data, such as medical records, you should solicit their permission before using the data (opt in). You must identify any other companies or business units to whom you may transfer the data for any purpose. You should state that those companies are required to meet all of the same principles and policies.

You should identify how a person can obtain a copy of the information you currently store about them. Your internal policies should be clear in the requirement to centrally register all data collected about individuals. You should identify how people can correct data that they believe is inaccurate and under what conditions you will accept their changes.

You must state that you effectively protect the data from being accessed by any unauthorized person. You should commit to meeting or exceeding the standard of due care continuously, or some other identifiable standard of security.

Data Location and Protection

This is a critical policy for Web application design. The information that is collected, stored, or used by a Web application can be very sensitive. It may include information on which your competitors would place a high value. Or it may provide an opportunity for your enemies to make your organization look bad.

An Internet Web server is any computer that can be accessed from a browser running on a computer via the Internet. *All* data stored on an Internet Web server is at high risk for theft or compromise. Therefore, it is imperative that your data location and protection policy clearly identify the types of data that may be stored on a server. Internet Web servers must be restricted to storing nonsensitive data.

But many Web applications need access to sensitive data. How do they get it if they do not store a copy? In the infrastructure design section below, we discuss how to segment the servers and the application so that data receives the protection it requires. But how much protection does each piece of data require? That level of understanding is the result of a successful data classification and risk assessment process. Once you know how much protection is needed, it is a simple matter of mapping the required security level to the infrastructure elements that provide security. But if no policy exists to dictate this process, Web applications will inevitably be designed and implemented that make security impossible.

Once the location of data is understood, the protections that must be implemented for that data can be specified. Each level of your data classification scheme should have its own location and protection specifications at the policy level. Protections are specified as an escalating series of mechanisms. An example of a table supporting such a policy is shown in Table 18–1.

Table 18–1   *Suggested Protection Mechanisms*

Policy Examples

Data Classification	Location Restrictions	Authentication	Authorization	Communications	Storage
Public	None	None	None	Open	Not encrypted but write controlled
Internal	Not on Internet Web server	Employee or contractor password	None	Open	Write controlled
Sensitive	External access via secured application through two firewall segments with different ports open	Employee, strong password	Role-based	Encrypted (weak)	Role-based access control for both read and write
Controlled	Not externally accessible unless isolated by at least two firewall segments with different ports open	Strong (multipart)	Role-based	Encrypted (strong)	Encrypted (weak)
Named User	Not shared server	Strong (multipart)	By name	Encrypted (strong)	Encrypted (strong)
User	Server	(multipart)		(strong)	(strong)

APPLICATION DESIGN ....

Once the policies are in place, the application design can begin. Both application and infrastructure design will take place in parallel, each feeding the other.

Authentication Requirements

Although we can describe generic levels of authentication quite easily, each application must be evaluated for the most suitable technology within the policy-dictated requirements. That evaluation needs to take into account the various audiences that might use the application, as well as the cost of managing the authentication solution. In addition, you should have a sense of overall authentication strategy. PKI is an expensive solution for some applications. But if the cost will be borne by other, more critical applications, it may become the best answer for an application that otherwise would not justify the investment.

Authentication solutions for Web applications run the gamut from unauthenticated through passwords, third-party tokens, SSL2, SSL3, and PKI. Each solution has its place. The most commonly used authentication methods for Web applications are passwords and SSL2. Applications that are very sensitive or that handle very high-value transactions may use either SSL3 or PKI.

Any change in authentication requirements after the initial application design will cause project delays and increased costs. This security decision needs to be made early.

Authorization and Scalability

Control over what screens can be seen—and who can read, write, or delete items of data—is exercised by the application. Most application programs contain relatively stable business logic, but ever-changing authorization rules. By externalizing the authorization process to a separate processing engine, the program code can be simplified and long-term maintenance costs significantly reduced. The products that provide this service also provide other useful capabilities.

Web applications run on computer servers that, like all computers, have performance limits. As the number of users grows and the number of screens displayed by the application increases with new development, the Web server becomes overloaded. Increasing the size and power of the computer can handle this growth for a while. Eventually, the workload needs to be split across multiple computers. Because of the limitations on Web application design, spreading an existing application across multiple processors can demand complex redesign of the application logic.

· ·

Maintaining Session Knowledge

Web applications do not maintain a session, or state knowledge. SSL or PKI may create a reusable tunnel that carries limited state information regarding authentication. All other aspects of application state, such as authorization, must be maintained by the application.

Fortunately, the authorization engines marketed today handle both of these situations well. External authorization is stored in a directory and accessed by a combination of Web server extensions and application calls. Support for growth in the number of computers handling the applications is built in. A set of applications can be split across computers and either duplicated or separated, as the workload dictates, without any impact on application design or logic. Management of the authorization tables can be done centrally or by individual application owners, using simple tables of control statements.

The decision of whether to use these authorization engines, also known as *Web SSO processors,* has a significant impact on application design and project budgeting. The decision must be made early.

Secure Code

The application coding practices that the development team uses are absolutely critical to the security of the application, once it is in production use. Many of the Web site defacements that are published in the press, as well as a large percentage of the more serious security breaches, are caused by inappropriate coding practices. Books have been written on secure coding practices, and tools are available to test code for correct implementation. Here are a few guidelines:

- **Error-check all inputs.** Hackers cause program failures by sending unexpected data types. Once a program has crashed, the hacker may be able to take control of the computer.

- **Every program must provide for recovery from errors.** Recovery routines are mandatory in every program element. Failure to recover in CGI exit routines is the most common way for hackers to compromise a server.

- **Input buffers should be separated from code and have controlled lengths.** Buffer overflows are the most reliable method of taking control of a computer. Input lengths must be carefully enforced. Ideally, the input buffers should not be adjacent to executable code.

INFRASTRUCTURE DESIGN . . . .

The Web application will run on a set of computers known as *Web servers*. Those servers and the associated network and security mechanisms that support and protect them constitute the infrastructure of the application. The design of the infrastructure is as important as the design of the application.

The DMZ of the Firewall

Chapter 5, "Firewalls," describes how the multiple interfaces of a firewall can provide filters, controls, and reporting on many different network connections at the same time. The primary purpose of the firewall is to stop information packets that do not represent valid and appropriate requests. The firewall does this by comparing each packet being transferred between your network and the Internet (or two sections of your own network) with a set of rules that you specify, defining what is appropriate and what is not. Packets that fail the rule are dropped and never reach any destination beyond the firewall. Packets that pass the rules are sent onward to their intended destination by the firewall.

The primary method of configuring firewall interfaces for Web applications is referred to as the *DMZ*, or demilitarized zone. The Web servers are said to be in a DMZ because every packet that needs to involve resources from inside your network must first go into a server in this DMZ and be processed there, invoking an application that has authority to communicate to the internal network resources.

A DMZ is formed by assigning one firewall interface to the Internet and another to a dedicated network link that will be used only for servers accessed from the Internet. The DMZ is a set of rules in the firewall that limit the paths that packets can take. Any packet arriving at the firewall from the Internet will be sent onward only if its destination is one of the servers on that DMZ network link. Those servers in the DMZ may have limited rights to send packets back through the firewall and into your internal network. But no packet can arrive at the firewall from the Internet and be allowed straight into the internal network.

As application complexity grows, many DMZ segments may be created to enforce a multilevel security model that provides appropriate but different levels of security for Web servers, application servers, and database servers. Also, separate DMZ segments may be created to isolate high-security applications from low-security ones. The design of the DMZ structure may have implications for application design. That is why the infrastructure and the application must be designed concurrently. Figure 18–1 illustrates how the information flows using the DMZ. The DMZ is formed by the firewall, in the center of the figure, which regulates traffic to different virtual networks.

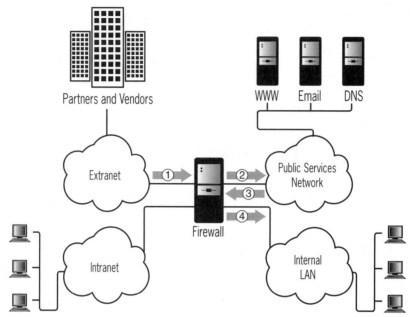

Figure 18–1
Information flow through the DMZ.

Here are the steps, as shown in the figure:

1. A request is sent from a computer on the Internet to a network address assigned to your company.

2. Your firewall intercepts the request. It tests the incoming packet to ensure that it is addressed to a computer in your DMZ and that it arrived on an expected "port" number. If NAT is being used, it translates the address used by the Internet into the internal address used on your DMZ. The request is sent to the server in the DMZ.

3. The request starts an application on the Web server. That application determines that data is needed from an application that runs on a computer that is inside the internal network. It addresses a message to that computer on the internal network. The firewall intercepts it.

4. The firewall checks that the message has a "from" address assigned to the DMZ and that it arrives on the firewall interface connected to the DMZ. It checks that the "to" address is within the internal network and that the message is assigned to an expected "port." If everything is cor-

rect, the firewall forwards the message to its destination on the internal network. It is possible that another NAT could take place before forwarding.

5. *(not shown)* The application on the internal network server returns the requested data to the DMZ Web server. The Web server returns a response to the original requester. In both cases, the firewall intercepts the message and checks its rules before allowing the message to be sent on.

This is the simplest case of a DMZ design. Applications that require high security will typically be designed using separate application servers that are outside of the internal network. The Web servers provide the formatting and control to service an incoming request. The business logic of the application runs on a separate application server. The database that stores all of the actual data being manipulated by the business logic is frequently on a third server. Each of these application segments may run on more than one server to support high availability and high transaction loads.

To optimize security, each set of servers should be isolated. The Web servers are separated from the Internet by a firewall, as shown previously in Figure 18–1. The application servers are isolated from the Web servers by another pass through the firewall. The rules for connecting from the Internet to a Web server must be significantly different from the rules for connecting from the Web server to the application server. The database servers may be in yet a third DMZ segment, isolated from the application servers by a firewall interface. Again, the rules for connecting from an application server to a database server must be different from those that allow connections from the Web server to the application server. The resulting DMZ structure is shown in Figure 18–2.

Some applications will connect from the application DMZ directly into the internal servers to complete a transaction. The firewall rules can become quite complex. Testing the configuration regularly is important. Testing is described in the security operations section later in this chapter.

In a large company with many Web applications, this configuration may be repeated three, four, or more times to house applications that require separation from one another. Each segment of each DMZ may have 50 or 100 servers within it. A properly designed application and infrastructure can support that level of scalability without compromising security.

Server Connectivity

For the firewall DMZ infrastructure to be effective, there must be no way to bypass the firewall. This means that all server connections must be along physical or logical network segments that pass through the firewall. Physical segments are pieces of wire that can be traced. Logical segments are those created by the advanced "level 2"

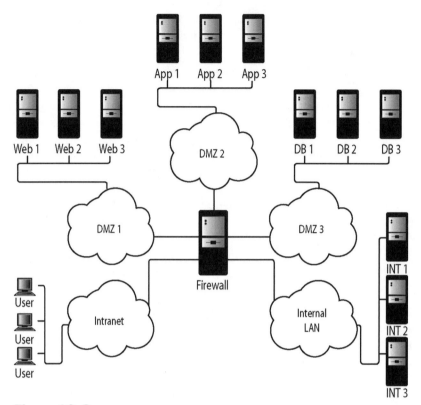

Figure 18–2
Information flow through a complex DMZ.

switches that are being used in some organizations to configure a logical network on the physical wires. In either case, the connectivity of all of the devices must be reviewed carefully. This is a significant issue for management consoles that might be connected to these servers so that they can be controlled from a central point.

One solution is to create a parallel network via a set of wires that connects the servers in the DMZ to management consoles, but those consoles are not connected to the internal network in any way. Another solution is to use VPNs to ensure that the connection from the server to the console is tightly secured. A firewall would allow the VPN traffic through to only the console on the internal network.

Operating System Configuration

The firewalls need to let some traffic through. It is hoped that this traffic will be only appropriate packets. But firewall rules cannot determine which packets are good and which are bad. They can only follow rules about addresses and ports. If a message arrives from what appears to be a valid address, sent to a valid address within your DMZ, and identified as a valid port (typically port 80, the HTTP port), the firewall will pass it through to its destination.

That destination server must be able to deal with whatever arrives from the firewall. Many arriving packets will be from hackers. Assuming that you have designed and coded your application well and designed and implemented your DMZ correctly, the weakest point is the operating system configuration and maintenance. We will discuss maintenance in the next section of this chapter. Operating system configuration generally takes place when a server is installed. Most server operating systems have hundreds of settings that can influence the level of security. No matter how well trained your system administrator may be, it is imperative that you use a reference document that has been created for this purpose. An example of such a document is the U.S. Navy's "Information Technology for the 21st Century" (IT-21) specification for secure configuration of Microsoft Windows NT 4 servers. It can be downloaded from the Internet at *www.hq.navy.mil/IT-21/about.html*. Similar documents are available for virtually all operating systems from many consulting and security publishing companies.

SECURITY OPERATIONS . . . .

Once your Internet connection is active and the Web applications are running successfully, it is time to start the processes that constitute continuous operations. Some of these are automated. Others are entirely manual. If the processes are not performed, your security will be incomplete and will lessen with time. Eventually, you will be compromised.

Virus Scanners and Content Filters

Anything entering your Web site may be carrying malicious code. If you allow the transfer of any data into the Web site, you must be running virus scanners and content filters. As more sophisticated models are used for application design, this will become a common problem. In this area, it is much better to be safe than sorry.

Vulnerability Scanners

One of the most effective ways to test your Web site security is via vulnerability scanners. Your technical staff can use them, or you can contract for outside providers to perform the scan and provide you with the results. Do both! It is worth it.

Intrusion Detection Tools

For all but the simplest publishing application, intrusion detection is vital. Simple, low-value sites can use just network intrusion detection. Once the Web applications are vital to your business or its image, host intrusion detection become important. Do both!

Change Control Process

Every change made to your Web site, whether it is to the application or the infrastructure, is critical. Any change could accidentally open a security hole. For security to be effective, changes must be reviewed, scheduled, and tested.

 SHOULD YOU BUY HACKER INSURANCE?

Hacker insurance first appeared in the late 1990s in response to information security threats. The idea is that, if you suffer a loss due to security breach, the insurance will pay for your losses. Unfortunately, although this is a good idea, it is not very good in implementation.

First, most of the losses covered by hacker insurance are already covered by your other business insurance. Second, the criteria describing loss to security breach are not sufficiently defined, making it very difficult to make a claim. Finally, the actuarial tables for these types of losses have no basis because there is not a history of losses on which to build good tables. This makes hacker insurance a speculative business for the insurance companies and bad business for the insured.

Although our recommendation is to steer clear of hacker insurance now, it may become valuable in the coming years. Business insurers are starting to exclude the very losses covered by hacker insurance in new policies, so it will be necessary to buy additional coverage in the future. Also, as time passes, more data is gathered on these threats, stabilizing the actuarial tables and clarifying the criteria for claims.

Bear in mind that losses to computer security breach will be covered only if you have good protection in place. Therefore, a good security program, protection, and monitoring technology will be necessary. See Chapter 19 for more information regarding fiduciary duty and avoidance of liability.

Operating System Maintenance

New vulnerabilities are discovered every week. Some operating systems, such as Windows NT and Linux, have hundreds of flaws found every year. Every discovery becomes an opportunity for hackers to compromise your Web site. Patches issued by the software publisher must be applied to all Internet-exposed operating systems regularly. Your system administration staff should review published fixes weekly. Urgent ones should be installed every week. Others should be installed on a monthly cycle.

MORE THAN THE SUM OF ITS PARTS . . . .

To be secure, Web sites must be designed and operated in a secure manner. The application design, infrastructure design, and operations are all critical to maintaining security. Ignoring this can cause severe brand damage to your organization. Numerous companies have been driven into bankruptcy as a result of a single serious compromise of their Web sites. Do not be the next.

SUMMARY . . . .

Connection to the Internet is a business imperative. Implementing security for Web-connected business requires writing good security policies, designing secure applications, implementing a secure infrastructure, and operating in a secure manner.

Defining an appropriate use policy will guide your efforts to define good and bad Internet usage. Privacy policy will protect your business from liability associated with new laws.

Applications should be designed with appropriate authentication to control access and an appropriate level of encryption. They should be implemented to resist buffer overflows and recover gracefully from errors.

Your infrastructure should include a firewall-protected DMZ for your Internet-facing services and isolation for your internal networks. Your operating systems should be configured securely and protected with monitoring, including regular vulnerability scans, intrusion detection, and virus scans.

Part 4

Odds and Ends

19 Legal Issues

In this chapter . . .

- Criminal Prosecutions

- Tort Litigation

- Standard of Due Care

- Liability

- Evidentiary Issues

- Law Enforcement Organizations

- Government Regulation of Security

Legal issues are inevitable when dealing with information security. In this chapter, we'll explore the legal issues surrounding information security, the ethical responsibilities of security professionals, some facts and trends regarding tort litigation, the changing standard of due care, and the role of liability in information security. In some instances, the standard of due care has been dictated by government regulations. These will also be covered. For more detailed information, see the resources section at the end of this chapter.

INTRODUCTION

There are several legal issues that crop up in information security and go beyond using the law to prosecute computer criminals. When law enforcement, lawyers, and judges are involved, you need to worry about things such as rules of evidence, bad publicity, and loss of intellectual property. These are some of the questions you might have:

- What constitutes criminal behavior on computers?
- What computer laws are on the books?
- Are the controls you put in place legal?
- Are you able to "attack back?"
- Are you legally responsible if someone breaks into your company and uses your systems to attack another company?
- What evidence do you need to prosecute someone?

COMPUTER CRIME LAWS

Computer misuse is certainly unethical but when does it cross the boundary into breaking the law? The criminal code of the United States, Title 18, lays out the basic laws defining what constitutes a computer crime. The entire text can be downloaded at *www.usdoj.gov/criminal/cybercrime/1030_new.html*. Key provisions include the following:

Title 18 USC Section 1030 (a) (1) Espionage statute. Unauthorized access to a computer, obtaining classified or restricted information that could be used to the injury of the United States

Title 18 USC Section 1030 (a)(2) Confidentiality statute. Unauthorized access to a computer and obtains:

(a)   financial or credit card information

(b)   information from any department of agency of the United States

(c)   information from any protected computer if access was from out of state or out of country

Title 18 USC Section 1030 (a)(3) Trespass on government computer. Unauthorized access to a U.S. government computer or access to any computer used by the government in a way that affects its use

Title 18 USC Section 1030 (a)(4) Property protection statute. Unauthorized access to a protected computer with intent to defraud and further that intended fraud, exceeding $5,000 in any one-year period

Title 18 USC Section 1030 (a)(5) Integrity/availability statute. DoS attacks and unauthorized access to a computer, causing damage and loss of information or prevents authorized access, with a loss of $5,000 or more over a one-year period

Title 18 USC Section 1030 (a)(6) Password trafficking. Traffic any password or similar information for gaining unauthorized access to a computer with intent to defraud if such trafficking affects interstate or foreign commerce or if the computer is used by the U.S. government

Title 18 USC Section 1030 (a)(7) Extortion provision. Using computer communications from out of state or out of country to extort money or anything of value

One of the keys to determining whether you can call on law enforcement is the $5,000 damage limit. If you can't demonstrate a $5,000 loss, no crime has been committed. This can be hard to show when your Web site has been defaced or one of your computers crashes and needs to be rebooted.

Many of the legal aspects of computer crime are currently focused on fighting criminal rings operating online and not necessarily breaking into your network. Typically, this means catching online pornographers or pedophiles. Significant emphasis in law enforcement training focuses on traditional data forensics. This involves recovering deleted files—avoiding hot-keys that destroy data on seized equipment—and is generally directed toward static information on computers. Computer crime puts special requirements on the legal system in this regard.

For example, the Fourth Amendment is designed to limit search and seizure to the narrow scope of relevant evidence. Current practice under Fourth Amendment protection provides that law enforcement can search only for pecific items in places allowed by the warrant. For example, warrants are usually issued for specific items (such as a Heisman trophy), and the search is limited to that one item. Everything else on the premises should remain untouched.

However, most computer warrants go directly against that tenet. When a computer is searched, it is very hard to take just the files you want, leaving everything else. This is primarily because you don't know what's relevant until you've had a chance to look at all of it. The result is usually seizure of an entire computer. Using the search of a house as a twisted metaphor for a computer-based search, we would take all the contents of a house and search through them, over time, looking for the specific items of the search.

LAW ENFORCEMENT/
CRIMINAL PROSECUTIONS . . . .

As we discussed, many incidents of computer misuse do not actually break laws. Even when laws are broken, law enforcement is stretched to the limit to deal with the incidents. To date, public law enforcement has been mostly ineffectual in dealing with computer-related crimes. There simply haven't been enough officers who understand computers, digital evidence, and the complexities of cybercrime.

 KEY POINT

There simply haven't been enough officers who understand computers, digital evidence, and the complexities of cybercrime.

This is changing rapidly, and significant strides have been made. The authorities understand the lack of trained people and, every year, are committing more resources to training through federal training academies and at the state level. Organizations include the High Technology Crime Investigators Association (HTCIA), the National Consortium for Justice Information and Statistics (SEARCH), and the National White Collar Crime Center. More about these organizations is presented later in this chapter.

It remains an uphill battle. Unfortunately, the situation is exacerbated by the fact that officers who improve their computer skills leave for better-paying jobs in the private sector as fast as they get trained. Even if there were enough trained officers, computer crime does not have sufficient priority at the local, state, or federal levels to address the growing need.

Law enforcement, although coming up to speed rapidly, won't be able to handle all computer security issues and may not be required to shoulder the lion's share of the burden in the first place. Civil authorities have been given regulatory and administrative powers, and professional disciplinary boards have been formed to deal with regulated industries. Although they may have taken little action to date in the area of e-commerce, in the absence of sufficient law enforcement resources or a tested regulatory conflict resolution system, the massive amounts of civil litigation will materialize to fill the enforcement vacuum.

TORT LITIGATION ·

Moving forward, many factors will affect the number of civil lawsuits. Historically, better technology has always resulted in an increase in legal liability and the number of lawsuits. The Y2K situation has resulted in an army of computer-savvy litigators who couldn't even use email just a few years ago. Although corporations remain reluctant to prosecute computer criminals, continued losses will put them in a defensive position as they deal with negligence lawsuits relating to imperfect security controls.

KEY POINT

Civil litigation will have a more significant impact on information security issues than criminal law over the next few years.

Negligence Litigation

Given a reasonable claim that losses were sustained in an environment where poor security measures were present and that the actual cause is difficult to determine, the temptation will be great to sue anyone in the chain of causation who can reasonably be blamed for a security lapse. The result is an increase in the number of lawsuits against security professionals who are arguably negligent.

Negligence can be proven in many different ways:

- Failure to disclose information regarding security risks
- Failure to use the latest technologies
- Failure to use extreme vigilance in establishing policy
- Failure to operate technology properly

Better Technology

The better technology gets, the more lawyers like it, because it results in job security. Several historical examples indicate increased litigation for liability and professional malpractice as better and safer technology is made available. Liability can be assigned when ignorance and/or negligence are present in applying new technologies to avoid foreseeable risks.

In other words, as better protection, such as intrusion detection, comes along, you had better be using it when you get hacked, or you may be held liable for negligence.

KEY POINT

As better protection, such as intrusion detection, comes along, you had better be using it when you get hacked, or you may be held liable for negligence.

Industry and technology examples abound:

- Shipping and radios
- Railroads and automobile crossings
- Highways and cattle guards
- Airplanes and air traffic control
- Surgery and new materials and procedures

The seminal example of this is the T.J. Hooper case. In this 1930s case, a tugboat company was sued for the loss of a coal ship and its cargo because the tugboat in question did not have one of those new-fangled radio things. In the 1930s, the shipboard radio was a known and rapidly developing communications technology but it was not considered an actual industry standard or legal requirement against which safety would be measured. However, the ruling went against the tugboat company for failing to use the new technology.

The Hooper case is still revolutionary today in the context of information security because many administrators and security professionals still do not understand that simply complying with generally accepted custom may not be sufficient to avoid liability. This is especially true when catastrophic failure results in large damages.

Corporate Reluctance to Prosecute

Companies are already reluctant to report security incidents because of the risks to their reputations and brand equity. Notwithstanding the prediction of a significant increase in lawsuits in the private sector, most companies are reluctant to prosecute computer criminals. Executives and shareholders alike are averse to the risks of bad publicity, lost productivity, liability, and disclosure of intellectual property during the discovery or trial process. There are attendant risks for the loss of good will among customers and shareholders when there are accusations of failure to disclose material facts or active misrepresentations regarding known risks.

ATTACKING BACK . . . .

Products have become available that allow companies that are "attacked" over the Internet to track and trace the source of the attacks. Some of these tools provide the ability to attack the attacker. This is not a good idea, for several reasons. The laws concerning this practice are unclear. You could be held responsible for damages under the very same laws intended to protect you. Spoofing IP addresses can make the attacker look like someone they are not. If you attack an innocent company because you believe they are the source of an outside attack on your company, you are perpetuating the misuse and could be held liable.

LIABILITY WHEN YOUR NETWORK
IS USED TO ATTACK OTHERS . . . .

A relatively new threat that has appeared is this concept of being used as a "zombie" for a hacker's attacks. Essentially, being a zombie means that your computer is hacked and an a remotely controlled agent is installed. This agent can be used for hacking, sniffing, or DoS attacks on other enterprises. The legal question raised is, are you liable if your computer is used to attack other computers? The answer is decided on a case-by-case basis, usually driven by civil litigation and heavily weighted toward your adherence to the standard of due care.

One famous example of this is *Nike v. FirstNet Online*. FirstNet is a Scottish ISP that was the victim of an Australian activist group, S11. S11 hacked Nike and redirected the Nike Web site traffic to S11, causing over 1.25 million requests routed through FirstNet over a 46-hour period in June 2000. The hack cost FirstNet about $37,500. FirstNet sued Nike for the loss, not S11. Greg Lloyd Smith, the ISP's managing director, was quoted as saying, "The fact that Nike failed to ensure adequate security measures for their Web address caused considerable damage to our company and denial of services to our online clients. Nike should be held liable for all resulting losses."

STANDARD OF DUE CARE . . . .

The *standard of due care* is a term that describes customary and usual precautions that should be taken by vendors to protect their customers. It is both determined and applied by a judge during a trial to ascertain liability. Essentially, if a company does everything they can that is both normal and customary, it is less likely to be liable for damages in a lawsuit. The problem is that the judge determines the definition of "normal and customary" at the time of any incident.

One of the clear messages you should be receiving in this chapter is that customary compliance may no longer be good enough. Following are some legal analyses that should act as food for thought on your responsibilities.

Responsibilities

In protecting our corporate infrastructures, we implement what Professor Mark Grady calls *durable and nondurable precautions*. Durable precautions are things such as security applications (firewalls, intrusion detection systems, and so on) and hardware (filtering routers, for example). Nondurable precautions include policies, procedures, and management controls. Professor Grady argues that nondurable precautions are as relevant as durable precautions.

In his article, "Why are People Negligent? Technology, Nondurable Precautions, and the Medical Malpractice Explosion," Professor Grady presents Grady's Law of Nondurable Precautions:

> The better and the safer technology becomes, when something goes seriously wrong, the more we presume human error on attending nondurable precautions.

The T.J. Hooper tugboat case was interpreted by Lance Rose in *NetLaw: Your Rights in the Online World.* Rose has written some pretty good advice into his analysis of this landmark case:

> First, it means that the system operators charged with security responsibility cannot ignore new security developments. They must keep up with the industry, and when new security tools come along that appear appropriate to the security risks and needs of the system, look into them. Second, while it is instructive to keep up with the security procedures used by other system operators, it is dangerous to ignore an effective security tool just because others are ignoring it.

As time passes, previously adopted security systems do not even retain their original effectiveness. System operators need to keep up with new developments just to keep security from slipping behind last year's security levels; improving system security over time is an extra responsibility. Under these circumstances, it seems the system operators need to keep up with security procedures; for systems with sensitive security, concern is even greater than for tugboat owner Hooper.

The responsibilities are clear. We believe you can take from this that installing an intrusion detection system is not good enough. You actually have to have a policy and procedures for using it effectively. Be aggressive about staying up to date with the latest innovations if you want to provide maximum protection for your organization from liability.

 KEY POINT

> Implementing information security is not good enough. You actually
> have to have a policy and procedures for using it effectively.

EVIDENTIARY ISSUES . . . .

Independent of the discussion regarding the risks and advantages of prosecuting computer criminals, there remains a number of issues surrounding evidence in legal proceedings.

The Web is a global phenomenon, so law enforcement and the legal system regularly have to deal with more than one country. Each country is going to have its own rules and procedures for handling computer forensic evidence. Intrusion cases that cross international borders are even more complicated because governments are reluctant to turn over legal evidence to noncitizens. Evidence must pass certain tests of viability even before the specific requirements of the legal system need be addressed.

Rules of Evidence

The *Federal Rules of Evidence* governs the admissibility of evidence in the United States. Evidence must pass the test of admissibility and weight. Admissibility is a set of legal rules applied by the judge. The rules of admissibility are extensive. There is an excellent reference available at *www.law.cornell.edu/rules/fre/overview.html*. Here are some examples of factors that affect admissibility:

Live Witness. Documents typically need to be delivered by the people responsible for creating them. Sommer points out that this rule has been substantially eroded because it was recognized that it would be impractical to require every clerk who has created an entry in a ledger to appear in court.

Expert Opinion. Opinions may be delivered only by identified experts.

Best Evidence. This is the rule that favors an original over a copy. Once again, Sommer points out that this has been significantly eroded because of computer-generated evidence.

Illegally Obtained. In criminal cases, evidence obtained illegally or "unfairly" may be inadmissible.

Hearsay (Audit Logs)

Hearsay stops people from testifying about things that they've heard. For example, Bob tells Alice that Charlie has confessed to a crime. Alice may testify only that she had a conversation with Bob about Charlie. She may not testify to the confession because she has no evidence herself that Charlie has confessed.

Hearsay is one of the important rules that control the admittance of audit logs into evidence. Logs are hearsay. They attest to the actions of an individual in an indirect manner so, generally speaking, they should not be allowed into evidence. Federal Rule of Evidence 803 provides a number of exceptions to the hearsay rule. Rule 803 (6) provides for activity logs under certain conditions. It states:

> **Records of regularly conducted activity.** A memorandum, report, record, or data compilation, in any form, of acts, events, conditions, opinions, or diagnoses, made at or near the time by, or from information transmitted by, a person with knowledge, if kept in the course of a regularly conducted business activity, and if it was the regular practice of that business activity to make the memorandum, report, record, or data compilation, all as shown by the testimony of the custodian or other qualified witness, unless the source of information or the method or circumstances of preparation indicate lack of trustworthiness. The term "business" as used in this paragraph includes business, institution, association, profession, occupation, and calling of every kind, whether or not conducted for profit.

This means that collecting logs has to be part of your everyday business routine if you hope to use them in a court of law. In the United States, the judge evaluates expert evidence before it is presented to a jury. Expert evidence is covered by Federal Rule of Evidence 702, which states:

If scientific, technical, or other specialized knowledge will assist the tier of fact to understand the evidence or to determine a fact in issue, a witness qualified as an expert by knowledge, skill, experience, training, or education, may testify thereto in the form of opinion or otherwise.

A case law interpretation of Rule 702 was provided by *Daubert v. Merrell Dow* in 1993. This case involved a drug that caused birth defects and produced four validity tests for expert evidence. One of four tests must be passed for the evidence to be presented to a jury:

1. The theory or technique must have been tested.
2. The error rate of a method must be acceptable.
3. A method must have been published in a peer-reviewed journal.
4. The technique must have gained widespread acceptance.

"Legal proof" is very different from "scientific proof." Scientific proof is based in scientific investigation, whereas legal proof is more about the rules of admissibility and what can be convincingly presented in court. The latter requirement of convincing presentation essentially renders proof subjective.

Historically, much computer evidence has been entered into court without much trouble because judges figured "hey, it came from the computer so it must be trustworthy." In other words, nobody in the legal arena had the technical knowledge to discredit the information. This situation is changing rapidly as the judges and lawyers deal with more of these cases.

After evidence has been admitted, it must then be assessed for weight. This is essentially whether the judge or jury believes the evidence. There are few guidelines here except what is convincing and well presented. Evidence should be authentic, accurate, and complete for it to pass any standard of weight.

Accuracy

There are many types of evidence that may be brought to court, including real, testimonial, documentary, expert, and derived. When forensic evidence is admitted, a lawyer must demonstrate both accuracy of the process that created the data and accuracy of the content of the evidence.

Raw event logs are considered documentary and will likely survive most challenges for accuracy if they are derived from reliable, secure sources. Also, they will have the most quality and authenticity because of the detail they contain.

KEY POINT

Raw event logs are considered documentary and will likely survive the most challenges for accuracy if they are derived from reliable, secure sources.

Tools that do not provide the collection of raw events will be subject to intense cross-examination in any legal setting. If your intrusion detection tool stores only alerts that were generated from analysis of raw data (event logs or TCP/IP data), without the raw data to back up the conclusion, the veracity of the detection may immediately be called into question. How do you know that your intrusion detection tool did not just make a mistake and generate this alert? Where is the data that caused the alert?

Charts, reports, and analyses, such as those presented in Chapter 8, "Intrusion Detection," are considered derived evidence because they are created from the raw event logs. Although charts may not have the same detail as raw event logs, they are still vital to explaining the meaning and interrelationships of the raw events.

Chain of Custody

Forensic evidence has additional requirements to survive challenges in court, including a clear chain of custody. This means that there should be a record of everything that happened to a piece of evidence up to the day it was presented in court.

Transparency

Any forensic method presented in court must be transparent. This means it must be tested or testable by a third-party expert. Methods that rely on secrecy to prevent the creation of countermeasures have trouble passing this test. For example, most security software developers want to hide the weaknesses in their mechanisms so that computer criminals cannot develop a way to circumvent their method. These weaknesses are precisely what defense lawyers attack when defending their clients.

The onus is on the good guys to create mechanisms that are transparent and effective. That's okay because "security by obscurity" is never a good policy. It should be assumed that attackers are going to know every aspect of your protection mechanisms in detail.

Case Study

For an example of evidence in practice, Peter Sommer uses a hacking case in which Richard Pryce in London attacked the U.S. Air Force (USAF) Rome Labs in 1994. This was the story of a hacker with the alias "Datastream Cowboy," who used a "blue box program" on his computer to access a free phone directory facility in Bogotá, Colombia, where he dialed into a Seattle-based ISP that offered free shell accounts. He ran a collection of widely available hacking tools to attack mainly *.mil* sites until he was eventually caught.

The tale that Sommer tells in his account of the story is fascinating reading, and we won't tell the entire story here. However, we will relate the basics and some highlights that relate specifically to intrusion detection systems. It is important to remember that this happened in 1994, before the time of any widely available intrusion detection systems. Certain rudimentary tools were used to capture IP packets but they pale in comparison with today's commercial tools.

Computer-derived evidence included data from his computer, his phone logs, IP traffic from Rome Labs, and logs from the targeted computers. The most complicated question that all this forensic evidence was required to answer was, can you link the person Richard Pryce, sitting in Bow Street Court, London, to the individual using the hacker alias *Datastream Cowboy* attacking United States military computers in Texas, beyond a reasonable doubt?

Sommer, instructed by defense lawyers, was asked to test the quality of the forensic evidence in the case, including:

- Data on the hard disk of Pryce's computer
- Logs of phone activity from Pryce's home
- Activity at the Bogotá telephone exchange
- Evidence from the ISP
- Network monitoring tools (network-based evidence)
- Evidence from the target computer (host-based evidence)

Sommer makes several points about the veracity of the evidence. There are a few notable points for this discussion. The exhibits from the ISP showed a break in the chain of custody. The printouts were of email of the original logs, not the logs themselves. The dates of the emails showed that a significant amount of time had passed since the original events. Sommer goes on to say that there were no descriptions of antitamper controls. Finally, the person producing the logs was not the person who collected the logs, violating the rule of hearsay that would have rendered all the logs inadmissible.

The exhibits from the network-monitoring tools produced printouts that were very similar to other USAF monitoring evidence. The USAF would not release the source of its monitoring tool, violating the standard of transparency. Sommer also states that the USAF was understandably reluctant to disclose the topography of its network, showing the monitoring points that would prevent it from proving completeness of its monitoring coverage.

One of the most damning indictments was of the evidence gathered from target machines. The argument is quite simple: These machines were attacked; how can you believe anything on them?

Sommer states that none of these arguments was ever tested in court. Pryce accepted the British equivalent to a plea bargain, and there never was a trial. He does point out that his brief "prosecution assassination" exercise shows how even "a well-thought-out investigation can become vulnerable when subject to the hostile scrutiny in the adversarial atmosphere of a legal proceeding."

ORGANIZATIONS . . . .

The following are law enforcement-related organizations that are at the vanguard of dealing with computer crime issues. As stated earlier, many resources are being spent in training and disseminating information to get the entire legal system up to speed.

National White Collar Crime Center

The National White Collar Crime Center provides a national support system for the prevention, investigation, and prosecution of economic crimes. These multijurisdictional white-collar crimes include investment fraud, telemarketing fraud, boiler-room operations, securities fraud, commodities fraud, and advanced-fee loan schemes.

From 1978 to 1992, the Center was called the *Leviticus Project*—a multistate association of law enforcement, prosecution, and regulatory agencies that banded together to fight criminal activity, first in the coal industry and subsequently in the oil, natural gas, and precious metals industries.

In 1992, the Center's board of directors (an elected group representative of the entire membership) expanded the mission of the Center to include all economic crimes. The Center's mission also includes providing investigative support services to assist in the fight against economic crime, operating a national training and research institute focused on economic crime, developing partnerships with public and private agencies to address economic crime issues, and developing the Center as a national resource in combating economic crime.

The Center provides services to its local and state law enforcement, prosecution, and regulatory agency members located throughout the United States. These include:

- Information sharing
- Case funding
- Training
- Research

The Center maintains computerized databases that contain case and investigative information on individuals and organizations suspected of involvement in economic crimes.

Trained Center staff conduct analytical services in areas such as financial analysis, check analysis, qualitative compilations, and background information assistance to specific member agency investigations. Certain member agency investigative expenses are reimbursed through the Center after careful monitoring by the Center's elected board of directors. The Center also provides specialized training at locations across the country on a variety of current white-collar crime topics.

National Cybercrime Training Partnership

The NCTP is a partnership of federal, state, local, and international law enforcement organizations formed to promote training at all levels of law enforcement in the battle against high-technology crime. The mission of the NCTP is guidance and assistance to local, state, and federal law enforcement agencies in an effort to ensure that the law enforcement community is properly trained to address electronic and high-technology crime.

Over 50 agencies work together to improve training through the following activities:

- Develop and promote a sound electronic and high-technology crime long-range strategy for police work in the 21st century, including interagency and interjurisdictional cooperation, information networking, and technical training.
- Educate the public about the issues associated with electronic and high-technology crime.
- Focus the momentum of the entire law enforcement community to ensure that proposed solutions are fully implemented.

The partnership meets these goals through the following activities:

- Develop and establish guidelines for new training programs.
- Create and maintain a clearinghouse ("knowledge base") to provide points of contact to investigators, prosecutors, and trainers on technical, legal, and policy issues.
- Support research and development of cybertools for criminal justice agencies through NCTP partners.
- Enhance communication among partner agencies.
- Develop a secure communications network for criminal justice agencies that provides a common platform and protocol among the NCTP community.

High-Technology Crime Investigators Association

The HTCIA is a professional organization comprised mostly of law enforcement dedicated to the field of criminal investigations involving advanced technologies and security within government, business and industry. The local chapters gather once a month to network, exchange ideas and notes, and listen to a speaker. The topics range from technologies to techniques to vendor products.

Selected objectives from the HTCIA bylaws include:

- To promote a representative, centralized organization to collect, collate, coordinate, and distribute data, information, ideas, knowledge, methods, and techniques by any suitable means in order to improve efficiency, promote uniformity in investigative methods, and develop matters of mutual interest to the membership of HTCIA
- To publish and distribute books, pamphlets, periodicals, papers, and articles supportive of activities and purposes of HTCIA
- To conduct surveys, studies, hold conferences, symposiums, seminars, and forums
- To arrange for the presentation of lectures and papers on matters and problems of interest
- To foster, promote, encourage, study, research, facilitate discussion, collect, and disseminate information of service or interest to the members of HTCIA or the public at large

- To conduct such other related activities as may be necessary, desirable, or incidental to gaining recognition of accomplishments in the field of criminal investigations involving advanced technologies and security within government, business and industry

The annual HTCIA International Training Conference was held in San Diego in September 1999. U.S. Attorney General Janet Reno spoke to the conference about training issues, budget increases, computer evidence issues, encryption, and legislative actions surrounding computer crime. One thing she stressed repeatedly was her appreciation for all the hard work by law enforcement nationwide and the federal government's commitment to dealing with computer crime. The text of her speech is available at *www.usdoj.gov/ag/speeches/1999/agsandiego92099.htm*.

Mitch Dembin, Chief of the General Crime Section and Supervisory Assistant U.S. Attorney, is the president of the local San Diego chapter of the HTCIA. He makes sure that the meetings and events are interesting and informative. One of the authors of this book has been a member of the San Diego chapter since 1998. In that time, I have seen attendance and interest almost double. Most of the attendees carry guns and badges, so I feel very safe at the meetings.

GOVERNMENT REGULATION OF INFORMATION SECURITY . . . .

Courts determine liability using the standard of due care, discussed earlier in this chapter. Due care is generally accepted to be the behavior of a normally trained and skilled practitioner within an industry. That level of care has been labeled as insufficient for some purposes and industries, and in an effort to improve the attention to information security, the U.S. government has taken a number of actions to set minimum standards well above those that are commonly accepted. As a result, your firm may be subject to civil fines or even selective criminal prosecution by simply not having met these new government mandates for security. Some mandates are international. Others are United States mandates only but industry-specific. If you suspect that your firm is covered by any of the initiatives listed below, you should involve your corporate counsel in your security planning efforts immediately.

European Data Privacy Initiatives and U.S. Department of Commerce Safe Harbor

In 1998, the European nations decided to protect the privacy of their citizens. Various national laws enacted by mid-2000 made it a criminal act to store personal data about any European citizen in a computer that was either (a) insecure or (b) located in a country that did not provide mandatory privacy and security protections. The United States has never required either privacy or security, and on July 1, 2001, it became illegal for almost any U.S. company to hold personal data about a European citizen. This applies to your prospects, your customers, and your employees. Personal data means home addresses or telephone numbers, as well as anything else that might be more sensitive. For most U.S.-based companies with European operations, it is now a criminal act to have a centralized human resources employee list.

Most, but not all, U.S. companies can be exempted from prosecution in Europe by enrolling in a program run by the U.S. Department of Commerce called the *Safe Harbor program*. To enroll, your company must commit to the six privacy principles required by European law. If you enroll in Safe Harbor and violate the principles, you are subject to prosecution by the U.S. Federal Trade Commission and state agencies. If you do not enroll and violate the principles, your corporate officers are subject to criminal prosecution in Europe. The six principles are:

1. **Notice.** You must tell people what you are collecting about them and how you will use it.

2. **Choice.** For the simplest class of data, such as name and address, you must give people the option to be removed from your proposed uses (opt-out). For more sensitive classes of data, you must solicit their permission before using the data (opt-in).

3. **Transfers.** You may not transfer personal data to any other company unless that company is required to meet all of the same principles and policies.

4. **Access.** You must tell anyone who asks what the current records about them contain.

5. **Security.** You must protect the data from being accessed by any unauthorized person.

6. **Data Integrity.** You must provide a method for correcting data that has been identified (and verified) as being incorrect.

The Gramm-Leach-Bliley and Health Insurance Portability and Accountability Acts

One U.S. industry does not have to register under Safe Harbor in order to be protected. The GLB act requires that all financial industry firms or companies that store financial industry-related information must comply with specific privacy and security regulations as of July 1, 2001. Those regulations meet all of the criteria covered by the six principles documented by the European community. By complying with GLB, a U.S. firm becomes compliant with European law. Most financial industry firms are audited by an agency of the U.S. government. Those auditors are now enforcing compliance.

The HIPAA provides the same level of accountability for the health care industry. However, HIPAA does not take full effect until 2003. Health care companies with European operations should investigate the Safe Harbor program.

Government Information Services Reform Act

U.S. federal agencies are required to establish formal information security programs, using guidelines published by the NIST. The law requiring this is the Government Information Services Reform Act (GISRA). The NIST program outline for information security is well thought out. As a new standard of due care emerges, we expect that it will be closely modeled on the NIST program.

Going Forward

There is strong bipartisan support in the U.S. Congress and in the White House for increased regulation of privacy and computer security. If the current regulations do not cover you, the next batch may. Establishing a security program and making appropriate investments can avoid liability now and can prepare for future mandates to be met more efficiently.

SUMMARY . . . .

Cybercrime is an important focus of law enforcement but it is only now getting the training necessary to deal with the problem effectively. In the meantime, civil litigation will probably increase with considerably more lawsuits about liability. Case law has shown that corporations are responsible for using the latest technologies to protect themselves and may be liable for damages if they do not.

Security officers need to determine the standard of due care for their industry and regularly track their corporation's adherence to that standard.

There are several law enforcement-affiliated organizations working both to combat computer crime and improve training. These organizations have conferences and Web sites that are used to bring people together and to improve law enforcement's response to computer crime.

Cyberlaw also may cover the minimum set of security controls that you must implement to meet the standards that will be accepted by regulators, government agencies, and courts.

RESOURCES . . . .

Daubert v. Merrell Dow Pharmaceuticals, Inc., 113 S.Ct. 2786 (1993).

Grady, Mark. "Why are People Negligent? Technology, Nondurable Precautions, and the Medical Malpractice Explosion," 82 *Northwestern U. L. Rev.* 293 (1988).

Nike v. FirstNet on *www.cnn.com/2000/TECH/computing/07/04/nike.v.nsi.idg/*

Rose, Lance. *Your Rights in the Online World.* McGraw-Hill. Berkeley, CA, 1995.

Smith, Fred. "Ethical Responsibilities and Legal Liabilities of Network Security Professionals," *Proceedings of the 13th Annual Computer Security Applications Conference*, San Diego, CA, December 1997, pp. 239–250.

Smith, Fred and D. Bailey. "Computer Security and the Millennium," *Proceedings of the 14th Annual Computer Security Applications Conference*, Phoenix, AZ, December 1998, pp. 129–133.

Sommer, Peter. "Evidence from Cyberspace: Downloads, Logs and Captures," in *Journal of Financial Crime* 5JFC2, pp. 138–152. 1997.

Sommer, Peter. "Intrusion Detection Systems as Evidence," *Proceedings of RAID98*, Louvain-la-Neuve, 1998.

Sommer, Peter. "Digital Footprints: Accessing Computer Evidence," *UK Criminal Law Review* (Special Edition, December 1998, pp. 61–78).

www.iir.com/nwccc/nwccc.htm

www.law.cornell.edu/rules/fre/overview.html

www.nctp.org

www.usdoj.gov/ag/speeches/1999/agsandiego92099.htm

www.usdoj.gov/criminal/cybercrime/1030_new.html

20 Putting It All Together

In this chapter . . .

- The Importance of Communication

- Understanding Your Company's Business

- Protecting Yourself

This book is a reference and a guide to the pieces of security. Those pieces have to be put together properly for effectiveness, and there are some requirements for success that aren't obvious. In this final chapter, we discuss how to be successful in a corporate environment. This chapter is directed toward Corporate Information Security (CIS) people. However, it will have significant value for business managers who have to work with them.

COMMUNICATION (AGAIN) . . . .

Communication is the most important element for success in a corporate environment. One of the most common challenges to implementing effective information security can be the failure of management/business and security/technology to communicate and understand the organization's security needs and requirements. If CIS cannot effectively communicate security issues, needs, and requirements, management will ignore, forget, or fail to understand the relevance of the security message.

When CIS tries to communicate with business unit managers, the executive management, or the board of directors, there are frequently breakdowns in understanding. It is likely that those outside of CIS who are responsible for security have the following issues:

- CIS does not understand its business as well as it should.
- CIS does not understand management's concerns.
- CIS does not work as closely or collaboratively with business units as it should.

If CIS works closely and collaboratively with business units, business needs will be understood. When business needs are understood, security needs can be determined. CIS can present a tailored security message that covers management's security concerns and identifies additional areas worthy of management consideration. Following this advice and improving your communications will have at least two benefits:

- It makes your job easier by helping people understand security.
- Business management will be more likely to release the purse strings and implement organizational change.

Remember to apply different techniques to different audiences, defined by levels on the organizational totem pole.

Line Managers. Give them in-depth information. For example, provide actual examples of Windows NT registry attacks and their impact on the system. Deliver a 50-page report.

Business Unit Managers. Give them less detailed information. For example, mention the existence of Windows NT attacks and the impact on their business unit. Deliver a 20-page report.

Executives. Be brief, with lots of pretty pictures and graphs. For example, mention that Windows NT may be at risk and the effect this would have on shareholder value. Deliver a three-page report with four additional pages of pictures and graphs.

Line managers require the most information. Due to their proximity to the "trenches," they typically know more about current technologies. They need to be sure that they understand the issues almost as well as you do before they can act on them and push them ahead of other tasks.

Business unit managers require detail but not as much as line managers. They have multiple responsibilities and are often spread thin. They trust their line managers and are looking for the nod from a line manager before they act on it and push it up to executive management.

Executives require the least detail and the most impact information. Their time is at a premium, and they don't have time to waste on understanding a whole bunch of technological detail. It's not that they don't want to, it's that they have many responsibilities, and they are dealing with more than one issue at any given time. Get to the point, and be clear and concise. Pictures and graphs make it easier for anyone to understand something. Use lots of them with executives. Never talk to an executive about security issues for more than 15–20 minutes unless he or she wants to. Typically, your briefs will be 10,000-foot views of a security situation.

The executive is depending on his or her midlevel managers for guidance and feedback. However, always be prepared to go into as much detail as the executive wants. Presentations have been made to executives who couldn't tell the difference between sending email and Web surfing but have insisted on receiving abnormally in-depth detail about some obscure security nuance. They do this to keep you on your toes and even sometimes to rattle you. Whatever their intention, you will look good if you are prepared and have the answers to their questions.

Here's some advice on preparing for questions from any manager: Anticipate, anticipate, anticipate. No matter who is asking the question, strive to understand enough about their business, their concerns, and their personalities to know what types and levels of answers they require in order to make decisions about their business. Be prepared for So what? and Why should I care? rebuttals. Having immediate and understandable answers to these questions can be very compelling.

UNDERSTAND YOUR COMPANY'S BUSINESS . . . . .

Understanding a manager's business is vital to implementing successful security. If your company makes garbage disposals, you had better understand the garbage disposal business. If your company makes airplanes, you need to know the aviation business. In all cases, you should understand the supply chain, the mission-critical processes, the partners, and the value of data. The best way to understand business needs is to take on the attitude that good security is a result of a collaborative effort between security and business. You might be the security guru but you can't know everything.

Advice on Politics

If you are in CIS, you may have the final say on security matters. However, the path to success is to solicit and review feedback from business units. One way to communicate is to assist business units, providing security insight and oversight by conducting technology security assessments. In some cases, you may know from the beginning that something is a very bad idea. Instead of shooting down the project, present your concerns and lay out the facts. Then solicit feedback and request business unit assistance in solving the problem. Try very hard not to say that something is not possible or is a bad idea.

To that end, it is a good idea to network and meet other people in other organizations. Take people out to lunch or breakfast. You will learn about the other business units in your company. This will help you to understand the dynamic aspect of operational security. As an added bonus, you will educate someone about security and gain an ally.

Know the lay of the land and pick your battles carefully. Security can be a sensitive and highly charged topic. Regardless of your communications skills, there may be times when the only way to resolve an issue will be through conflict. You must be sure that a battle is worth fighting before you commit to making people angry. You may lose the battle and lose precious credibility. You may win the battle in a Pyrrhic victory. Don't commit to battle unless you are prepared. Never do anything that would prevent you from graciously yielding if the battle goes against you.

PROTECT YOURSELF . . . .

One of the primary jobs of a security person is to provide security information to executives and business units about security matters. Save memos and copies of emails, and document every time you notify, inform, and/or give advice about security issues within the realm of security to a superior or a business unit manager. If you speak to someone on the phone or at a meeting and discuss a security issue, follow up with a memo or an email that summarizes what the other person said and what you said. Your job is to advise and inform. In many cases, management might not give you the authority to act.

Develop risk acceptance forms for business managers. Determine the risk and advise the business unit managers. If you believe the risk is unacceptable and the business unit manager has the political clout to contradict you, have the business unit manager accept the responsibility by signing a risk acceptance form. Just make sure that the risk and potential impacts are faithfully documented on the risk acceptance form.

ADVICE FOR A SMALL BUSINESS

There is probably no person in your organization who spends all of the work day involved in information security. Use the information from this book to help identify qualified consultants in your geographical area. If possible, try to write down a first draft of a security policy before bringing the consultant in. Get the management team within your company to participate in a brainstorming session to decide what security policies would be appropriate for your corporate culture.

Have the potential consultants provide you with a proposal that shows how they would secure your computers, based on the policy you wrote. Analyze their proposals with the material you learned in this book.

ADVICE FOR A MID-SIZED BUSINESS

Your information security is probably run from within your network management group. You should establish responsibility for security policy and process outside of that group, even if it is a part-time assignment for an otherwise occupied manager. Most mid-sized organizations should have at least one manager assigned full time to security.

Security standards for application design teams are critical if your company expects growth. And a risk assessment process that connects security policy to the business managers is essential.

ADVICE FOR A LARGE ENTERPRISE

Large organizations must have a security program that ties together policy, process, and technology in support of information security. Architectural standards for security must be established. Security metrics should be in place to measure the success of the security program.

To be enterprise-class, an IT organization must have a minimum of three people dedicated to security policy and process management at a headquarters (central IT) level. Most enterprise IT organizations, of course, have many more people assigned to security than that. Depending on the industry and some other factors, such as labor management relations, security should cost a fixed percentage of the complete IT investment. That is, for every dollar spent on information technology, there should be three to eight cents spent on information security.

A FINAL WORD

Here are the highlights from the book, in case you missed them.

- Security is a process, not a destination.
- If business units work effectively with security people to define effective requirements, you will end up with effective security.
- Start with policy and remember that a small, effective policy is better than a comprehensive one that can't be understood or implemented.
- People are more important than technology in the creation of effective security.
- Effective security involves protection, detection, and response.

Security is vital in today's environment. The authors wish you well in creating effective security in your organization.

Glossary

Access Control

Process and mechanisms to control access to information (e.g., passwords, privileges).

Access Rule

A specific check that enforces access control. For example, human resources data may be accessed by administrators, executives, or anyone in the human resources department.

Applet

A small computer program downloaded from the Internet to perform special functions. Applets may include malicious code, such as viruses, and are a threat.

Appropriate Use

A policy that defines how computers should and should not be used. For example, the Internet should be used for business pur-

poses only. Personal use is acceptable outside normal business hours.

Assessment

A review of policies and system configuration to identify vulnerabilities and readiness. There are several types of assessments, including vulnerability assessment and security audits. *See also* Risk Assessment.

Attack

Any action that results (intentionally or unintentionally) in a violation of security policy.

Audit

The process of comparing anything with the set of such things that are allowed. In this book, *audit* is used to describe the process of comparing the current security posture with an industry standard posture (security audit) and is also used to describe the comparison of any recorded set of actions against those considered allowable by current security policies.

Audit Policy

A security policy that dictates the set of actions that will be traced or recorded as they occur for later audit analysis, typically via a host intrusion detection program.

Authentication

The process of confirming that you are who you claim to be. Identification and authentication usually go together. You identify yourself by entering a username. You authenticate yourself by entering a password that only you would know, confirming that you must be who you claim to be.

Authorization

The process of determining the list of secured resources that you are allowed to access and the types of access (read, update, delete, etc.) permitted.

Biometrics

An authentication mechanism where a unique physical characteristic (e.g., retina pattern, palm/fingerprint, facial structure) is used to confirm that you are who you claim to be.

Black Hat

A malicious hacker with significant technical knowledge to overcome sophisticated access control mechanisms. Also a popular computer security conference series, "The Black Hat Briefings."

Certificates

Encrypted electronic records that provide strong authentication of machines (*See* Virtual Private Network) or individuals (*See* Public Key Infrastructure).

Computer Emergency Response Team (CERT)

The group inside your company responsible for coordinating response to identified security threats and breaches. Also, a consortium of national groups responsible for coordinating worldwide response for national and global threats, such as the Code Red worm.

Configuration Control

The process of detecting and eliminating elements of computer or network configurations (e.g., settings) that are not compliant with current security policy.

Content Filter

A filter on Internet and email traffic going in and out of your enterprise. Content filters can identify threatening email attachments (e.g., the Nimda worm) or suspicious communications, using key words such as *bomb*, *kill*, or *Project X*.

Data Classification

The process of categorizing data within your enterprise into useful groups and sensitivity levels.

Demilitarized Zone (DMZ)

The part of your network that is open to access from the Internet, such as Web servers. The DMZ is protected at a different level than the internal "back office" data, which is usually restricted from any type of outside access.

Denial of Service (DoS)

A threat that manifests itself in a loss of some resource, such as processing power, disk space, or access to a computer entirely.

Digital Signature

A use of certificates that creates a special encrypted data file (the signature) that can be used to guarantee that the file it is associated with comes from the certificate owner and has not been modified since the signature was created.

Encryption
The process of scrambling data so that it is not understandable by third parties. Usually used in the transmission of data over unprotected networks (such as the Internet) to protect the integrity and security of the data or to store data so that no one retrieving it without authorization can read it.

Extranet
A computer-to-computer connection between two companies, using Web-based technologies. A prior generation of such connections, using less flexible technology, is known as *electronic data interchange* (EDI).

False Positives
An intrusion detection alert that is raised when no threat is present. Reducing false positives is a desirable trait in intrusion detection and monitoring systems.

Firewall
A computer/operating system/application (or an appliance preconfigured with all three components) that allows flexible filtering of all communications passing through it via the specification of access rules.

Forensics
Postprocessing of computer data to identify or investigate threats.

Hacker
Traditionally, anyone who investigates the internal processes of computers. In recent years, the press has used the term exclusively to describe black hat hackers.

Host-Based Intrusion Detection System (IDS)
A system that looks for the presence of threats and suspicious indications in computer logs and other static information on computers themselves. Host-based IDS is particularly suited for finding insider misuse and threats. (*See also* Network-Based IDS.)

Intrusion Detection
Monitoring for the existence of ongoing threats, such as intrusion originating outside the enterprise or internal misuse.

Intrusion Prevention
An access control method using intrusion detection methods to identify threats and stop them before they can cause loss.

Kerberos
A technology created at Massachusetts Institute of Technology that allows strong authentication without shipping passwords over the network.

Macro Virus
A type of computer virus that is attached to another data file, such as a document or a spreadsheet, and that works its malicious actions by running as a macro supported by the program that opens the file.

Managed Security Services (MSS)
Services provided by a vendor organization on an ongoing basis in support of your computer operations.

Misuse
When an authorized user abuses his or her privileges to cause harm or otherwise to do something he or she is not supposed to do.

Network Address Translation (NAT)

A capability typically found in firewalls to connect computers inside your organization to the Internet without revealing the IP addresses of your computers. The firewall sends every request from inside your network out to the Internet, using the firewall IP address, then sends the responses to the computer inside your network that originated the request. This allows the computers inside your network to use addresses that would not be valid if those computers were directly connected to the Internet.

Network-Based Intrusion Detection System (IDS)

An intrusion detection mechanism that looks for patterns of misuse in network traffic flowing between computers. Network-based IDS is well suited for detecting outsider threats, such as hackers breaking in from the Internet. (*See also* Host-Based IDS.)

Operating System

The underlying program (Linux, Windows, UNIX) that runs the computer. All applications (word processor, spreadsheet, Web server) run on top of the operating system. Operating systems are one of the keys to secure computing.

Policy

Any documented and communicated statement that separates what is allowed from what is not.

Privacy

The requirement, whether market-driven, legislated, or moral, to protect information about individuals from misuse or inappropriate disclosure.

Public Key Infrastructure (PKI)

A set of technologies that provide key management for encryption so that communications can be secure, even though they use insecure networks, such as the Internet.

Risk Assessment

The process of matching security policy and enforcement to the needs of the business.

Secure Shell (SSH)

A UNIX command processor that accepts encrypted communications so that "hackers" cannot issue commands.

Secure Socket Layer (SSL)

A set of encryption technologies used principally by Web servers to secure communications with an end user's browser.

Security Operations Center (SOC)

The computer operations function that monitors the security environment using intrusion detection, vulnerability assessment, configuration management, and other technologies to detect actual or attempted attacks. In large companies, the SOC should always be separate from other operations functions so that the SOC can monitor the actions taken by operations and system/network administration.

Security Policy

Policy that governs security-related issues.

Single Signon (SSO)

The ability of an end user to connect to all authorized computer applications by presenting a single user account name and password once. It is sometimes possible to accomplish this for a limited subset of computer applications. New applications designed around a coherent security architecture support SSO. Older applications, or those without such an architecture, cannot.

Smart Cards

A credit-card-sized device with an embedded computer chip, memory, operating system, and application program(s). As used in this book, the smart card holds a certificate and related information, allowing an end user to authenticate.

Social Engineering

A threat that is perpetrated by an individual, fooling your staff members into believing that he or she is someone in authority within your organization and getting them to reveal mission-critical or sensitive information. For example, a person calls an employee and claims to be a computer system administrator. When this person has the employee's trust, he or she asks for the employee's password.

Threat

A theoretical attack.

Trojan

An applet that, once downloaded, hides itself inside your operating system. Typically, the Trojan records key strokes and sends them over the Internet to its author in order to steal your user account names and passwords.

Virtual Private Network (VPN)

A technology that allows end users to connect over the Internet to your corporate network with almost as much security as if they were at their computers inside your office building.

Virus Controls

A set of technologies that scan files and network messages for possible viruses. Virus controls are effective only if they are implemented at every desktop, every mail server, and every application or file server running Microsoft or Apple operating systems. Some virus controls are also available for other operating systems.

Vulnerability

A "hole" in your security that can lead to an unauthorized break-in from the Internet or to internal misuse.

Vulnerability Scanner

An application that checks each of the computers in your enterprise for vulnerabilities so that they can be tracked and corrected.

White Hat

A hacker with significant technical knowledge who uses his or her understanding of computer threats and hacking techniques to secure computers.

Worm

A computer virus that spreads from one computer to another, using vulnerabilities and networked applications. The name comes from the idea that each infected computer becomes a segment in the "worm."

Index

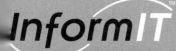